Building Psychological Resilience in Military Personnel

Building Psychological Resilience in Military Personnel

Theory and Practice

edited by Robert R. Sinclair and Thomas W. Britt

American Psychological Association • Washington, DC

Chapters 6, 8, 9, and 10 were authored/coauthored by employees of the United States government as part of official duty and are considered to be in the public domain.

Published by
American Psychological Association
750 First Street, NE
Washington, DC 20002
www.apa.org

To order
APA Order Department
P.O. Box 92984
Washington, DC 20090-2984
Tel: (800) 374-2721; Direct: (202) 336-5510
Fax: (202) 336-5502; TDD/TTY: (202) 336-6123
Online: www.apa.org/pubs/books
E-mail: order@apa.org

In the U.K., Europe, Africa, and the Middle East, copies may be ordered from
American Psychological Association
3 Henrietta Street
Covent Garden, London
WC2E 8LU England

Typeset in Goudy by Circle Graphics, Inc., Columbia, MD

Printer: Maple Press, York, PA
Cover Designer: Mercury Publishing Services, Rockville, MD

The opinions and statements published are the responsibility of the authors, and such opinions and statements do not necessarily represent the policies of the American Psychological Association.

Library of Congress Cataloging-in-Publication Data

Building psychological resilience in military personnel : theory and practice / edited by Robert R. Sinclair and Thomas W. Britt.
    pages cm
  Includes bibliographical references and index.
  ISBN 978-1-4338-1331-3 — ISBN 1-4338-1331-9 1. Psychology, Military. 2. Resilience (Personality trait)—Study and teaching. 3. Soldiers—Mental health services—United States. 4. Soldiers—United States—Psychology. 5. War—Psychological aspects. I. Sinclair, Robert R. II. Britt, Thomas W., 1966-
  U22.3.B85 2013
  355.001'9—dc23

                                    2013001884

British Library Cataloguing-in-Publication Data

A CIP record is available from the British Library.

Printed in the United States of America
First Edition

http://dx.doi.org/10.1037/14190-000

CONTENTS

v

CONTRIBUTORS

Amy B. Adler, PhD, U.S. Army Medical Research Unit-Europe, Walter Reed Army Institute of Research, Heidelberg, Germany

Thomas W. Britt, PhD, Clemson University, Clemson, SC

Oscar A. Cabrera, PhD, U.S. Army Aeromedical Research Laboratory, Fort Rucker, AL

Colonel Carl A. Castro, PhD, U.S. Army Medical Research and Materiel Command, Fort Detrick, MD

Danielle Charbonneau, PhD, Royal Military College of Canada, Kingston, Ontario

Rhonda L. Cornum, PhD, MD, Uniformed Services University, Bethesda, MD

Marilyn Nicole Deese, MS, Centenary College, Shreveport, LA

Neil Greenberg, MD, FRCPsych, Royal Navy (UK) and King's College Academic Centre for Defence Mental Health, London, United Kingdom

Steve M. Jex, PhD, Bowling Green State University, Bowling Green, OH

Jason Kain, PhD, Fors Marsh Group, Arlington, VA

Paul B. Lester, PhD, Research Facilitation Team, Office of the Deputy Under Secretary of the Army, Monterey, CA

Allister MacIntyre, CD, PhD, Royal Military College of Canada, Kingston, Ontario

Sharon McBride, PhD, Comprehensive Soldier Fitness Program, Arlington, VA

Anna C. McFadden, BS, Clemson University, Clemson, SC

Julie C. Merrill, MS, Military Psychiatry Branch, Center for Military Psychiatry and Neuroscience, Walter Reed Army Institute of Research, Silver Spring, MD

Damian O'Keefe, PhD, St. Mary's University, Halifax, Nova Scotia, Canada

Celina M. Oliver, PhD, Portland State University, Portland, OR

Kalifa K. Oliver, PhD, Clemson University, Clemson, SC

YoungAh Park, PhD, Kansas State University, Manhattan

Lyndon A. Riviere, PhD, Military Psychiatry Branch, Center for Military Psychiatry and Neuroscience, Walter Reed Army Institute of Research, Silver Spring, MD

Josef I. Ruzek, PhD, National Center for PTSD, Training and Dissemination Division, Veterans Affairs (VA) Palo Alto Health Care System and Stanford University, Palo Alto, CA

Robert R. Sinclair, PhD, Clemson University, Clemson, SC

Edward M. Vega, PhD, Trauma Recovery Program, Atlanta Veterans Affairs (VA) Medical Center, Atlanta, GA

Melissa C. Waitsman, PhD, Research Transition Office, Center for Military Psychiatry and Neuroscience, Walter Reed Army Institute of Research, Silver Spring, MD

Julia M. Whealin, PhD, National Center for PTSD, Pacific Islands Division, Veterans Affairs (VA) Pacific Islands Health Care System and the University of Hawaii School of Medicine, Honolulu

Kathleen M. Wright, PhD, U.S. Army Medical Research Unit-Europe, Walter Reed Army Institute of Research, Heidelberg, Germany

FOREWORD

Rarely in the history of war have the nations conducting the war actually cared about those doing the fighting. The only names recorded of those killed in battle were those of the nobility. And when laymen rose to the rank of general or admiral, their names too would be recorded. The enlisted who were killed or who fought remained anonymous, their names unknown. In the United States and other modern democracies, all of this has changed. Today, the names of all service members killed are immortalized on monuments or tributes. Their names and photos appear in newspapers, on television, and on the Internet. Those killed are brought back to life when we preserve their identity. They are no longer anonymous.

Care for the wounded became a national responsibility after World War II, as care for the severely wounded shifted from charities to the nation. Although most modern democracies developed national health care systems to ensure health care for all of their citizens, both civilians and military, in the United States a national health care system was created for military veterans only. At first, the focus was on those veterans who were physically wounded, yet now we focus just as much on the psychologically wounded. A natural extension of our focus on the care of the wounded is to identify how we may prevent or lessen these injuries, both physically and psychologically.

In terms of preventing psychological injuries of war, the concept of resilience was borrowed from the fields of child psychology and psychiatry, where nearly all of the early work on resilience was conducted. Few researchers in the field of military resilience actually appreciate the implications of this important lineage. Very early on, it was recognized that resilience is something not only desirable but also essential for normal psychological development. Thus, from a national strategic security perspective, we require a healthy, resilient population, and we should be working collaboratively to achieve this by focusing on ensuring that our children are healthy and resilient. Waiting until our young men and women join the military to introduce resilience building is in many respects too late, yet building resilience is still essential to ensure a high-performing military.

Efforts to exclude the less resilient from serving in the military represent a narrow and flawed understanding of what resilience is and the potential for resilience building to enhance the strength of a military. We must focus on the strengths that every individual possesses rather than the weaknesses. We must focus on team building and leadership and avoid adopting an individualistic and elitist model that harkens back to the medieval mind-set. The field of military resilience holds the promise to fundamentally transform the military in ways that are just now being imagined; to limit this potential by focusing efforts on identifying and excluding those we deem less resilient will certainly retard this potential. The contents of this book rightly focus on achieving these goals by addressing two major areas: understanding the nature and determinants of resilience in military settings, and describing methods and techniques for building resilience. Although it can be argued that resilience is a somewhat nebulous construct that has many definitions, the present volume tackles this problem by attempting to inform an improved definition for the betterment of both military personnel and their families. As advances in military resilience are realized, we must never forget that military service is fundamentally about preparing for and fighting and winning our nation's wars, which is achieved through teamwork and leadership.

Colonel Carl A. Castro, PhD
Director, Military Operational Medicine Research Program
U.S. Army Medical Research and Materiel Command
Fort Detrick, Maryland

ACKNOWLEDGMENTS

We wish to acknowledge the important contributions made by Donald McCreary of Defence Research and Development Canada and Maureen Adams of the American Psychological Association. Don had the original idea for this book and identified many of the authors who contributed chapters. We are grateful to Don for his vision in conceiving of the need for this volume and his leadership in getting it off the ground. Maureen played a critical role in helping us shape Don's vision into this final product. Without them, this book would not have been possible.

Building Psychological Resilience in Military Personnel

1

INTRODUCTION: THE MEANING AND IMPORTANCE OF MILITARY RESILIENCE

THOMAS W. BRITT, ROBERT R. SINCLAIR, AND ANNA C. McFADDEN

Combat deployments in Iraq and Afghanistan at the beginning of the 21st century have demonstrated the toll that exposure to traumatic events can take on a service member's psychological and physical functioning. Up to 30% of military personnel returning from combat in Afghanistan and Iraq have been identified as suffering from psychological problems (Hoge, Auchterlonie, & Milliken, 2006; Hoge et al., 2004). As further evidence of the severe mental health consequences of the wars, 281 confirmed suicides across all branches of the armed services were reported by the Department of Defense in 2010. Of that total, 147 suicides and 413 suicide attempts were reported by the U.S. Army. Of those who committed suicide, roughly 62% had a history of deployment, with a smaller percentage (14.3%) having experienced direct combat (Kinn et al., 2011).

Deployed military personnel are exposed to a much wider range of acute and chronic stressors than is the general population. Personnel engaged in

http://dx.doi.org/10.1037/14190-001
Building Psychological Resilience in Military Personnel: Theory and Practice, R. R. Sinclair and T. W. Britt (Editors)

combat operations face a wide range of traumatic or potentially traumatic events, including being shot at, knowing someone who has been injured or killed, seeing dead bodies or human remains, witnessing atrocities, and seeing ill or injured civilians (including children). Combat exposure has been associated with a high risk of developing different mental health problems, including post-traumatic stress disorder (PTSD), depression, and substance abuse/dependence (e.g., Hoge et al., 2004; Kessler, Sonnega, Bromet, Hughes, & Nelson, 1995). Additionally, soldiers experienced an increase in combat exposure from 2009 to 2010 in Operation Iraqi Freedom and Operation Enduring Freedom (Joint Mental Health Advisory Team 7, 2011), placing them at even greater risk of developing such problems.

Combat deployments affect not only service members but their families as well. Lester et al. (2010) found that at-home female civilian parents reported increased symptoms of global distress, anxiety, and depression at a greater rate than the community norm, but anxiety levels were lower for those whose spouse had recently returned. Furthermore, wives of deployed U.S. Army soldiers have been found to be at increased risk for mental health diagnoses (e.g., anxiety, depression, sleep and adjustment disorders) and to make more medical visits for their diagnosis (Mansfield et al., 2010). Gorman, Eide, and Hisle-Gorman (2010) found that while a parent was deployed, children were 11% more likely to be seen in an outpatient mental or behavioral health care setting. Additionally, diagnoses of pediatric behavioral disorders increased by 18%, and diagnoses of pediatric stress disorders increased by 19%.

Given that military personnel deployed to combat environments experience multiple traumatic events that are likely to compromise health, well-being, and performance, military psychologists have developed great interest in understanding the factors that are associated with resilience in the face of these incredible demands. Colloquially, resilience is often viewed as the ability to "bounce back" following stressful events. Researchers have attempted to develop more precise definitions of resilience, but a universally accepted definition has not been adopted. Instead, resilience has been defined and measured in many different ways (Fikretoglu & McCreary, 2012; Meredith et al., 2011). As discussed in more detail later in this chapter, in the present volume we define resilience as *the demonstration of positive adaptation after exposure to significant adversity.*

The present volume embodies two major goals. The first is to bring together researchers who have studied resilience among military personnel and their families to highlight the ways resilience has been defined and describe the factors that contribute to resilience in these important populations. Although multiple definitions of resilience have been offered, enough commonality exists among them to provide the reader with some clarity regarding what constitutes resilience. Furthermore, the chapters in the present volume identify a number of personal, social, and unit factors that have been posited to predict resilience in military personnel and their families. Therefore, the reader should come away with a better understanding of how resilience is conceptualized and assessed, as well as a great awareness of the factors that predict resilience among military personnel and their families.

The second major goal for the volume is to highlight applied interventions that have been developed to increase levels of resilience in service members and their families. The reader will see that although researchers differ on their precise definitions of resilience, a consensus exists regarding the factors that contribute to positive adaptation in the face of adversity (e.g., realistic optimism, flexible coping strategies, effective communication). Several training programs have been developed to enhance those factors associated with resilience. Although the evaluation of these training programs is just beginning, researchers and practitioners are starting to obtain evidence that resilience can be enhanced through training and interventions. The reader will have a better appreciation for what these training programs target and how they are expected to increase the resilience of military personnel and their families.

In the remainder of this introduction, we first discuss the proliferation of definitions of resilience, provide a justification for the definition of resilience we use in the present volume, and highlight how that definition applies to military personnel and their families. We then provide a framework for understanding the determinants of resilience in military personnel and their families, along with a brief description of how the chapters in this volume fit within this framework. Finally, we illustrate how the present volume is related to but distinct from other books that have recently been published within the fields of military and deployment psychology. This discussion highlights how the present volume is relevant to multiple audiences, including researchers in the field of military psychology and psychiatry, clinicians who treat military personnel with mental health problems, leaders and policymakers within the armed services, and members of the general public who have an interest in understanding and promoting resilience in the face of extreme levels of stress.

DEFINING RESILIENCE

Most people have at least some informal understanding of the term *resilience*. However, informal definitions do not always involve the level of consensus necessary to drive good science. Resilience is one of many terms (e.g., *engagement*, *sustainability*, *diversity*, *dynamics*) that researchers use in different ways and with varying levels of precision, leading to studies of very different phenomena under the same broad label. Such terminological diversity leads to research "silos," which represent a substantial barrier to the advancement of science because they slow the rate at which knowledge can accumulate about a phenomenon. Thus, it is important to search for some level of consensus on what researchers mean by the term *resilience*.

In a recent review of the conceptual and measurement issues in resilience, Fikretoglu and McCreary (2012) took on the challenging but important task of defining resilience and clarifying several conceptual issues related to the resilience construct. They traced the historical development of the resilience concept from research examining children who were able to overcome adversity (e.g., having a schizophrenic or alcoholic parent, living in an economically disadvantaged environment) to the current emphasis on identifying the processes through which personal and environmental factors contribute to healthy functioning under adversity.

Fikretoglu and McCreary (2012) reviewed a number of definitions of resilience (see also Meredith et al., 2011, for a table of 104 definitions of resilience). They noted that most highlighted an individual showing signs of positive adaptation after having gone through adversity, which they identified as the two defining characteristics of resilience. However, Fikretoglu and McCreary noted that prior researchers have been inconsistent in how they treat the two main components of the definition of resilience: how to quantify going through "adversity" and what precisely is meant by "positive adaptation."

In the present volume, we concur with the defining characteristics identified by Fikretoglu and McCreary (2012) and define resilience as the demonstration of positive adaptation in the face of significant adversity. Our definition highlights that resilience is a response to stressful circumstances (e.g., a demonstration of positive adaptation), rather than a trait, disposition, or capacity residing within the individual. Although certain personality traits (e.g., hardiness, optimism) may be associated with resilience (see Chapter 2 of this volume), these traits do not constitute resilience itself. To further justify our definition of resilience, we address how the key components of the definition (significant adversity and positive adaptation) have been addressed by researchers investigating resilience among military personnel and their families.

The first question to be addressed in applying our definition to military personnel and their families involves what constitutes significant adversity. Fikretoglu and McCreary (2012) noted that some researchers have defined adversity in terms of exposure to a single traumatic event with a relatively short duration (Bonanno, Westphal, & Mancini, 2011), whereas other authors have defined adversity in terms of exposure to multiple stressful events that may or may not have reached the threshold of being traumatic (Luthar, Cicchetti, & Becker, 2000). When studying resilience among military personnel, researchers have highlighted that service members are often exposed to multiple traumatic events during a combat deployment and at the same time have to continuously deal with an underlying malevolent environment (Castro & Adler, 2011). Therefore, the chapters in the present volume discuss resilience within the context of exposure to multiple discrete traumatic events (e.g., combat exposure), as well as more continuous and low-level stressors (e.g., length of deployment, living in an austere environment). Given the stressors encountered by military personnel and their families, there is little doubt that they are frequently exposed to significant adversity.

A more challenging aspect of the definition of resilience guiding the present volume is how researchers have conceptualized positive adaptation. Fikretoglu and McCreary (2012) noted that authors have focused on the extent and duration of psychological distress following exposure to stressful events, as well as on which domains should be assessed when confirming that adaptation has occurred. With regard to the extent and duration of distress-related indices of adaptation, Mancini and Bonanno (2010) argued that resilience exists when the individual is exposed to a highly stressful event and shows only "mild-moderate" signs of distress that do not interfere with the individual's overall level of functioning before he or she returns to a baseline level of distress. Fikretoglu and McCreary noted the lack of precision regarding this definition's ability to adequately distinguish between various levels of severity, in terms both of level of distress and of level of functional impairment.

With regard to the duration of time that psychological distress is experienced, Fikretoglu and McCreary (2012) noted that researchers have yet to offer specific requirements for how quickly individuals must return to baseline functioning before they can be classified as resilient. Within the context of resilience in military personnel, Fikretoglu and McCreary noted that PTSD-related psychological distress does not become fully apparent until some months following combat exposure (Bliese, Wright, Adler, Thomas, & Hoge, 2007). Therefore, charting the course of recovery among military personnel may include nonlinear components.

The authors in the present volume have not provided specific cutoff scores to clearly indicate when an individual has adapted positively following exposure to significant adversity; nor have these authors followed military personnel and their families for repeated assessments after exposure to significant adversity and assessed the proportion of service members who return to baseline levels of functioning to index positive adaptation. Instead, researchers frequently compare the symptoms of military personnel who have experienced significant adversity based upon a hypothesized protective factor, such as positive leadership or a particular personality trait, and examine whether the protective factor results in lower symptoms under high levels of adversity. Researchers are beginning to assess both psychological distress and functional impairment when examining how personality factors (i.e., optimism) might protect service members from the negative consequences of combat exposure (Thomas, Britt, Odle-Dusseau, & Bliese, 2011).

Fikretoglu and McCreary (2012) noted that prior researchers have differed in terms of the specific domains in which individuals have to demonstrate positive adaptation to be considered resilient. For example, should only those individuals demonstrating adaptation in all life domains (e.g., family, work, job, psychological health) following adversity be classified as resilient, or is adaptation required only in domains related to psychological health? Within the context of resilience among military personnel, Adler, Britt, Castro, McGurk, and Bliese (2011) noted that service members face transition challenges in multiple domains following a combat deployment and that adaptation may occur in some of these domains but not others. In the chapters included in the present volume, most authors have addressed positive adaptation in terms of decreased psychological and physical symptoms in the face of significant adversity.

In summary, our definition of resilience is consistent with the broader research literature on the construct, and it does a good job of cutting across resilience as considered by the different authors of the present volume. The authors in the present volume are consistent in viewing resilience as the demonstration of positive adaptation in the presence of significant adversity, but they differ in the types of adversity addressed and how positive adaptation is defined.

A FRAMEWORK FOR STUDYING RESILIENCE

Given the magnitude of the stressors military personnel face, it would seem especially important to investigate those factors that promote resilience in this group, and we might expect to see a large and well-developed literature on resilience in military samples. However, a review of the literature reveals that this is not necessarily the case. Using PsycINFO, we conducted key term searches on the terms *resilience* and *resilience AND military*, limiting the search to articles published in peer-reviewed journals in each year between 2000 and 2010. As shown in Table 1.1, resilience has received a great deal of interest from psychological scholars, with more than 4,000 citations between 2000 and 2010. Moreover, the number of citations has increased each year, with the exception of a slight dip between 2005 and 2006. The increase was fairly dramatic over the course of the decade, with 130 studies in 2000 and 679 in 2010.

TABLE 1.1
Resilience Citation Counts in PsycINFO: 2000–2010

Year	Resilience[a]	Resilience and military[b]
2010	679	36
2009	600	19
2008	593	22
2007	519	17
2006	354	11
2005	362	11
2004	333	5
2003	241	5
2002	197	3
2001	152	4
2000	130	3

Note. [a]PsycINFO search on the key term *resilience* was limited to articles published in peer-reviewed journals in the indicated year. [b]PsycINFO search on the key terms *resilience* and *military* was limited to articles published in peer-reviewed journals in the indicated year.

The military studies show some different trends. First, there were only 136 studies on resilience in the military over the course of the decade, a small percentage of the cumulative total. However, 94 of the 136 (69%) references were in the last 4 years of the decade, indicating a strong trend of growing interest in the topic. These data should be viewed as illustrative rather than definitive because different key term searches might reveal different patterns of results and would no doubt reveal more citations on pertinent topics; additionally, it is important to note that the review does not include data sources not indexed in PsycINFO. But the results clearly show widespread and growing research interest in the topic of resilience. Although there are relatively few military studies overall, there appears to be rapid growth in military research on resilience in the last few years. Notable research trends within the study of military resilience include the identification of personality traits associated with resilience, the role of coping strategies and positive emotions in increasing resilience, and ways to build resilience. These research trends are represented in the chapters comprised by the present volume.

Figure 1.1 presents an organizing framework for the key questions we set out to address in this book. This framework is based on the soldier adaptation model (Bliese & Castro, 2003), a meta-theoretical framework often used as a guide for military stress research. The framework presents a representation of resilience-related processes where soldiers' appraisal and coping responses influence the outcomes the soldiers experience from potentially demanding events (e.g., combat). This process is influenced both by the individual characteristics of the soldiers and by characteristics of their

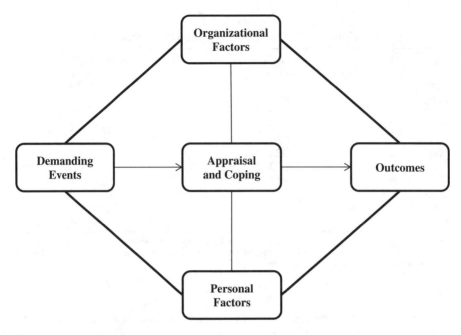

Figure 1.1. A framework for the study of military resilience.

organization, including their particular units and the broader military environ-ment. Each of these boxes includes numerous factors, and our goal here is not to describe specific hypotheses about the possible relationships among all of these factors. Rather, we highlight how the different chapters in the present volume address different aspects of this overall model.

With regard to the section of the model addressing how organizational factors influence how demanding events impact important outcomes, several chapters in our volume examine how organizational attributes such as unit cohesion, leadership, and climate serve as risk or protective factors for soldiers' mental health (e.g., Chapters 3, 4, and 5). In these chapters, the benefits of such factors as high unit cohesion and strong leadership for the demonstration of resilience are hypothesized to be a function of the effects of the organiza-tional factors on the ways in which military personnel appraise and cope with the stressful demands they encounter. For example, Chapters 3 and 4 high-light how high levels of unit cohesion enable military personnel to appraise highly stressful events in a more adaptive manner and how such levels of unit cohesion provide them with social resources to cope with the demands they encounter.

Considering the section of the model addressing personal factors, several chapters in the volume examine how factors residing within the individual contribute to resilience, including personality traits, morale, attitudes, and beliefs (Chapters 2, 3, and 6). As is the case with organizational factors, chapter authors emphasizing personal factors associated with resilience highlight appraisal of and coping with stressful events as important mediators of how these factors confer resilience. For example, Chapter 2 highlights how personality variables such as hardiness ultimately influence resilience through their association with adaptive appraisals and coping strategies.

Finally, the chapters in the present volume that focus on interventions and training to increase resilience attempt either to increase the personal and organizational factors that have been associated with resilience (Chapters 6, 7, and 8) or to directly affect the appraisals and coping strategies that are enacted upon exposure to demanding conditions (Chapter 9). Therefore, all of the chapters herein touch upon at least one of the elements in Figure 1.1, and the model provides a useful framework for organizing the different approaches to resilience being presented. More information is provided in the next section on the unique issues addressed in each of the chapters.

THE PRESENT VOLUME

Both the research and the citation data we have reviewed demonstrate what most readers probably already recognize: The topic of resilience is of considerable importance in the military context. Three other books published by the American Psychological Association have taken on similar topics, and we encourage readers to review all three. Adler, Bliese, and Castro (2011) edited a book titled *Deployment Psychology: Evidence-Based Strategies to Promote Mental Health in the Military*. Similarly, Moore and Kennedy (2010) published an authored volume titled *Wheels Down: Adjusting to Life After Deployment*. Finally, Ruzek, Schnurr, Vasterling, and Friedman (2011) published an edited book titled *Caring for Veterans With Deployment-Related Stress Disorders: Iraq, Afghanistan, and Beyond*. All of these books address issues related to mental health and military deployments, and thus they and this book have some similar features. However, there also are important differences. The Moore and Kennedy book has a primary audience of military service members who have experienced deployments, rather than an academic or practitioner audience. The Adler et al. book focused on evidence-based mental health interventions related to the deployment transition process. Ruzek et al. (2011) focused on stress-related disorders commonly experienced by deployed military personnel rather than on resilience per se.

As discussed above, this book was designed to accomplish two goals. First, we wanted to summarize the current state of the literature on military resilience, with particular regard to defining resilience and discussing personal, social, and organizational factors that influence resilience within the military work context. The first half of the book addresses this set of issues, with chapters that offer reviews of concepts, models, and measures related to resilience. Most of this literature emphasizes resilience in occupational settings rather than in other contexts, such as child development. From a theoretical perspective, these chapters may be viewed as identifying antecedents of resilience that are significant in the military context. From a practical perspective, they may be viewed as identifying some of the critical processes that military organizations must address in order to develop and maintain resilience in military personnel.

Second, we wanted to discuss practical programs to develop and maintain resilience among military personnel. Several military organizations are currently implementing intervention programs that have the expressed or implicit goal of developing resilience. The second half of the book describes some of these programs, as well as some best practices and critical concepts in resilience-related intervention. Although our primary focus is on the military, we are confident that the lessons learned from the research and programs reviewed are widely applicable to other settings, particularly to other workers (e.g., law enforcement, paramedics, nurses) who face potentially traumatic stressors.

As noted above in the section on defining resilience, one of the potentially confusing issues about resilience concerns whether it is an element of one's character, a particular pattern of reaction to adverse circumstances, or both. Although the term *resilience* is relatively new and somewhat less frequently studied than other aspects of the stress-response process, individual differences in reactions to stressors have a long research history in psychology. No discussion of resilience would be complete without some discussion of resilience-related personality traits. In Chapter 2, Sinclair, Waitsman, Oliver, and Deese review research on several models of traits potentially related to resilience. Some of these models have received a great deal of attention from military researchers; others have received almost none. Sinclair et al. point out that these models share similarities that are not always widely recognized, and they show that each model contributes some unique ideas to the understanding of dispositional aspects of resilience.

In Chapter 3, Britt and Oliver discuss unit morale and cohesion as critical influences on both unit functioning and soldier resilience. These constructs have a long history of attention by military scholars, although perhaps with less of a historical focus on how they might be related to mental health concerns. Britt and Oliver address this gap by providing a detailed review of each construct, presenting a theoretical rationale linking each to resilience, and offering a research agenda for future studies on morale and cohesion.

Several decades of industrial/organizational (I/O) psychology research shows how situational features at work (sometimes referred to as work organization or work design) can influence outcomes such as job attitudes, performance, and retention. More recently, occupational health psychology (OHP) has begun to address some of the health-related implications of these factors. However, I/O and OHP have paid somewhat less attention to mental health outcomes of interest to military scholars and military leaders (e.g., PTSD, depression). In Chapter 4, Jex, Kain, and Park bridge this gap by discussing three workplace situational factors related to resilience in the military: organizational culture, training programs, and social support. Jex et al. provide a conceptual discussion of each construct and illustrate some of the potential military applications of each.

Leadership is a critical issue in the military, and military scholars have contributed greatly to the understanding of leadership in civilian organizations. Military leaders face extreme situations where their lives, as well as the lives of civilians and members of their units, may be either threatened or saved by their actions. Although leadership is certainly among the most heavily studied topics in applied psychology (as well as other disciplines outside of psychology), the relationship between leadership and resilience has received much less attention in empirical literature, particularly in military settings. MacIntyre, Charbonneau, and O'Keefe address this issue in depth in Chapter 5, discussing how transformational and ethical aspects of leadership may be particularly influential on resilience.

The next set of chapters focuses more explicitly on resilience-related interventions and programs, discussing some of the current best practices and emerging issues with respect to military resilience. The early 21st century could be viewed as a resilience renaissance of sorts, as, largely in response to conflict in the Middle East, the U.S. military and nations contributing personnel to Operations Enduring Freedom and Iraqi Freedom have begun to examine training programs to promote and maintain resilience. As evaluations of these programs begin to appear in the empirical literature, scholars will make tremendous strides in understanding the nature of resilience. Such research will help both military and civilian organizations implement mental health-focused interventions.

Whealin, Ruzek, and Vega in Chapter 6 and Greenberg in Chapter 7 look at resilience-focused intervention programs from different vantage points. Greenberg organizes his discussion around the stages of the deployment cycle, indicating the particular needs and opportunities for intervention at each point of the cycle. Whealin et al. use stress appraisal models as a starting point for discussing interventions aimed at modulating the stress response associated with military stressors. It is interesting to read these chapters together, as they provide a long list of mental health interventions aimed at resilience and/or mental health, including, for example, pre- and postdeployment screening, rehearsal and exposure-focused programs, predeployment education, stress management programs, critical incident stress debriefing, cognitive behavioral therapy, and programs focused on easing the transition back from deployments and into civilian life. Taken together, these chapters provide military organizations with many possible resilience intervention strategies, albeit with varying degrees of empirical support in the military context. Both chapters also highlight some practical considerations with implementing these programs in the unique culture of the military.

Although most resilience research focuses on individuals, Wright, Riviere, Merrill, and Cabrera in Chapter 8 address resilience in military families. Military families face demands that are quite different from those faced by workers in most other occupations, including periods of long separation when service members deploy, challenges of reintegrating service members into families when they return from deployments, and frequent relocations as personnel receive new duty assignments. Wright et al. highlight the point that such changes create many challenges for service members' families. They also discuss the need for additional attention to *family resilience*, in relation both to family constructs and processes and to programs intended to help families cope with the military lifestyle.

In Chapter 9, Lester, McBride, and Cornum discuss the Comprehensive Soldier Fitness (CSF) program. CSF has generated a great deal of interest among applied psychologists, as it represents one of the largest (if not the largest) empirically driven mental-health-related intervention programs that has ever been attempted. Lester et al. provide a valuable overview of the empirical and conceptual foundations of the program, describe the core components of the current CSF program, and respond to some of the criticisms that have been raised about the program. Although CSF was designed to respond to specific concerns about resilience in the U.S. Army, the program has far-reaching implications for soldiers' postmilitary lives, as well as for similar interventions in civilian contexts. CSF is itself a data-driven program. But implementing CSF in a military setting provides the capacity to conduct large-scale assessments of program effectiveness, and we expect the lessons learned from CSF to exert a powerful influence on future resilience research and practice.

We conclude the volume with two chapters focused on the future of resilience research. Chapter 10 consists of commentary from Amy Adler, one of the leading military mental health researchers in the world. Adler offers her unique insights into resilience-related research and intervention, with an eye toward identifying critical but understudied topics related to military resilience. She reinforces and expands on the discussion from other authors about the unique aspects of resilience in the military context as well as some of the potential unanticipated consequences of focusing on resilience. One of the central points she raises is that the military is a unique occupational context for developing and sustaining resilience; she illustrates how a "one size fits all" approach may not work for resilience-focused interventions. She also discusses the dark side of resilience, highlighting potential unintended consequences of and limits to the benefits of focusing on resilience, such as increasing the stigma members feel about seeking treatment for mental health problems. She concludes by highlighting several issues that require further attention from researchers and practitioners, with respect both to designing resilience interventions that meet the needs of military personnel and to conducting solid scientific investigations of those interventions.

In Chapter 11, the volume editors discuss several current themes and future needs in military research. In particular, they address issues that, in their view, are important to military resilience research and have not been effectively addressed to date. Such issues include the need for continued refinement and clarification of the construct of resilience, attention to the relative importance of various personal and situational factors in understanding resilience, continued investigation of the validity of resilience-focused training programs, and the need for greater attention to resilience-related issues as veterans return home and reintegrate into their communities and into the civilian workforce.

REFERENCES

Adler, A. B., Bliese, P. D., & Castro, C. A. (Eds.). (2011). *Deployment psychology: Evidence-based strategies to promote mental health in the military.* Washington, DC: American Psychological Association. doi:10.1037/12300-000

Adler, A. B., Britt, T. W., Castro, C. A., McGurk, D., & Bliese, P. D. (2011). Effect of transition home from combat on risk-taking and health-related behaviors. *Journal of Traumatic Stress, 24,* 381–389. doi:10.1002/jts.20665

Bliese, P. D., & Castro, C. A. (2003). The soldier adaptation model (SAM): Applications to behavioral science peacekeeping research. In T. W. Britt & A. B. Adler (Eds.), *The psychology of the peacekeeper: A multinational perspective* (pp. 185–203). Westport, CT: Praeger.

Bliese, P. D., Wright, K. M., Adler, A. B., Thomas, J. L., & Hoge, C. W. (2007). Timing of postcombat mental health assessments. *Psychological Services, 4,* 141–148. doi:10.1037/1541-1559.4.3.141

Bonanno, G. A., Westphal, M., & Mancini, A. D. (2011). Resilience to loss and potential trauma. *Annual Review of Clinical Psychology, 7,* 511–535. doi:10.1146/annurev-clinpsy-032210-104526

Castro, C. A., & Adler, A. B. (2011). Reconceptualizing combat-related posttraumatic stress disorder as an occupational hazard. In A. B. Adler, P. D. Bliese, & C. A. Castro (Eds.), *Deployment psychology: Evidence-based strategies to promote mental health in the military* (pp. 217–242). Washington, DC: American Psychological Association. doi:10.1037/12300-009

Fikretoglu, D., & McCreary, D. R. (2012). *Psychological resilience: A brief review of definitions, and key theoretical, conceptual, and methodological issues* (Technical Report 2012-012). Toronto, Ontario, Canada: Defence R&D Canada.

Gorman, G. H., Eide, M., & Hisle-Gorman, E. (2010). Wartime military deployment and increased pediatric mental and behavioral health complaints. *Pediatrics, 126*, 1058–1066. doi:10.1542/peds.2009-2856

Hoge, C. W., Auchterlonie, J. L., & Milliken, C. S. (2006). Mental health problems, use of mental health services, and attrition from military service after returning from deployment to Iraq or Afghanistan. *JAMA, 295*, 1023–1032. doi:10.1001/jama.295.9.1023

Hoge, C. W., Castro, C. A., Messer, S. C., McGurk, D., Cotting, D. I., & Koffman, R. L. (2004). Combat duty in Iraq and Afghanistan, mental health problems, and barriers to care. *The New England Journal of Medicine, 351*, 13–22. doi:10.1056/NEJMoa040603

Joint Mental Health Advisory Team 7. (2011). *Operation Enduring Freedom 2010 and Afghanistan*. Retrieved from http://www.armymedicine.army.mil/reports/mhat/mhat_vii/J_MHAT_7.pdf

Kessler, R. C., Sonnega, A., Bromet, E., Hughes, M., & Nelson, C. B. (1995). Post-traumatic stress disorder in the National Comorbidity Survey. *Archives of General Psychiatry, 52*, 1048–1060. doi:10.1001/archpsyc.1995.03950240066012

Kinn, J. T., Luxton, D. D., Reger, M. A., Gahm, G. A., Skopp, N. A., & Bush, N. E. (2011). *Department of Defense suicide event report: Calendar year 2010 annual report*. Tacoma, WA: National Center for Telehealth and Technology.

Lester, P., Peterson, K., Reeves, J., Knauss, L., Glover, D., Mogil, C., . . . Beardslee, W. (2010). The long war and parental combat deployment: Effects on military children and at-home spouses. *Journal of the American Academy of Child & Adolescent Psychiatry, 49*, 310–320. doi:10.1016/j.jaacap.201.01.003

Luthar, S. S., Cicchetti, D., & Becker, B. (2000). The construct of resilience: A critical evaluation and guidelines for future work. *Child Development, 71*, 543–562. doi:10.1111/1467-8624.00164

Mancini, A. D., & Bonanno, G. A. (2010). Resilience to potential trauma: Toward a life span approach. In J. W. Reich, A. J. Zautra, & J. Hall (Eds.), *Handbook of adult resilience: Concepts, methods, and applications* (pp. 258–282). New York, NY: Guilford Press.

Mansfield, A. J., Kaufman, J. S., Marshall, S. W., Gaynes, B. N., Morrissey, J. P., & Engel, C. C. (2010). Deployment and the use of mental health services among U.S. Army wives. *The New England Journal of Medicine, 362*, 101–109. doi:10.1056/NEJMoa0900177

Meredith, L. S., Sherbourne, C. D., Gaillot, S., J., Hansell, L., Ritschard, H. V., Parker, A. M., & Wrenn, G. (2011). *Promoting psychological resilience in the U.S. military*. Retrieved from http://www.rand.org/pubs/monographs/MG996.html

Moore, B. A., & Kennedy, C. H. (Eds.). (2010). *Wheels down: Adjusting to life after deployment*. Washington, DC: American Psychological Association.

Ruzek, J. I., Schnurr, P. P., Vasterling, J. J., & Friedman, M. J. (Eds.). (2011). *Caring for veterans with deployment-related stress disorders: Iraq, Afghanistan, and beyond.* Washington, DC: American Psychological Association. doi:10.1037/12323-000

Tedeschi, R. D., & McNally, R. J. (2011). Can we facilitate posttraumatic growth in combat veterans? *American Psychologist, 66,* 19–24. doi:10.1037/a0021896

Thomas, J. L., Britt, T. W., Odle-Dusseau, H., & Bliese, P. D. (2011). Dispositional optimism buffers combat veterans from the negative effects of warzone stress on mental health symptoms and work impairment. *Journal of Clinical Psychology, 67,* 866–880. doi:10.1002/jclp.20809

I

UNDERSTANDING RESILIENCE: PERSONAL AND ORGANIZATIONAL DETERMINANTS

2

PERSONALITY AND PSYCHOLOGICAL RESILIENCE IN MILITARY PERSONNEL

ROBERT R. SINCLAIR, MELISSA C. WAITSMAN,
CELINA M. OLIVER, AND MARILYN NICOLE DEESE

People differ considerably in how they respond to potentially stressful events. Although some develop serious mental and physical health problems, others report few or no adverse effects. Some may report personal growth following exposure to stressors (Tedeschi & McNally, 2011), and experiencing adversity may be important for optimal functioning (Seery, 2011). Veterans of combat deployments show all of these patterns. They have higher rates of mental health problems than comparable civilian populations do (Hoge et al., 2004), and those with mental health problems are more likely to engage in maladaptive behaviors, such as reckless driving, substance use, and aggression (Riviere, Merrill, Wilk, Edens, & Adler, 2010; Thomas et al., 2010). However, the same studies show that most service members exposed to traumatic events do not report severe mental health problems. In other words, even as rates of reported mental problems are distressingly high, substantial

We gratefully acknowledge David Cadiz, Carie McClendon, Nisreen Pedhiwala, Brett Roberts, and Michelle Tamanaha for their assistance in the preparation of this chapter.

http://dx.doi.org/10.1037/14190-002
Building Psychological Resilience in Military Personnel: Theory and Practice, R. R. Sinclair and T. W. Britt (Editors)

numbers of combat-exposed military personnel still appear to be resilient. Thus, there is a need for continued examination of risk factors for mental health problems and for research focused on why most service members do not develop mental health problems when exposed to stressors.

Personality factors likely play a critical role in explaining these differences. However, until relatively recently, personality has not received much attention from military researchers interested in resilience. Moreover, the general applied personality literature resides in multiple silos, such that researchers aware of concepts from one body of research might not be aware of how similar ideas have been studied under different labels. With these concerns in mind, our general goals in this chapter are to review several personality concepts and models likely to be related to military resilience and to discuss several issues that, in our view, need more attention in this literature.

The scientific literature on personality and the stress-response process is vast. In a recent electronic search, we found over 5,000 references with the keywords *personality* and *stress* and nearly 4,000 references with the keywords *personality* and *health*. A complete review of this literature is well beyond the scope of this chapter. Rather, we seek to highlight some central themes in the literature in order to better understand individual differences in resilience in the military context. In doing so, we seek to address what Block (1995) referred to as the jingle and jangle fallacies in personality research. Block noted that personality research is characterized by multiple researchers using the same term to describe different ideas (the "jingle fallacy") and by researchers using multiple terms to refer to the same core idea (the "jangle fallacy"). The jingle and jangle fallacies are important concerns in resilience research, although there also appears to be some convergence on core understandings about individual differences in resilience. We review several models that reflect this convergence to varying degrees and offer several directions for continued research on personality and resilience.

As noted in Chapter 1 of this volume, the definition of resilience continues to be a vexing problem for resilience research, largely because the term *resilience* is used in many different ways. This is particularly true with regard to the relationship between personality and resilience. As we discuss in detail below, some authors define resilience as a specific personality trait or cluster of traits, whereas others view resilience as a particular pattern of outcomes following exposure to stressful circumstances. In this chapter we adopt a view consistent with the definition offered in Chapter 1, that resilience reflects positive adaptation following exposure to adversity. Thus, in our view, personality traits and processes are antecedents of resilience rather than elements of resilience. We would expect personality to help explain differences between people who, when exposed to traumatic stressors, show few adverse health outcomes and those who, when exposed to traumatic stressors, experience adverse health outcomes. We note that the traits we review are not uniquely important to resilience; they are also likely related to patterns such as recovery and growth as well as other work outcomes such as job performance and job attitudes.

PERSONALITY, MILITARY STRESSORS, AND RESILIENCE

Funder (2001) defined *personality* as "an individual's characteristic patterns of thought, emotion, and behavior, together with the psychological mechanisms behind those patterns" (p. 2). Historically, many aspects of personality were assumed to be set in stone by early adulthood. Applied to resilience research, this suggests a general approach of studying personality traits as unchanging risk/protective factors that influence people's reactions to stressors. However, research indicates that people often continue to experience at least some personality changes throughout their lives (Roberts & Del Vecchio, 2000), at least in part due to work experiences (Roberts, Wood, Caspi, & Moffitt, 2008). Thus, it is important to recognize that Funder's definition encompasses a wide array of constructs that vary in their assumed stability over time, susceptibility to developmental change, heritability, and cross-situational stability. Accordingly, the scientific study of personality encompasses a wide range of approaches, including evolutionary models focusing on common patterns of behavior across the human species, biologically based traits reflecting inherited behavioral tendencies, characteristic ways in which people respond to situations, and even personal life stories (McAdams & Pals, 2006).

The soldier adaptation model (SAM; Bliese & Castro, 2003) provides a useful framework for conceptualizing the multiple potential effects of stressors on military personnel and, thus, for constructing general propositions about how personality traits might be related to resilience. The SAM includes three central components: potential stressors, strains, and outcomes. *Potential stressors* are events that require an adaptive response. For deployed soldiers, potential stressors include demands such as separation from family, physical danger, boredom, and extended work hours (Adler, Litz, & Bartone, 2003). *Strains* are the set of negative responses to stressors. Strains may be cognitive (e.g., distractibility, memory impairment), affective (e.g., irritability, emotional exhaustion), physical (e.g., fatigue, insomnia), or behavioral (e.g., withdrawal, substance abuse). Finally, *outcomes* refers to the consequences of strain including physical illness, decreased performance, accidents, injuries, and poor morale.

Drawing from cognitive appraisal models of stress (e.g., Lazarus & Folkman, 1984), the SAM framework suggests that people experience higher levels of strain when the perceived demands of an event exceed an individual's coping resources and/or when individuals choose maladaptive coping responses. Service members with higher levels of resilience-related traits should be less likely to appraise events as stressful, should have less intense negative emotional reactions to stressors, should perceive higher levels of social support when under stress, and should be more likely to choose effective coping strategies (Mancini & Bonanno, 2009).

Although it has received less attention in applied psychological research, reappraisal, a process through which individuals come to reevaluate potential stressors after a period of time has passed, is also discussed by Lazarus and Folkman (1984). Reappraisal may be particularly important in the study of military resilience. For example, once they have returned home after a deployment, service members may appraise their deployment experiences differently than they would in the heat of the moment. Some may see their deployment experiences as beneficial; others may conclude that the same experiences were threatening or harmful. As we discuss below, some research shows that resilience-related personality traits likely play a role in the reappraisal process (Britt, Adler, & Bartone, 2001).

Researchers have drawn from three broad approaches to identify traits potentially related to resilience: all-inclusive taxonomies, such as the five-factor model; composite trait models, which integrate several traits but are not necessarily intended to encompass all aspects of personality; and single traits, which either stem from the all-inclusive or composite models or have evolved as relatively separate research traditions. We provide an overview of each approach and a selective discussion of research from each body of literature.

Inclusive Taxonomies: The Five-Factor Model

The five-factor model of personality (FFM, Big Five model, OCEAN model) is the most widely used broad personality framework. The FFM emerged from the lexical tradition in personality research, which suggests that the fundamental dimensions of personality are encoded in terms people use to describe themselves and others (Wiggins, 1996). After decades of study, lexical researchers concluded that most personality-related variation between individuals can be captured by five broad dimensions: neuroticism, extraversion, agreeableness, openness to experience, and conscientiousness, with each broad dimension composed of several specific facets (Costa & McRae, 1992). High scorers on *neuroticism* (i.e., low emotional stability) tend to be impulsive, self-conscious, and prone to negative emotions such as depression, anger, and anxiety. *Extraverts* tend to experience more positive emotions and to be outgoing, assertive, and energetic. *Agreeable* people are more trusting, helpful, modest, and kind. People with higher levels of *openness to experience* tend to be more imaginative, humorous, and interested in arts, culture, and unconventional ideas. Finally, *conscientious* people are hardworking, organized, responsible, self-disciplined, and dutiful.

The FFM has widespread, although not complete (cf. Block, 1995), acceptance among personality and organizational psychologists. Reasons for its popularity include the substantial empirical support for FFM traits as predictors of work behavior (Sinclair & Tucker, 2006) and the availability of many well-validated FFM instruments. Heritability research also suggests a strong genetic contribution to each FFM dimension (Bouchard & McGue, 2003), and evidence continues to accumulate regarding the biological basis of the FFM traits (McAdams & Pals, 2006), supporting their treatment as "core" individual differences. Although all of the FFM dimensions may be related to stress and health outcomes of service members, we focus our discussion on three of the FFM traits with strong and conceptually distinct relationships to stress and health outcomes: neuroticism, extraversion, and conscientiousness.

People who score higher on measures of neuroticism are typically described as being emotionally reactive and prone to experience negative affect (NA). Lahey (2009) characterized the importance of neuroticism to public health as "profound" (p. 241), given the size of the literature linking neuroticism to mental and physical health outcomes, health behaviors, and stress reactivity in a wide range of populations. George (1992) suggested two effects of trait NA on stress. People who are higher in NA seem to be more susceptible to stimuli that generate negative emotions, and, as a result, they are more likely to experience strong negative reactions to demanding events. Because individuals with high NA can be unpleasant to work with, they may also have less coworker support and experience more stressful interpersonal relationships (Smith & Zautra, 2002). A growing body of military literature has implicated neuroticism as a factor linked to posttraumatic stress disorder (PTSD) among military veterans (Engelhard & van den Hout, 2007; Rademaker, van Zuiden, Vermetten, & Geuze, 2011; Talbert, Braswell, Albrecht, Hyer, & Boudewyns, 1993) as well as health behavior (Booth-Kewley & Vickers, 1994) and other stress-related outcomes (Roesch, Aldridge, Vickers, & Helvig, 2009).

Whereas people higher in neuroticism are more likely to experience NA, extraverts are disposed to experience positive emotional states/positive affect (PA). High PA affects health outcomes through several pathways: Those who experience more positive emotional states are typically more self-confident, have stronger social support and higher quality social relationships, choose more adaptive coping responses, and have better physical health (Lyubomirsky, King, & Diener, 2005). Research also has established that PA and NA are distinct—people may be high or low on both, either, or neither of these traits (cf. Watson, Clark, & Tellegen, 1988). One explanation for this distinction is that PA and NA reflect different biologically based motivational systems that concern susceptibilities to rewards (PA) and punishments (NA; George, 1992). Military studies have shown that extraverts are more likely to experience positive emotions (Roesch et al., 2009), engage in better health behavior

(Booth-Kewley & Vickers, 1994), and have more favorable mental health outcomes (Eurelings-Bontekoe, Verschuur, Koudstaal, van der Sar, & Duijsens, 1995; Sümer & Sümer, 2007). Although this literature is sparse, these findings track with a large body of research on the benefits of PA and a growing body of civilian research linking positive emotions to resilience (Mancini & Bonanno, 2009).

Conscientiousness is increasingly recognized as an important factor in health-related studies, including those in a military context (e.g., Booth-Kewley & Vickers, 1994; Marshall, Wortman, Vickers, Kusulas, & Hervig, 1994; Sümer & Sümer, 2007). There are several reasons to expect that conscientiousness should be related to resilience. First, conscientious individuals tend to be hardworking and persistent. Persistent individuals are more likely to view job demands as challenges than as threats and are therefore less likely to withdraw from demanding situations (Hochwarter, Kent, & Perrewé, 1993). Conscientious individuals typically have higher levels of self-control, which helps them regulate their activities while under stress (Baumeister, 2001). Finally, conscientious individuals are more likely to engage in healthy patterns of behavior (Bogg & Roberts, 2004). Individuals who are physically healthy and persistent and have strong self-control should be better able to withstand the negative effects of potentially stressful circumstances.

Composite Trait Models

Composite trait models, sometimes referred to as syndromes, examine clusters of traits that share some conceptual and empirical similarities but that are not all-inclusive frameworks. These models differ in their hypothesized effects on resilience and the extent to which they focus on modifiable attributes. Whereas the FFM traits are viewed as broad dispositional constructs, the composite traits reviewed below fit what McAdams and Pals (2006) described as *characteristic adaptations*, or typical ways in which people learn to respond to their environments that vary across cultures and situations. Three such models have received a great deal of attention, albeit with differing levels of focus on stress, health, and resilience. These models are core self-evaluations, hardiness, and psychological capital.

Core Self-Evaluations

Judge and colleagues (e.g., Judge, Locke, & Durham, 1997) proposed the idea of core self-evaluations (CSEs) and subsequently created a CSE measure (Judge, Erez, Bono, & Thoresen, 2003) as part of an effort to develop a dispositional explanation for job attitudes. Judge et al. (1997) described CSEs as a second-order construct reflecting four commonly studied individual differences:

self-esteem, generalized self-efficacy, locus of control, and emotional stability. CSE research uses three basic inclusion criteria for such traits as part of CSE: They are self-evaluative in nature (i.e., rather than being descriptions of behaviors), they are fundamental (i.e., central) to the self-concept, and they are broad in scope rather than being domain/role-specific evaluations (cf. C.-H. Chang, Ferris, Johnson, Rosen, & Tan, 2012). Indeed, a large literature supports C.-H. Chang et al.'s (2012) view that the constituent parts of CSE are typically highly correlated with each other and show similar patterns of relationships to job satisfaction. Subsequent research has also linked CSE to several other outcomes, including stronger attachment to one's organization, better job performance, and higher life satisfaction (C.-H. Chang et al., 2012). C.-H. Chang et al. also described some of the concerns and controversies related to CSE; interested readers will find their review to be a useful guide to the CSE literature.

The general conceptual link between CSEs and stress appraisals is straightforward. Individuals with higher CSEs feel in control of their lives, are optimistic about their future, believe they can successfully complete tasks, and are less prone to negative emotions. Judge et al. (1997) proposed that such individuals should have more favorable appraisals of their job situation and themselves, and these appraisals should be related to how they respond to situations they appraise as stressful. Luria and Torjman (2009) found, consistent with this view, that Israeli Defense Forces recruits with higher CSEs reported less perceived stress following exposure to intense stressors. Their study is one of only a few that has investigated CSE as a composite trait in relation to stressors and health and is the only one we are aware of that used a military sample. However, each of the four CSE traits has been extensively studied in stress and health research, including many studies in the military context. We discussed neuroticism/emotional stability above; we discuss the other components below.

Self-Esteem. Self-esteem is a general evaluation of one's self-worth. Individuals with low self-esteem are thought to be more susceptible to negative effects from work stressors (Brockner, 1988). Depending on the key terms selected, literature searches on terms such as *stress*, *health*, and *resilience* reveal anywhere from hundreds to thousands of studies investigating self-esteem as a protective health factor, including some studies showing mental health benefits of self-esteem interventions (e.g., Greenberg et al., 1992). Conversely, low self-esteem has been shown to be a risk factor for PTSD and is associated with diminished well-being for military veterans, regardless of their PTSD status (Kashdan, Uswatte, Steger, & Julian, 2006). Other research has shown that service members with low self-esteem perceive the transition from military to civilian life as being more stressful (Gowan, Craft, & Zimmerman, 2000). A loss of self-esteem has also been shown to mediate the relationship between service members' traumatic exposure and traumatic reactions (Slobodin, Caspi, Klein, Berger, & Hobfoll, 2011).

Self-Efficacy. People with high self-efficacy believe they have the ability to successfully complete tasks or goals and have the capabilities required to exert control over events in their lives (Bandura, 1986). As a result, they tend to experience less stress in high-demand situations, because they see themselves as able to cope successfully (Bandura & Wood, 1989). Self-efficacious individuals are also more likely to view potential threats as challenges or as opportunities for accomplishment. This enables them to remain task oriented in the face of pressing demands, failures, or setbacks, because they maintain confidence in their ability to ultimately succeed (Parker, Williams, & Turner, 2006). The literature on beneficial work outcomes of self-efficacy is large, and several military studies have shown that service members with higher self-efficacy are less likely to experience adverse reactions to stressors (Jex & Bliese, 1999; Jex, Bliese, Buzzell, & Primeau, 2001; Stetz, Stetz, & Bliese, 2006).

Locus of Control. Locus of control refers to the extent to which people judge themselves to be in control of events in their lives. People with an internal locus of control believe they can affect their world through their actions, whereas people with an external locus of control believe there is little they can do to affect the outcomes they receive. People with an external locus of control are more likely to appraise potentially stressful events as threatening and are less likely to engage in adaptive problem-focused coping. Not surprisingly then, an internal locus of control is associated with higher subjective well-being, favorable job and life attitudes, motivation, and career success (DeNeve & Cooper, 1998; Ng, Sorensen, & Eby, 2006). Military studies also show that external locus of control is a risk factor for PTSD following combat exposure (Al-Turkait & Ohaeri, 2008; McKeever, McWhirter, & Huff, 2006; Solomon, Mikulincer, & Avitzur, 1988; Solomon, Mikulincer, & Benbenishty, 1989).

Hardiness

Hardiness is a cognitively oriented composite personality trait reflecting the way people typically interpret potentially stressful events. Hardy individuals are generally thought to be more resilient because of the adaptive ways they tend to view events (Kobasa, 1982; Maddi, Kahn, & Maddi, 1998). Hardiness has a straightforward link to stress appraisal, as hardy individuals are thought to be less likely to appraise events as stressful (i.e., primary appraisal) and more likely to believe they have the resources to cope with demands (i.e., secondary appraisal). Although little hardiness work has focused on reappraisal, hardiness may be associated with the tendency to come to see demanding events as beneficial over time. For example, Britt et al. (2001) found that hardiness was associated with perceiving that a deployment involved meaningful work and ultimately to experiencing greater benefits from the deployment experience.

The popularity of hardiness in the military literature is undoubtedly due in part to the connotations associated with the term and the military's cultural emphasis on mental toughness. However, empirical research also strongly supports the role of hardiness in the stress-response process. For example, a recent meta-analysis by Eschleman, Bowling, and Alarcon (2010) showed that higher levels of hardiness were associated with lower levels of many stressors and negative health outcomes and were positively related to perceptions of support, role performance, and adaptive coping styles. Another appealing aspect of hardiness is its changeable nature; scholars have argued that hardiness may be increased through effective leadership (Bartone, 2006) or training programs (Maddi, 2007; Maddi et al., 1998).

Hardiness is conceptualized as having three components—commitment, control, and challenge—although researchers often combine measures of these components into a single hardiness score. The control construct in the hardiness literature shares a great deal of overlap with the CSE features of locus of control and self-efficacy, which we discussed previously. However, the commitment and challenge facets of hardiness contribute some different content to our discussion of personality and resilience.

Commitment. In hardiness literature, commitment reflects the nature of one's relationship with other people and the ability to find meaning and purpose in events. High levels of commitment enable individuals to be invested in all aspects of their lives, because they see activities as interesting and worthwhile. Commitment engenders feelings of excitement along with a strong sense of community and provides the motivation to remain engaged during difficult times. Individuals who are low in commitment tend to feel alienated from others and detached from their circumstances. Events seem difficult or pointless to them.

Service members with high levels of commitment are likely to perceive themselves as connected to others (e.g., unit members) and are more likely to see their mission as having an important purpose. This can be a critical influence on mental health for service members on deployments, who need to believe that their efforts and sacrifices are both meaningful and valuable to others (Bartone, 2005). Past research confirms the importance of commitment to mental health in comparison both with other components of hardiness and with other traits, such as those in the FFM (cf. Eschleman et al., 2010).

Challenge. Individuals high in challenge are characterized by cognitive flexibility and tolerance for ambiguity, which allows them to easily integrate unexpected or otherwise stressful events. Challenge generates a zest for seeking new or difficult experiences, because potentially stressful events are seen as opportunities for personal growth rather than as threats. People with high levels of challenge are thought to enjoy learning to respond to the unexpected and exploring their surroundings in an ongoing search for new and interesting experiences. They also expect that life can and will change, a belief that may foster personal growth and development (Kobasa, Maddi, & Courington,

1981). Although some reviews have questioned the construct validity of the challenge component (Hull, Van Treuren, & Virnelli, 1987), Eschleman et al. (2010) concluded that there was sufficient meta-analytic evidence of its incremental validity beyond both other hardiness components and FFM measures.

In the military context, several studies have shown that higher levels of hardiness are generally associated with better mental and physical health outcomes (Bartone, 1999; Bartone, Ursano, Wright, & Ingraham, 1989; Britt et al., 2001; Carston & Gardner, 2009; Dolan & Adler, 2006; Florian, Mikulincer, & Taubman, 1995; King, King, Foy, Keane, & Fairbank, 1999; Skomorovsky & Sudom, 2011; Sutker, Davis, Uddo, & Ditta, 1995). Although there is some inconsistency across these studies in the measures of hardiness used and in the outcomes studied, results generally support the importance of hardiness in relation to the health and well-being of military personnel. Few military studies have directly compared hardiness with other trait models, but Eschleman et al. (2010) reported meta-analytic evidence (mostly from civilian studies) that hardiness predicts outcomes above and beyond measures of the FFM. Skomorovsky and Sudom (2011) reported similar evidence in a military sample. Still other military studies have linked hardiness to performance outcomes in various demanding military contexts (Bartone, Roland, Picano, & Williams, 2008; Eid & Morgan, 2006; Johnsen, Eid, Pallesen, Bartone, & Nissestad, 2009; Westman, 1990).

Psychological Capital

Psychological capital (PsyCap) is a relatively new concept developed as part of the emerging literature on positive organizational behavior. According to Luthans (2002), this literature involves the study of "human resources strengths and psychological capacities that can be measured, developed, and effectively managed" (p. 59). Luthans defined PsyCap as a composite of four traits that reflect such human strengths: hope, optimism, resilience, and self-efficacy. Luthans, Avolio, Avey, and Norman (2007) described PsyCap as "state-like" in that though it is relatively stable, it may also be developed through interventions or experience. Thus, PsyCap reflects the idea of personality as characteristic adaptations, as discussed by McAdams and Pals (2006). PsyCap has received less attention from military researchers, who appear to favor other conceptual frameworks (e.g., hardiness). However, PsyCap introduces three characteristics that are not represented in hardiness or CSE research: hope, optimism, and the trait of resilience.

Hope. Hopeful people believe they can accomplish their goals (agency) and are able to identify several ways they can do so (pathways; Luthans et al., 2007). Hope involves the will to move toward a goal, the ability to identify subgoals that facilitate reaching the larger goal, and the capability to plan alternative routes to the goal (Snyder et al., 1991).

Many studies have linked hope to better performance and to recovery from health problems, but few studies have focused on military personnel or on resilience as a specific trajectory of health outcomes. In a qualitative study, Huff (2002) described the central role of hope in Vietnam veterans' reactions to their combat experiences. Irving, Telfer, and Blake (1997) found that combat veterans reported lower levels of hope than other samples did but also that hope appeared to play an important role in their recovery from PTSD. These studies, although limited, suggest that hope may facilitate resilience among service members.

Optimism. People who are high in optimism have a positive outlook about the future and make positive attributions about the causes of events (Luthans et al., 2007). Optimists habitually believe that negative events are caused by external factors (i.e., not their own personal qualities), by temporary rather than enduring influences, and by factors that are limited in scope rather than by global, all-encompassing characteristics. Although unrealistic optimism in the face of overwhelming stress may be unhealthy, many studies have linked dispositional optimism with better health (E. C. Chang, 2001), and some military research has linked dispositional optimism to posttraumatic growth (e.g., Feder et al., 2008). Thomas, Britt, Odle-Dusseau, and Bliese (2011) also recently found that soldiers higher in optimism were less likely to report symptoms of PTSD under high levels of combat exposure than were soldiers low in optimism.

Resilience. Luthans et al. (2007) defined resilience as the ability to adapt "in the face of significant risk or adversity" (p. 546). Thus, Luthans et al. used a trait definition of resilience. Trait resilience is associated with better job attitudes as well as better health outcomes (Snyder, 2002). One important concern about resilience as defined in PsyCap research is the apparent circularity of definition, in that resilient people are essentially defined as those who are resilient.

The number of published studies on PsyCap has grown exponentially in recent years, particularly in studies of job attitudes and job performance. A meta-analysis by Avey, Reichard, Luthans, and Mhatre (2011) summarized much of this literature and demonstrated that PsyCap has important relationships with job attitudes (e.g., satisfaction, commitment), job performance, and retention-related outcomes. Notably, Avey et al. reported results of only three studies linking PsyCap to well-being and four studies linking PsyCap to stress/anxiety.

To our knowledge, the only study of PsyCap in the military context was conducted by Schaubroeck, Riolli, Peng, and Spain (2011). They found, in a sample of soldiers deployed to Iraq, that higher PsyCap was associated with lower stress appraisals and that the protective effects of PsyCap for outcomes such as anxiety and somatic complaints were stronger for soldiers in units with higher levels of combat exposure. Although there is relatively little research on PsyCap as it relates to health and well-being, three lines of evidence suggest its importance. In particular, (a) studies of the individual components of PsyCap show they are related to health outcomes, (b) the individual components of PsyCap are typically highly correlated (e.g., Luthans, Avey, & Patera, 2008), and (c) the small body of existing literature supports the importance of PsyCap for occupational health. PsyCap remains an understudied construct in the military literature, although with a growing body of empirical support, including some research showing that it may be improved through intervention (Luthans et al., 2008). Future military research should continue to focus on the potential protective effects of PsyCap and investigate its utility in military resilience interventions. One could argue that although its conceptual foundations differ, the Comprehensive Soldier Fitness program discussed in Chapter 9 represents just such an effort.

Other Traits

Several other streams of trait literature deserve at least a brief mention. These traits vary in their conceptual links to resilience, their overlap with other models we reviewed, and the extent to which they have been studied in military samples. Yet, all of them have links to mental health, and all should be examined in future military resilience research. They include Type A behavior pattern, proactive personality, and self-enhancement.

Type A Behavior Pattern

Sulsky and Smith (2005) described Type A people as "identified by certain personality traits such as impatience, competitiveness, and hostility" (p. 165). People characterized as Type A are thought to be highly reactive to stressors, particularly social stressors. As such, Type A is sometimes referred to as the "coronary-prone personality," given the strong links between the hostility component of Type A and heart disease and cardiovascular health (Booth-Kewley & Friedman, 1987; Miller, Smith, Turner, Guijarro, & Hallet, 1996). As with other models we have discussed, questions may be raised about whether Type A personality contributes to resilience above and beyond other traits. For example, the hostility component of Type A personality closely resembles some facets of agreeableness (e.g., low trust) and neuroticism (e.g., angry hostility) in the FFM. Research is needed to examine whether Type A personality intensifies negative reactions to combat stressors and whether Type A contributes to resilience-related outcomes above and beyond other traits discussed above.

Proactive Personality

Proactive individuals are self-motivated, comfortable taking initiative, and future oriented (Parker et al., 2006). They constantly scan the environment to anticipate stressors and take action to lessen the impact of those stressors through one of three avenues: (a) preventing the stressor from occurring; (b) addressing the stressor early, while it is still easily resolved; or (c) accumulating resources to allow for effective coping (Bateman & Crant, 1993). To date, most research on proactive personality has focused on job performance. However, proactive personality is, by definition, associated with adaptive coping styles, which are one of the proximal outcomes of many resilience-related traits.

Self-Enhancement

Bonanno and colleagues have described the protective role of trait self-enhancement with regard to trauma exposure (e.g., Bonanno, Rennicke, & Dekel, 2005; Gupta & Bonanno, 2010). Drawing from older literature on socially desirable responding, they characterized trait self-enhancement as a dispositional tendency to present a positively biased view of one's self. They proposed that such positive self-perceptions are adaptive when individuals have to deal with potentially traumatic events, in part because such events present severe threats to one's self and one's worldview. Thus, people with stronger opinions of themselves are thought to be better able to withstand traumatic stressors. Taken as a whole, this research strongly supports the role of trait self-enhancement in resilience. However, one important question to address in further research concerns the relative contributions of self-enhancement and other resilience-related constructs such as CSE. For example, the protective effects of CSE could reflect high scorers' unrealistically positive self-views.

QUESTIONS, CONCERNS, AND DIRECTIONS

The literature on individual differences related to resilience is enormous. Indeed, our review only scratched the surface of a literature that is large, rapidly growing, and messy. In addition to the traits we discussed, several other individual differences, including coping styles and attachment patterns, likely play a role in resilience. The jingle and jangle fallacies described by Block (1995) still reverberate through this literature; many similar concepts have multiple names, and different ideas sometimes fall under the same general label. As Block noted with regard to the personality literature as a whole, these issues represent serious obstacles to the cumulative advancement of scientific understanding of resilience. They can be addressed in part by avoiding the temptation to find new labels for existing ideas and by construct validity studies establishing the relationships among various traits. Research also is needed to sort out which factors contribute to resilience and which factors are either unimportant or redundant. But there are several other questions that should be addressed in subsequent resilience research.

Is Resilience a Trait or an Outcome of Traits?

One of the most important concerns in military resilience literature is the lack of consensus on whether resilience is a single trait, a collection of traits, or an outcome of traits. Resilience reflects a lack of adverse outcomes following a stressor and may be distinguished from other trajectories, such as recovery (i.e., a decline in functioning followed by a return to baseline), thriving/posttraumatic growth (e.g., increases in functioning after an event), survival with some impairment, and succumbing (cf. Carver, 1998). In this approach, personality traits are thought to explain why an individual follows a particular trajectory. Although some military research has investigated individual differences between trajectories (e.g., Dekel, Mandl, & Solomon, 2011), this research is in its nascent stages.

Other studies have treated resilience as a specific trait, with most typically defining resilience as a characteristic reflecting the ability to "bounce back" following exposure to stressors. This idea appears in literature on psychological capital (discussed above) as well as other studies on health outcomes (e.g., Smith et al., 2008). Whereas Bonanno (2004) defined resilience as a lack of disruption to functioning, the resilience-as-trait model defines resilience as declines in functioning followed by recovery (i.e., as a dispositional ability to bounce back). Resilience presumably reflects faster recovery, although temporal aspects such as how fast one needs to recover to be classified as resilient are often not addressed.

Finally, many studies have treated resilience as a collection of traits, typically operationalized as a second-order factor reflecting the shared variance among a particular set of first-order trait measures. This approach is evident in the CSE and PsyCap literatures discussed above and is at least implicit in the hardiness literature. These three composite trait models each offer the advantage of reasonable levels of consensus within the literature on construct definition. However, many other studies have used different subsets of the traits reviewed above, with varying degrees of comprehensiveness or theoretical/empirical justification for their choices.

At one end of the spectrum, researchers sometimes study small subsets of the traits discussed above. For example, Schok, Kleber, and Lensvelt-Mulders (2010) operationalized resilience as a combination of self-esteem, optimism, and perceived control. This approach of studying a small set of resilience-related traits is fairly typical of much of the existing research on personality and health. Lee, Sudom, and McCreary (2011) represent the other end of the spectrum: They studied a broad list of measures, including the FFM as well as dispositional affect, dispositional optimism, hardiness, mastery, and self-esteem. Both of these studies, like much of the research on the composite traits discussed above, ultimately concluded that a single dimension captured much of the variation between resilience-related traits. This dimension also closely resembles what FFM researchers have referred to as *alpha*—a higher order combination of conscientiousness, neuroticism, and agreeableness (Digman, 1997; van der Linden, Nijenhuis, & Bakker, 2010).

Marshall et al. (1994), using a long list of health-related individual differences, found three factors that they labeled *optimistic control*, *anger expression*, and *inhibition*. Their optimistic control dimension resembles much of the content described above, with measures of optimism, hopelessness, self-esteem, anxiety, and life purpose (which resembles commitment in the hardiness literature). Anger expression focused on how people express emotions, particularly negative emotions. Inhibition reflected rational/inward expression of emotions and introspectiveness. One implication of Marshall et al.'s research is that factor-analytic studies showing a general personality factor related to resilience may be heavily influenced by researchers' choices of input variables. Researchers who choose a more diverse set of traits are likely to find more than one general personality factor.

As our review suggests, researchers have taken different approaches to studying the relationship between resilience and personality. Much of the resilience-related military research equates resilience with the personality traits thought to be antecedents of favorable mental health outcomes. The problem with this approach is that it equates the particular set of outcomes of traits with the inherent qualities of the traits themselves. For example, resilience-related traits such as a propensity to view events in a positive light, self-discipline/control, and emotional stability are studied as elements of "integrity" in industrial/organizational research focused on reducing counterproductive workplace behavior (Ones & Viswesvaran, 2001). In terms of labels, the distinction between integrity and resilience almost entirely concerns the outcomes of interest; the theoretical mechanisms associated with the two are very similar. When different research traditions use different labels for the same phenomena, the end result is increased difficulty in accumulating generalizable conclusions from empirical research. Resilience researchers cannot solve this problem independently, but we can contribute by clearly differentiating resilience-related traits from resilience-related outcomes as we build theoretical models and conduct empirical research. We also can resist the temptation to coin new terminology without at least carefully considering whether a concept is covered in existing literature.

Under What Conditions Are First- and Second-Order Factor Models Appropriate?

Discussions of bandwidth and fidelity issues in personnel selection suggest that broad traits predict broad outcomes and that narrow traits may be more useful for predicting narrow outcomes (cf. Hogan & Roberts, 1996). Resilience may be conceived of either as a broad-bandwidth outcome (consisting of a person's general mental health following exposure to stressors) or as a narrow-bandwidth outcome (such that people might simultaneously show resilient patterns for some outcomes and nonresilient patterns for others). The broad-bandwidth conception is probably more common; it implies that broader personality measures might be more useful predictors. However, narrow trait measures could be more useful for predicting specific resilience-related outcomes. For example, neuroticism might be more strongly related to emotional aspects of resilience, whereas conscientiousness might be more strongly related to motivational aspects of resilience. As Hogan and Roberts (1996) highlighted with regard to job performance, careful consideration of nature of the criteria under investigation is an important issue for this literature.

Are Resilience-Related Traits Interchangeable?

Mancini and Bonanno (2009) explained that "resilience can be achieved through a variety of means. There are multiple risk and protective factors . . . and it is the totality of these factors . . . that determines the likelihood of a resilient outcome" (pp. 1819–1820). This raises interesting questions about the relative contributions of different traits. For example, does having high levels of one resilience trait and low levels of another lead to the same expected outcome as having moderate levels of each, or is having high levels of one sufficient to provide stress-buffering effects?

Much of the trait literature emphasizes structural issues concerning the extent to which various resilience-related traits load on one or more general resilience-related factors. This frames the basic research question as whether or not to aggregate multiple traits. However, an alternate perspective would be that multiple resilience-related traits are interchangeable, such that people need enough of one resource to solve a problem but not necessarily high levels of several of them. This suggests a possible alternative to the focus on first- versus second-order factor models in much of the relevant research. Moreover, resilience-related traits may be interchangeable with other resources, such as social support.

How Important Is Prior Trauma?

Another issue that requires further attention from military researchers concerns the interrelationship of personality traits and prior trauma history with regard to the development of PTSD. Some studies have shown that after controlling for prior traumatic experiences, personality traits do not buffer against the development of PTSD (e.g., Solomon & Mikulincer, 1990). Other studies have found that traits predict PTSD outcomes even when prior trauma is controlled (e.g., McKeever et al., 2006). Still other studies have shown that stressors predict subsequent development of resilience-related traits (e.g., Vogt, Rizvi, Shipherd, & Resick, 2008), implying that personality mediates the relationship between prior trauma and subsequent PTSD risk. Although PTSD researchers have long recognized that trauma exposure can have lifelong positive or negative effects on veterans' mental health (cf. Aldwin, Levenson, & Spiro, 1994; Elder & Clipp, 1989), this issue is not always incorporated into empirical studies and may be critical to understanding how service members react to stressors. Future research should examine multiple combinations of traits, prior exposures, and mental health outcomes in order to gain a more comprehensive understanding of the conditions under which traits do and do not have protective effects.

Are Resilience-Related Traits Domain-Specific or General?

Most personality trait measures refer to a person's general pattern of thoughts, feelings, and/or behaviors. In contrast, domain-specific personality measures are tailored to reflect one's thoughts, emotions, and/or behaviors in a particular role (i.e., work, school, family). Personnel selection research has shown that using a job-specific frame of reference (i.e., asking people about their typical behavior in a work role) improves the predictive validity of personality measures in personnel selection systems (Hunthausen, Truxillo, Bauer, & Hammer, 2003); using a work-role-specific frame of reference reflects the theoretical assumption that behavioral expression of a trait is context specific. For military personnel, the demand constraints and expectations of their occupation are likely considerably different from those of other roles (e.g., parent, spouse), making it likely that domain-specific measures might be superior predictors of resilience.

Others have taken the position that traits conceptualized as global should be operationalized globally. For example, CSE researchers have contended that to be considered core traits, CSEs should be conceptualized globally (C.-H. Chang et al., 2012; Judge et al., 1997). Thus, we encourage further investigation of whether domain-specific measures predict certain kinds of outcomes more effectively, as well as continued consideration of the theoretical implications of various aggregation choices.

How Applicable Is Military Resilience Research to Combat Deployments?

One of the important caveats to consider is that many of the military studies cited above are frequently conducted in a training context, such as basic training or training for special assignments (e.g., Special Forces). It is unclear whether resilience-related findings from the training context apply to the demands of actual combat and peacekeeping deployments, which involve stressors such as seeing friends killed, being in firefights, or encountering dead bodies. Research needs to address the extent to which findings may be generalized from training to deployment settings or from civilian employees to military samples. These concerns may be less important for some issues, such as the strength of correlations among various personality traits, but critical for others, such as the predictive validity of traits. One could also argue for a narrower view that studies of resilience should include exposure to a traumatic event and longitudinal efforts to follow individuals over time in order to study individual differences in reactions to resilience.

Conclusion

How should the military apply concepts from personality-based resilience? It is perhaps more important than ever to select individuals with resilient personalities as well as to afford less resilient people the opportunity to screen themselves out of extremely demanding occupations (e.g., by providing realistic job previews). It follows that organizations also should provide continual training to develop and maintain resilience. Sinclair and Tucker (2006) distinguished between developmental and compensatory trait training. *Developmental trait training* consists of an intentional focus on developing a particular personality trait. For example, researchers have made some progress in hardiness training (cf. Maddi, 2007; Maddi et al., 1998), as well as in the development of psychological capital (Luthans et al., 2008), but the great potential of such work for military resilience remains relatively untapped. In contrast, *compensatory trait training* involves teaching people skills to compensate for maladaptive aspects of their personalities or to capitalize on personal strengths. Some aspects of the army's Comprehensive Soldier Fitness program described by Lester et al. in Chapter 9 could be viewed as compensatory trait training.

Finally, we note that the increasing recognition among personality scholars that traits are subject to change throughout adulthood highlights the need for those working in applied settings to attend to all aspects of the work environment that may affect personality traits. Resilience research implies that organizations should take all possible realistic steps to encourage the development of characteristics such as self-confidence, hopefulness, purpose, and control, through their policies and the actions of organizational leaders.

REFERENCES

Adler, A. B., Litz, B. T., & Bartone, P. T. (2003). The nature of peacekeeping stressors. In T. W. Britt & A. B. Adler (Eds.), *The psychology of the peacekeeper: Lessons from the field* (pp. 149–167). Westport, CT: Praeger.

Aldwin, C. M., Levenson, M. R., & Spiro, A., III (1994). Vulnerability and resilience to combat exposure: Can stress have lifelong effects? *Psychology and Aging, 9*, 34–44. doi:10.1037/0882-7974.9.1.34

Al-Turkait, F. A., & Ohaeri, J. U. (2008). Prevalence and correlates of posttraumatic stress disorder among Kuwaiti military men according to level of involvement in the first Gulf War. *Depression and Anxiety, 25*, 932–941. doi:10.1002/da.20373

Avey, J. B., Reichard, R. J., Luthans, F., & Mhatre, K. H. (2011). Meta-analysis of the impact of positive psychological capital on employee attitudes, behaviors, and performance. *Human Resource Development Quarterly, 22*, 127–152. doi:10.1002/hrdq.20070

Bandura, A. (1986). *Social foundations of thought and action*. Englewood Cliffs, NJ: Prentice-Hall.

Bandura, A., & Wood, R. (1989). Effects of perceived controllability and performance standards on self-regulation of complex decision making. *Journal of Personality and Social Psychology, 56*, 805–814. doi:10.1037/0022-3514.56.5.805

Bartone, P. T. (1999). Hardiness protects against war-related stress in Army reserve forces. *Consulting Psychology Journal: Practice and Research, 51*, 72–82. doi:10.1037/1061-4087.51.2.72

Bartone, P. T. (2005). The need for positive meaning in military operations: Reflections on Abu Ghraib. *Military Psychology, 17*, 315–324. doi:10.1207/s15327876mp1704_5

Bartone, P. T. (2006). Resilience under military operational stress: Can leaders influence hardiness? *Military Psychology, 18*(Suppl. 3), S131–S148. doi:10.1207/s15327876mp1803s_10

Bartone, P. T., Roland, R. R., Picano, J. J., & Williams, T. J. (2008). Psychological hardiness predicts success in U.S. Army Special Forces candidates. *International Journal of Selection and Assessment, 16*, 78–81. doi:10.1111/j.1468-2389.2008.00412.x

Bartone, P. T., Ursano, R. J., Wright, K. M., & Ingraham, L. H. (1989). The impact of a military air disaster on the health of assistance workers: A prospective study. *Journal of Nervous and Mental Disease, 177*, 317–328. doi:10.1097/00005053-198906000-00001

Bateman, T. S., & Crant, J. M. (1993). The proactive component of organizational behavior: A measure and correlates. *Journal of Organizational Behavior, 14*, 103–118. doi:10.1002/job.4030140202

Baumeister, R. F. (2001). Ego depletion, the executive function, and self-control. In B. W. Roberts & R. Hogan (Eds.), *Personality psychology in the workplace* (pp. 299–316). Washington, DC: American Psychological Association. doi:10.1037/10434-012

Bliese, P. D., & Castro, C. A. (2003). The soldier adaptation model (SAM): Applications to behavioral science peacekeeping research. In T. W. Britt & A. B. Adler (Eds.), *The psychology of the peacekeeper: A multinational perspective* (pp. 185–203). Westport, CT: Praeger.

Block, J. (1995). A contrarian view of the five-factor approach to personality description. *Psychological Bulletin, 117,* 187–215. doi:10.1037/0033-2909.117.2.187

Bogg, T., & Roberts, B. W. (2004). Conscientiousness and health-related behaviors: A meta-analysis of the leading behavioral contributors to mortality. *Psychological Bulletin, 130,* 887–919. doi:10.1037/0033-2909.130.6.887

Bonanno, G. A. (2004). Loss, trauma, and human resilience: Have we underestimated the human capacity to thrive after extremely aversive events? *American Psychologist, 59,* 20–28. doi:10.1037/0003-066X.59.1.20

Bonanno, G. A., Rennicke, C., & Dekel, S. (2005). Self-enhancement among high-exposure survivors of the September 11th terrorist attack: Resilience or social maladjustment? *Journal of Personality and Social Psychology, 88,* 984–998. doi:10.1037/0022-3514.88.6.984

Booth-Kewley, S., & Friedman, H. S. (1987). Psychological predictors of heart disease: A quantitative review. *Psychological Bulletin, 101,* 343–362. doi:10.1037/0033-2909.101.3.343

Booth-Kewley, S., & Vickers, R. R., Jr. (1994). Associations between major domains of personality and health behavior. *Journal of Personality, 62,* 281–298. doi:10.1111/j.1467-6494.1994.tb00298.x

Bouchard, T. J., Jr., & McGue, M. (2003). Genetic and environmental influences on human psychological differences. *Journal of Neurobiology, 54,* 4–45. doi:10.1002/neu.10160

Britt, T. W., Adler, A. B., & Bartone, P. T. (2001). Deriving benefits from stressful events: The role of engagement in meaningful work and hardiness. *Journal of Occupational Health Psychology, 6,* 53–63. doi:10.1037/1076-8998.6.1.53

Brockner, J. (1988). *Self-esteem at work.* Lexington, MA: Heath.

Carston, M. C., & Gardner, D. (2009). Cognitive hardiness in the New Zealand military. *New Zealand Journal of Psychology, 38,* 26–34.

Carver, C. S. (1998). Resilience and thriving: Issues, models, and linkages. *Journal of Social Issues, 54,* 245–266. doi:10.1111/j.1540-4560.1998.tb01217.x

Chang, C.-H., Ferris, D. L., Johnson, R. E., Rosen, C. C., & Tan, J. A. (2012). Core self-evaluations: A review and evaluation of the literature. *Journal of Management, 38,* 81–128. doi:10.1177/0149206311419661

Chang, E. C. (Ed.). (2001). *Optimism and pessimism: Implications for theory, research, and practice.* Washington, DC: American Psychological Association.

Costa, P. T., & McRae, R. R. (1992). *Revised NEO Personality Inventory (NEO-PI–R) and NEO Five-Factor Inventory (NEO-FFI) professional manual.* Odessa, FL: Psychological Assessment Resources.

Dekel, S., Mandl, C., & Solomon, Z. (2011). Shared and unique predictors of post-traumatic growth and distress. *Journal of Clinical Psychology, 67,* 241–252. doi:10.1002/jclp.20747

DeNeve, K. M., & Cooper, H. (1998). The happy personality: A meta-analysis of 137 personality traits and subjective well-being. *Psychological Bulletin, 124,* 197–229. doi:10.1037/0033-2909.124.2.197

Digman, J. M. (1997). Higher-order factors of the Big Five. *Journal of Personality and Social Psychology, 73*, 1246–1256. doi:10.1037/0022-3514.73.6.1246

Dolan, C. A., & Adler, A. B. (2006). Military hardiness as a buffer of psychological health on return from deployment. *Military Medicine, 171*, 93–98.

Eid, J., & Morgan, C. A., III. (2006). Dissociation, hardiness, and performance in military cadets participating in survival training. *Military Medicine, 171*, 436–442.

Elder, G. H., Jr., & Clipp, E. C. (1989). Combat experience and emotional health: Impairment and resilience in later life. *Journal of Personality, 57*, 311–341. doi:10.1111/j.1467-6494.1989.tb00485.x

Engelhard, I. M., & van den Hout, M. A. (2007). Preexisting neuroticism, subjective stressor severity, and posttraumatic stress in soldiers deployed to Iraq. *Canadian Journal of Psychiatry/Revue canadienne de psychiatrie, 52*, 505–509.

Eschleman, K. J., Bowling, N. A., & Alarcon, G. M. (2010). A meta-analytic examination of hardiness. *International Journal of Stress Management, 17*, 277–307. doi:10.1037/a0020476

Eurelings-Bontekoe, E. H. M., Verschuur, M., Koudstaal, A., van der Sar, S., & Duijsens, I. J. (1995). Construction of a homesickness-questionnaire: Preliminary results. *Personality and Individual Differences, 19*, 319–325. doi:10.1016/0191-8869(95)00056-C

Feder, A., Southwick, S. M., Goetz, R. R., Wang, Y., Alonso, A., Smith, B. W., . . . Vythilingam, M. (2008). Posttraumatic growth in former Vietnam prisoners of war. *Psychiatry: Interpersonal and Biological Processes, 71*, 359–370. doi:10.1521/psyc.2008.71.4.359

Florian, V., Mikulincer, M., & Taubman, O. (1995). Does hardiness contribute to mental health during a stressful real-life situation? The roles of appraisal and coping. *Journal of Personality and Social Psychology, 68*, 687–695. doi:10.1037/0022-3514.68.4.687

Funder, D. C. (2001). *The personality puzzle* (2nd ed.). New York, NY: Norton.

George, J. M. (1992). The role of personality in organizational life: Issues and evidence. *Journal of Management, 18*, 185–213. doi:10.1177/014920639201800201

Gowan, M. A., Craft, S. L. S., & Zimmerman, R. A. (2000). Response to work transitions by United States Army personnel: Effects of self-esteem, self-efficacy, and career resilience. *Psychological Reports, 86*, 911–921. doi:10.2466/pr0.2000.86.3.911

Greenberg, J., Solomon, S., Pyszczynski, T., Rosenblatt, A., Burling, J., Lyon, D., . . . Pinel, E. (1992). Why do people need self-esteem? Converging evidence that self-esteem serves an anxiety-buffering function. *Journal of Personality and Social Psychology, 63*, 913–922. doi:10.1037/0022-3514.63.6.913

Gupta, S., & Bonanno, G. A. (2010). Trait self-enhancement as a buffer against potentially traumatic events: A prospective study. *Psychological Trauma: Theory, Research, Practice, and Policy, 2*, 83–92. doi:10.1037/a0018959

Hochwarter, W. A., Kent, R. L., & Perrewé, P. L. (1993). The impact of persistence on the stressor–strain and strain–intentions to leave relationships: A field examination. *Journal of Social Behavior and Personality, 8*, 389–404.

Hogan, J., & Roberts, B. W. (1996). Issues and non-issues in the fidelity–bandwidth trade-off. *Journal of Organizational Behavior, 17,* 627–637. doi:10.1002/(SICI)1099-1379(199611)17:6<627::AID-JOB2828>3.0.CO;2-F

Hoge, C. W., Castro, C. A., Messer, S. C., McGurk, D., Cotting, D. I., & Koffman, R. L. (2004). Combat duty in Iraq and Afghanistan, mental health problems, and barriers to care. *New England Journal of Medicine, 351,* 13–22. doi:10.1056/NEJMoa040603

Huff, M. B. (2002). Role of hope in the survival of Vietnam combat veterans. *Psychological Reports, 90,* 1191–1196.

Hull, J. G., Van Treuren, R. R., & Virnelli, S. (1987). Hardiness and health: A critique and alternative approach. *Journal of Personality and Social Psychology, 53,* 518–530. doi:10.1037/0022-3514.53.3.518

Hunthausen, J. M., Truxillo, D. M., Bauer, T. N., & Hammer, L. B. (2003). A field study of frame-of-reference effects on personality test validity. *Journal of Applied Psychology, 88,* 545–551. doi:10.1037/0021-9010.88.3.545

Irving, L. M., Telfer, L., & Blake, D. D. (1997). Hope, coping, and social support in combat-related posttraumatic stress disorder. *Journal of Traumatic Stress, 10,* 465–479. doi:10.1002/jts.2490100311

Jex, S. M., & Bliese, P. D. (1999). Efficacy beliefs as a moderator of the impact of work-related stressors: A multilevel study. *Journal of Applied Psychology, 84,* 349–361. doi:10.1037/0021-9010.84.3.349

Jex, S. M., Bliese, P. D., Buzzell, S., & Primeau, J. (2001). The impact of self-efficacy on stressor–strain relations: Coping style as an explanatory mechanism. *Journal of Applied Psychology, 86,* 401–409. doi:10.1037/0021-9010.86.3.401

Johnsen, B., Eid, J., Pallesen, S., Bartone, P. T., & Nissestad, O. A. (2009). Predicting transformational leadership in naval cadets: Effects of personality hardiness and training. *Journal of Applied Social Psychology, 39,* 2213–2235. doi:10.1111/j.1559-1816.2009.00522.x

Judge, T. A., Erez, A., Bono, J. E., & Thoresen, C. J. (2003). The Core Self-Evaluations Scale: Development of a measure. *Personnel Psychology, 56,* 303–331. doi:10.1111/j.1744-6570.2003.tb00152.x

Judge, T. A., Locke, E. A., & Durham, C. C. (1997). The dispositional causes of job satisfaction: A core evaluations approach. *Research in Organizational Behavior, 19,* 151–188.

Kashdan, T. B., Uswatte, G., Steger, M. F., & Julian, T. (2006). Fragile self-esteem and affective instability in posttraumatic stress disorder. *Behaviour Research and Therapy, 44,* 1609–1619. doi:10.1016/j.brat.2005.12.003

King, D. W., King, L. A., Foy, D. W., Keane, T. M., & Fairbank, J. A. (1999). Posttraumatic stress disorder in a national sample of female and male Vietnam veterans: Risk factors, war-zone stressors, and resilience–recovery variables. *Journal of Abnormal Psychology, 108,* 164–170. doi:10.1037/0021-843X.108.1.164

Kobasa, S. C. (1982). The hardy personality: Toward a social psychology of stress and health. In G. S. Sanders & J. Suls (Eds.), *Social psychology of health and illness* (pp. 3–32). Hillsdale, NJ: Erlbaum.

Kobasa, S. C., Maddi, S. R., & Courington, S. (1981). Personality and constitution as mediators in the stress–illness relationship. *Journal of Health and Social Behavior, 22*, 368–378.

Lahey, B. B. (2009). Public health significance of neuroticism. *American Psychologist, 64*, 241–256. doi:10.1037/a0015309

Lazarus, R. S., & Folkman, S. (1984). *Stress, appraisal, and coping.* New York, NY: Springer.

Lee, J. E. C., Sudom, K. A., & McCreary, D. R. (2011). Higher-order model of resilience in the Canadian Forces. *Canadian Journal of Behavioural Science/Revue canadienne des sciences du comportement, 43*, 222–234. doi:10.1037/a0024473

Luria, G., & Torjman, A. (2009). Resources and coping with stressful events. *Journal of Organizational Behavior, 30*, 685–707. doi:10.1002/job.551

Luthans, F. (2002). Positive organizational behavior: Developing and managing psychological strengths. *Academy of Management Executive, 16*, 57–72. doi:10.5465/AME.2002.6640181

Luthans, F., Avey, J. B., & Patera, J. L. (2008). Experimental analysis of a web-based training intervention to develop positive psychological capital. *Academy of Management Learning & Education, 7*, 209–221. doi:10.5465/AMLE.2008.32712618

Luthans, F., Avolio, B., Avey, J. B., & Norman, S. M. (2007). Positive psychological capital: Measurement and relationship with performance and satisfaction. *Personnel Psychology, 60*, 541–572. doi:10.1111/j.1744-6570.2007.00083.x

Lyubomirsky, S., King, L., & Diener, E. (2005). The benefits of frequent positive affect: Does happiness lead to success? *Psychological Bulletin, 131*, 803–855. doi:10.1037/0033-2909.131.6.803

Maddi, S. R. (2007). Relevance of hardiness assessment and training to the military context. *Military Psychology, 19*, 61–70. doi:10.1080/08995600701323301

Maddi, S. R., Kahn, S., & Maddi, K. L. (1998). The effectiveness of hardiness training. *Consulting Psychology Journal: Practice and Research, 50*, 78–86. doi:10.1037/1061-4087.50.2.78

Mancini, A. D., & Bonanno, G. A. (2009). Predictors and parameters of resilience to loss: Toward an individual differences model. *Journal of Personality, 77*, 1805–1832. doi:10.1111/j.1467-6494.2009.00601.x

Marshall, G. N., Wortman, C. B., Vickers, R. R., Kusulas, J. W., & Hervig, L. K. (1994). The five-factor model of personality as a framework for personality–health research. *Journal of Personality and Social Psychology, 67*, 278–286. doi:10.1037/0022-3514.67.2.278

McAdams, D. P., & Pals, J. L. (2006). A new Big Five: Fundamental principles for an integrative science of personality. *American Psychologist, 61*, 204–217. doi:10.1037/0003-066X.61.3.204

McKeever, V. M., McWhirter, B. T., & Huff, M. E. (2006). Relationships between attribution style, child abuse history, and PTSD symptom severity in Vietnam veterans. *Cognitive Therapy and Research, 30*, 123–133. doi:10.1007/s10608-006-9018-9

Miller, T. Q., Smith, T. W., Turner, C. W., Guijarro, M. L., & Hallet, A. J. (1996). A meta-analytic review of research on hostility and physical health. *Psychological Bulletin, 119*, 322–348. doi:10.1037/0033-2909.119.2.322

Ng, T. W. H., Sorensen, K. L., & Eby, L. T. (2006). Locus of control at work: A meta-analysis. *Journal of Organizational Behavior, 27*, 1057–1087. doi:10.1002/job.416

Ones, D. S., & Viswesvaran, C. (2001). Personality at work: Criterion-focused occupational personality scales used in personnel selection. In B. W. Roberts & R. Hogan (Eds.), *Personality psychology in the workplace* (pp. 63–92). Washington, DC: American Psychological Association. doi:10.1037/10434-003

Parker, S. K., Williams, H. M., & Turner, N. (2006). Modeling the antecedents of proactive behavior at work. *Journal of Applied Psychology, 91*, 636–652. doi:10.1037/0021-9010.91.3.636

Rademaker, A. R., van Zuiden, M., Vermetten, E., & Geuze, E. (2011). Type D personality and the development of PTSD symptoms: A prospective study. *Journal of Abnormal Psychology, 120*, 299–307. doi:10.1037/a0021806

Riviere, L. A., Merrill, J. C., Wilk, J. E., Edens, E. N., & Adler, A. B. (2010, August). *Health risk behaviors among U.S. soldiers*. Paper presented at the meeting of the American Psychological Association, San Diego, CA.

Roberts, B. W., Caspi, A., & Moffitt, T. E. (2003). Work experiences and personality development in young adulthood. *Journal of Personality and Social Psychology, 84*, 582–593. doi:10.1037/0022-3514.84.3.582

Roberts, B. W., & Del Vecchio, W. F. (2000). The rank-order consistency of personality traits from childhood to old age: A quantitative review of longitudinal studies. *Psychological Bulletin, 126*, 3–25. doi:10.1037/0033-2909.126.1.3

Roesch, S. C., Aldridge, A. A., Vickers, R. R., & Helvig, L. K. (2009). Testing personality-coping diatheses for negative and positive affect: A longitudinal evaluation. *Anxiety, Stress & Coping, 22*, 263–281. doi:10.1080/10615800802158419

Schaubroeck, J. M., Riolli, L. T., Peng, A. C., & Spain, E. S. (2011). Resilience to traumatic exposure among soldiers deployed in combat. *Journal of Occupational Health Psychology, 16*, 18–37. doi:10.1037/a0021006

Schok, M. L., Kleber, R. J., & Lensvelt-Mulders, G. M. (2010). A model of resilience and meaning after military deployment: Personal resources in making sense of war and peacekeeping experiences. *Aging & Mental Health, 14*, 328–338. doi:10.1080/13607860903228812

Seery, M. D. (2011). Resilience: A silver lining to experiencing adverse life events? *Current Directions in Psychological Science, 20*, 390–394. doi:10.1177/0963721411424740

Sinclair, R. R., & Tucker, J. S. (2006). Stress-CARE: An integrated model of individual differences in soldier performance under stress. In T. W. Britt, C. A. Castro, & A. B. Adler (Eds.), *Military life: The psychology of serving in peace and combat. Vol. 1: Military performance* (pp. 202–231). Westport, CT: Praeger Security International.

Skomorovsky, A., & Sudom, K. A. (2011). Psychological well-being of Canadian Forces officer candidates: The unique roles of hardiness and personality. *Military Medicine, 176*, 389–396.

Slobodin, O., Caspi, Y., Klein, E., Berger, B. D., & Hobfoll, S. E. (2011). Resource loss and posttraumatic responses in Bedouin members of the Israeli Defense Forces. *Journal of Traumatic Stress, 24*, 54–60. doi:10.1002/jts.20615

Smith, B. W., Dalen, J., Wiggins, K., Tooley, E., Christopher, P., & Bernard, J. (2008). The Brief Resilience Scale: Assessing the ability to bounce back. *International Journal of Behavioral Medicine, 15*, 194–200. doi:10.1080/10705500802222972

Smith, B. W., & Zautra, A. J. (2002). The role of personality in exposure and reactivity to interpersonal stress in relation to arthritis disease activity and negative affect in women. *Health Psychology, 21*, 81–88. doi:10.1037/0278-6133.21.1.81

Snyder, C. R. (2002). Hope theory: Rainbows in the mind. *Psychological Inquiry, 13*, 249–275. doi:10.1207/S15327965PLI1304_01

Snyder, C. R., Harris, C., Anderson, J. R., Holleran, S. A., Irving, L. M., Sigmon, S. T., . . . Harney, P. (1991). The will and the ways: Development and validation of an individual-differences measure of hope. *Journal of Personality and Social Psychology, 60*, 570–585. doi:10.1037/0022-3514.60.4.570

Solomon, Z., & Mikulincer, M. (1990). Life events and combat-related posttraumatic stress disorder: The intervening role of locus of control and social support. *Military Psychology, 2*, 241–256. doi:10.1207/s15327876mp0204_4

Solomon, Z., Mikulincer, M., & Avitzur, E. (1988). Coping, locus of control, social support, and combat-related posttraumatic stress disorder: A prospective study. *Journal of Personality and Social Psychology, 55*, 279–285. doi:10.1037/0022-3514.55.2.279

Solomon, Z., Mikulincer, M., & Benbenishty, R. (1989). Locus of control and combat-related post-traumatic stress disorder: The intervening role of battle intensity, threat appraisal, and coping. *British Journal of Social and Clinical Psychology, 28*, 131–144. doi:10.1111/j.2044-8260.1989.tb00823.x

Stetz, T. A., Stetz, M. C., & Bliese, P. D. (2006). The importance of self-efficacy in the moderating effects of social support on stressor–strain relationships. *Work & Stress, 20*, 49–59. doi:10.1080/02678370600624039

Sulsky, L., & Smith, C. (2005). *Work stress.* Belmont, CA: Thomson Wadsworth.

Sümer, H. C., & Sümer, N. (2007). Personality and mental health: How related are they within the military context? *Military Psychology, 19*, 161–174. doi:10.1080/08995600701386325

Sutker, P. B., Davis, J. M., Uddo, M., & Ditta, S. R. (1995). War zone stress, personal resources, and PTSD in Persian Gulf War returnees. *Journal of Abnormal Psychology, 104*, 444–452. doi:10.1037/0021-843X.104.3.444

Talbert, F. S., Braswell, L. C., Albrecht, I. W., Hyer, L. A., & Boudewyns, P. A. (1993). NEO-PI profiles in PTSD as a function of trauma level. *Journal of Clinical Psychology, 49*, 663–669. doi:10.1002/1097-4679(199309)49:5<663::AID-JCLP2270490508>3.0.CO;2-A

Tedeschi, R. D., & McNally, R. J. (2011). Can we facilitate posttraumatic growth in combat veterans? *American Psychologist, 66,* 19–24. doi:10.1037/a0021896

Thomas, J. L., Britt, T. W., Odle-Dusseau, H., & Bliese, P. D. (2011). Dispositional optimism buffers combat veterans from the negative effects of warzone stress on mental health symptoms and work impairment. *Journal of Clinical Psychology, 67,* 866–880. doi:10.1002/jclp.20809

Thomas, J. L., Wilk, J. E., Riviere, L. A., McGurk, D., Castro, C. A., & Hoge, C. W. (2010). Prevalence of mental health problems and functional impairment among active component and National Guard soldiers 3 and 12 months following combat in Iraq. *Archives of General Psychiatry, 67,* 614–623. doi:10.1001/archgenpsychiatry.2010.54

van der Linden, D., Nijenhuis, J., & Bakker, A. B. (2010). The general factor of personality: A meta-analysis of Big Five intercorrelations and a criterion-related validity study. *Journal of Research in Personality, 44,* 315–327. doi:10.1016/j.jrp.2010.03.003

Vogt, D. S., Rizvi, S. L., Shipherd, J. C., & Resick, P. A. (2008). Longitudinal investigation of reciprocal relationship between stress reactions and hardiness. *Personality and Social Psychology Bulletin, 34,* 61–73. doi:10.1177/0146167207309197

Watson, D., Clark, L. A., & Tellegen, A. (1988). Development and validation of brief measures of positive and negative affect: The PANAS scales. *Journal of Personality and Social Psychology, 54,* 1063–1070. doi:10.1037/0022-3514.54.6.1063

Westman, M. (1990). The relationship between stress and performance: The moderating effect of hardiness. *Human Performance, 3,* 141–155. doi:10.1207/s15327043hup0303_1

Wiggins, J. S. (1996). *The five-factor model of personality: Theoretical perspectives.* New York, NY: Guilford Press.

3

MORALE AND COHESION AS CONTRIBUTORS TO RESILIENCE

THOMAS W. BRITT AND KALIFA K. OLIVER

Any organization would want employees who are resilient in the face of multiple work demands. However, resilience is especially important for the military, as service members are faced with multiple traumatic stressors that can result in a host of psychological and physical problems (Adler, Litz, & Bartone, 2003; Driskell, Salas, & Johnston, 2006). In addition, military personnel face continued exposure to more insidious stressors that represent a generally volatile and negative work environment (e.g., difficult environmental conditions, high workload; King, King, Fairbank, Keane, & Adams, 1998). The inability of service members to successfully cope with stress has implications at multiple levels. Not only are service members more likely to develop problems such as posttraumatic stress disorder (PTSD), depression, alcohol abuse, and anger management problems (Hoge et al., 2004; Maguen, Suvak, & Litz, 2006), but the performance of the unit may also be affected, thereby potentially compromising the success of the overall mission.

http://dx.doi.org/10.1037/14190-003
Building Psychological Resilience in Military Personnel: Theory and Practice, R. R. Sinclair
and T. W. Britt (Editors)
Copyright © 2013 by the American Psychological Association. All rights reserved.

In the present chapter, we consider two constructs in military psychology that have a long history of being considered desirable attributes for service members to possess: morale and unit cohesion. We argue that the major reason for the perceived importance of morale and unit cohesion for the psychological functioning of service members is that these variables are presumed to help enhance the resilience of military personnel, thereby allowing service members to accomplish mission objectives in the face of extreme stress. Military leaders and scholars of military psychology have recognized the importance of both morale and unit cohesion as critical determinants of soldier functioning and performance during different types of military operations (Britt & Dickinson, 2006; Siebold, 2006). However, there is virtually no direct research linking morale and cohesion to resilience as conceptualized in the present volume.

In the present chapter, we first briefly describe current conceptualizations of morale and unit cohesion and describe the model of resilience guiding our thinking in the chapter. We then provide a theoretical discussion of why morale and unit cohesion should be related to resilience among military personnel. Given the lack of direct research on the role of morale and unit cohesion in resilience, we review indirect evidence linking the two constructs to resilience. Finally, we provide recommendations for the type of research needed to definitively examine how morale and cohesion are related to resilience and discuss the implications of the proposed research for interventions designed to enhance the resilience of military personnel.

MORALE, UNIT COHESION, AND RESILIENCE: CLARIFYING THE CONSTRUCTS

Morale

The concept of morale has a long history within military psychology (Manning, 1991). After reviewing the extant research, Manning (1991) defined *morale* as "the enthusiasm and persistence with which a member of a group engages in the prescribed activities of that group" (p. 455). Britt and Dickinson (2006) noted that prior researchers had offered many different definitions of morale, and they developed a definition based on a view of morale as a positive psychological variable indicative of enthusiasm and energy (see also Britt, 1997). Britt and Dickinson defined *morale* as "a service member's level of motivation and enthusiasm for achieving mission success" (p. 162). Morale has been conceptualized as a positive psychological resource that influences movement toward a goal (Britt, Dickinson, Moore, Castro, & Adler, 2007). We see morale as a type of positive affect, similar to Shirom's (2010) concept of vigor, that combines feelings of energy with feelings of enthusiasm for accomplishing salient tasks. Morale should therefore be related to task accomplishment and positive emotional responses to work. This relationship has been supported by Britt et al. (2007), who found that morale ratings of U.S. peacekeepers were prospectively related to perceived benefits of participating in the peacekeeping mission. Although morale may exist at the unit level, in the present chapter we focus on morale at the level of the individual service member. Britt et al. (2007) found little evidence of unit-level variability in morale (as revealed by a low intraclass correlation coefficient for unit on reports of morale).

Britt and Dickinson (2006) argued that the determinants of morale could be divided into four major areas: mission, leadership, unit, and individual. Each of these areas will be briefly described. Regarding mission-relevant predictors, they proposed that morale should be high when there is a clear purpose behind the mission, objectives are seen as achievable, service members perceive incremental success being made, and there is public support for the operation. With regard to leadership factors, morale should be high when leaders clarify mission objectives, instill high efficacy and trust, emphasize positive outcomes associated with mission success, and recognize personnel for superior performance. With regard to unit factors, morale should be high when individuals are part of a unit with high collective efficacy, thereby facilitating the belief that achieving mission objectives is a real possibility. As discussed in more detail below, although morale and unit cohesion should be related, we expect this relationship to be primarily a function of the relationship between unit cohesion and collective efficacy. That is, unit cohesion contributes to a stronger sense of collective efficacy (the unit's ability to accomplish tasks to achieve desired goals; see Jex & Bliese, 1999), which should result in higher morale.

Finally, it is clear there are individual differences in the extent to which military personnel report high versus low morale that are a function of personality factors or prior experiences that have nothing to do with the given mission or unit climate. Britt and Dickinson (2006) hypothesized that dispositional optimism, hardiness, and self-efficacy should be related to higher levels of morale. An optimistic individual is someone who believes "that the future holds positive opportunities with successful outcomes" (Burke, Joyner, Czech, & Wilson, 2000, p. 129). Given our view that morale is determined by an expectation that mission objectives are achievable, it makes sense that a service member's dispositional level of optimism would in part determine his or her level of morale during a military operation.

Bartone (1999) found that soldiers scoring higher on a measure of hardiness were less likely to develop psychological problems after exposure to war-related stressors. In addition, Britt, Adler, and Bartone (2001) found that higher levels of hardiness were related to a greater tendency to perceive a sense of meaning during a peacekeeping mission to Bosnia. Therefore, hardiness would be expected to relate to morale by providing service members with a sense of purpose and confidence during a military operation. Finally, *self-efficacy* refers to confidence in being able to execute the actions necessary to succeed in a given domain (Bandura, 2001), and service members who are confident in their ability to do their job, especially under difficult conditions, should report higher levels of morale.

Britt et al. (2007) conducted a longitudinal study among U.S. soldiers deployed to a peacekeeping mission in Kosovo to examine some of the hypothesized predictors of morale. They found that engagement in meaningful work during the deployment and confidence in unit functioning and leadership were both related to soldier morale during the deployment. They also found that morale during the deployment was related to perceived benefits of deploying months after the deployment was over. Although these results were obtained among soldiers participating in a military operation other than war, we would hypothesize that engagement in meaningful work and confidence in unit functioning and leadership would be related to morale in combat operations as well (Gal & Manning, 1987).

Unit Cohesion

Siebold (2006) defined *cohesion* as "the extent to which the group maintains its structure (pattern) or maintains an effective structure within its environment" (p. 190) and suggested that "cohesion develops to enable the human group to serve the basic need of its members through mutual give and take" (p. 193). Loosely defined, *team cohesion* is the degree to which the members of the team try to coordinate with, help out, and support each other in their efforts to carry out team goals. Cohesion helps to enhance efficiency, motivation, and flexibility among group members. Cohesion is "a state where a group of relatively similar individuals holds together to accomplish its purpose, especially when the group is under stress" (Siebold, 2006, p. 188). Cohesion can be described as the state in which a group is holding together, whereas the term *cohesiveness* is used to describe the strength of cohesion (Siebold, 2006).

Griffith (1988) described two types of cohesion: (a) affective cohesion (relating to interpersonal support) and (b) instrumental cohesion (relating to task performance). Within a military context, authors have discussed the importance of both types of cohesion for well-being and performance, with the latter being more strongly linked to performance (Siebold, 2006). Much has been written on the affective ties that develop between military personnel, and these ties may help sustain service members when they are faced with continued stressors (Manning & Fullerton, 1988). However, it is also critical that military personnel exhibit instrumental cohesion, so they can collaborate effectively to accomplish group goals.

Cohesion can be conceived as having two fundamental targets: (a) vertical cohesion (referring to superior–subordinate relations) and (b) horizontal cohesion (referring to peer relations; Siebold, 2006). The concept of cohesion is also based on properties of small groups and can be seen as serving both instrumental and affective needs. Researchers typically focus on horizontal cohesion, and vertical cohesion is dealt with by those studying leadership.

Siebold (2006) defined *military group cohesion* as

> a special type of cohesion in that typically the group exists as part of a large, long-lived, somewhat isolated, highly regulated, hierarchical organization from which the group member cannot easily leave or travel about. . . . These features of military groups make them different from many groups portrayed in the general behavioral and social science literature. (p. 185)

Given the consequences associated with military action, there are likely higher stakes associated with military group cohesion than with cohesion in civilian workplace settings.

The most widely researched predictor of cohesion is leadership. According to Siebold (2006), leaders are responsible for developing and promoting vertical cohesion between themselves and their subordinates, as well as for facilitating peer bonding between soldiers. Leaders are also responsible for building pride and support of the mission and goals at hand by integrating the service member to his or her larger units. Leaders help develop the infrastructure for cohesion by ensuring and enforcing rule clarity so that members of the group can achieve necessary mission goals as well as satisfy their needs, those of their peers, and the organization as a whole. Good leadership is fundamental to cohesion. A leader may be able to improve unit cohesion simply though altering the subunit and individual reward structure in a targeted area (Blades, 1986) or by diminishing the time lapse between exemplary performance and receipt of rewards for such actions (Siebold, 2006). Poor leadership of a unit may lead to poor unit cohesion.

Bass, Avolio, Jung, and Berson (2003) examined transformational and transactional leadership as predictors of unit cohesion and performance among light infantry platoons. They found that positive ratings of leadership were related to objective indicators of unit performance and that unit cohesion accounted for a portion of the relationship. These results suggest that quality leadership is related to higher unit cohesion, which then predicts better unit performance. Researchers using civilian samples have also revealed connections between positive ratings of leadership and unit cohesion (Callow, Smith, Hardy, Arthur, & Hardy, 2009; Sanders & Schyns,

2006). Siebold (2006) found that research on other predictors of cohesion is minimal. Most of the variables tested, including similarity of personal characteristics, degree of mutual interdependence, and length of time service members interacted with each other so as to have had similar experiences (e.g., Siebold & Lindsay, 1999), have had modest or insignificant correlations with cohesion. Cohesion is more commonly examined as a predictor and has been related to a number of outcome variables, including unit performance, service member's ability to handle stressful situations, reduction of disciplinary problems, and other positive outcomes (Siebold, 2006).

Resilience

Psychological resilience (herein referred to as *resilience*) is a relatively new concept that has come out from the growing recognition of the human ability to adapt and positively overcome stressful life interruptions and events. For our purpose in the present chapter, resilience is conceptualized as the ability to remain at or quickly return to an original state of psychological functioning following exposure to stressful and/or traumatic events. Therefore, the model of resilience guiding our analysis of morale and cohesion is that of Bonanno (2004), who defined *resilience* as

> the ability of adults in otherwise normal circumstances who are exposed to an isolated and potentially highly disruptive event, such as the death of a close relation or a violent or life-threatening situation, to maintain relatively stable, healthy levels of psychological and physical functioning. (p. 20)

Within the prototypical military context of service members participating in combat operations, Bonanno's (2004) approach can be used to examine changes in psychological function from predeployment to multiple points after deployment as a function of exposure to traumatic events during deployment. Bolton, Litz, Britt, Adler, and Roemer (2001) discussed the importance of examining psychological functioning prior to deployments, as 8% of service members typically meet criteria for PTSD at the pre-deployment time period, which thereby establishes a baseline for examining the impact of traumatic events that occur during combat deployments. In terms of exposure to traumatic events, Hoge et al. (2004) noted, most service members deployed to operations in Iraq and Afghanistan have encountered events such as being fired upon, having to fire on the enemy, or being exposed to death and disease. However, there is variability in the extent to which military personnel are exposed to traumatic experience during combat (Adler, Bliese, McGurk, Hoge, & Castro, 2009), and this variability should be considered when examining resilience following combat deployments. Operationally, resilience would be defined either as experiencing no decline in functioning or as experiencing relatively shorter and relatively less severe declines in the months following return from the operation.

THEORETICAL MECHANISMS AND EVIDENCE LINKING MORALE AND UNIT COHESION TO RESILIENCE

Figure 3.1 provides the overall model guiding our discussion of how morale and unit cohesion are expected to predict resilience for military personnel on different types of deployments. Unfortunately, no research of which we are aware has utilized a longitudinal design to establish morale and cohesion as predictors of resilience; our analysis is based largely on research indicating the importance of morale and unit cohesion as predictors of precursors to resilience, such as PTSD and other indexes of psychological functioning. We review this research in the next sections after discussing the mechanisms that theoretically link the key military constructs to resilience.

Morale as a Predictor of Resilience

As shown in Figure 3.1, morale is expected to be linked to resilience through the provision of psychological resources that help the military cope with the challenges of participating in stressful military operations (Britt, Adler, Bliese, & Moore, in press). These resources include greater

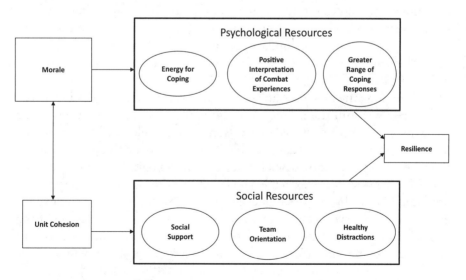

Figure 3.1. Theoretical model of how morale and unit cohesion are related to resilience.

energy for coping, a more positive interpretation of stressful deployments, and a greater range of options for coping with the consequences of combat exposure (Folkman & Moskowitz, 2000; Hobfoll, 2002). Frederickson and her colleagues have argued that positive affect increases the range of "thought–action repertoires," so that individuals experiencing more positive affect should think of more potential solutions for dealing with current life problems (Fredrickson, 1998; Fredrickson & Losada, 2005). Individuals high in morale may be similarly likely to generate a greater range of options for approaching work demands, which should enable them to function better when dealing with the consequences of stressful events.

Hobfoll (2002) reviewed the importance of resources in adapting to stressful life events. He noted that psychological and social resources are valued in their own right and can help individuals deal with the demands of especially taxing situations. Lazarus and Folkman's (1984) transactional model of stress suggests that these different resources should result in a more positive primary (initial) appraisal that the stressors encountered on a given deployment are manageable. In fact, it may even be possible that under conditions of high morale, the primary appraisal of operational demands such as engaging the enemy is seen as a challenge, as such events allow service members to contribute to the success of the overall mission.

Of course, for many stressors encountered by military personnel, the primary appraisal of the environment will be one of threat, and individuals will be required to engage in a secondary appraisal of whether they possess the resources to deal with the threat (Adler et al., 2003; Lazarus & Folkman, 1984). Under these circumstances, the motivational resources resulting from high morale should result in a more favorable secondary appraisal in which service members perceive an increased ability to cope with these stressful events. This enhanced secondary appraisal should ultimately lessen the psychological impact of the event (Lazarus & Folkman, 1984), resulting in greater resilience.

Therefore, the processes linking morale to resilience in military settings reside largely within the individual. High levels of morale are hypothesized to be associated with adaptive motivational states fueled by being involved in a meaningful mission that has the possibility of succeeding. We argue that these adaptive motivational states are psychological resources that are needed to cope with the extreme demands faced during military operations, and individuals who possess higher levels of these resources should experience less severe psychological consequences. This conceptualization of the relationship between morale and resilience is consistent with models that emphasize the individual having a coherent view of his or her reality that is imbued with purpose and meaning (Antonovsky, 1987; Richardson, 1993). Military personnel should adapt much better to a stressful deployment when they can derive a sense of meaning and purpose from their participation in the mission (Britt, 2003).

To fully examine the role of morale in the resilience of military personnel to the stressors of deployments, researchers would need to measure psychological functioning prior to the given deployment. Researchers would then need to measure exposure to stressful events during the deployment (or simply assume that all service members would likely be exposed to highly stressful events), as well as morale during the deployment. Psychological functioning would then have to be assessed at multiple points in time postdeployment.

As stated earlier, no research meeting these expectations has been conducted with morale. In fact, research within military psychology has been much more focused on morale as an outcome measure than on morale as a predictor of psychological functioning (Britt & Dickinson, 2006; Manning, 1991). In one of the few studies to examine the relationship between morale and psychological functioning, Britt et al. (2007) studied U.S. peacekeepers deployed to Kosovo. When soldiers were assessed at roughly the midpoint of their deployment, they completed a number of measures, including a measure of morale. They completed a postdeployment assessment 3 to 4 months after returning home that included a measure of PTSD symptoms and perceived benefits from deploying. Britt et al. (2007) found that morale during the deployment was negatively related to PTSD following the deployment and was positively related to perceived benefits from the deployment. These results suggest that morale was prospectively linked to reduced reports of psychological symptoms as well as to experience of psychological benefits from the deployment experience. Both of these outcomes would be expected to be associated with higher levels of soldier resilience.

More recently, Britt et al. (2013) examined morale as a moderator of the combat exposure–PTSD symptom relationship among soldiers who had returned from a long deployment to Iraq. Morale, combat exposure breadth and perceived stressfulness, and PTSD symptoms were assessed 4 months following the deployment, and PTSD symptoms were assessed again 6 months later. Morale interacted with both combat exposure breadth and combat exposure stressfulness to predict PTSD symptoms not only at 4 months postdeployment but also 6 months later. In a result supporting the argument that morale is an indicator of resilience, soldiers reporting high morale reported fewer symptoms of PTSD under high levels of combat exposure, both at 4 months and 10 months following their return home.

However, the ideal research design for establishing the role of morale in resilience would be to have pre-deployment information on the psychological functioning of the soldiers and to follow them for longer postdeployment. This type of design would enable researchers to assess whether morale predicts the increase of PTSD from predeployment to postdeployment and whether it is predictive of the length of time it takes soldiers to return to baseline levels of symptomatology postdeployment. This type of design could also assess the role of perceived benefits (a positive interpretation of the deployment experience) in allowing soldiers to bounce back from the stressful events encountered during the deployment.

Unit Cohesion as a Predictor of Resilience

As shown in Figure 3.1, unit cohesion is hypothesized to influence resilience through different processes than morale does. Unit cohesion captures the strength of the social ties within the unit and the ability for the unit to come together to accomplish mission objectives (Manning, 1991; Siebold, 2006), and it is therefore by definition an interpersonal or social construct. Within a military context, it is easy to see how the cohesiveness of unit members could influence the well-being and performance of service members. Mission success and well-being will be much higher when personnel come together out of a commitment to a shared purpose of accomplishing stated objectives. We hypothesize that unit cohesion should be related to resilience by providing service members with sources of support, by allowing service members to focus on the team as a unit, and by providing healthy distractions from the demands of combat. As discussed previously, units with high levels of cohesion have military personnel who are close to each other, support one another, and work well together (Siebold, 2006). We would argue that the impact of military unit cohesion on resilience should be especially strong. In fact, military historians and authors have for some time emphasized the importance of unit cohesion for the psychological functioning and performance of service members (see Manning, 1991).

We argue that, as was the case with morale, unit cohesion influences resilience through providing the service member with resources needed to cope with stressful events encountered on deployment. Whereas morale contributes to a service member's level of psychological resources, unit cohesion and the social support such cohesion provides contribute to a service member's social resources (Hobfoll, 2002). Military personnel who are part of a highly cohesive unit will have higher levels of social resources, which will better prepare them to confront the demands experienced when encountering stressful events on deployments. Affective cohesion within a unit should help service members cope emotionally with stressful events encountered on a deployment, and instrumental cohesion within a unit should help service members use problem-focused coping to confront demands that can be addressed through action (Lazarus & Folkman, 1984).

We also hypothesize that focusing attention on unit factors (e.g., determining who is responsible for what aspect of team functioning, providing fellow unit members with support) and engaging in healthy distractions will facilitate resilience. Ruminating on the characteristics of a negative event is an unhealthy way to cope with stressors (Nolen-Hoeksema, Parker, & Larson, 1994). We argue that when service members are focused on the unit (e.g., unit goals, unit functioning), they should be less likely to be self-focused and therefore less likely to ruminate on aspects of a stressful situation. In fact, long periods of isolation and inactivity during a deployment will likely give rise to increased rumination. Related to this idea is that of healthy distractions, where unit members come together when not participating in mission-relevant activities to let off steam, joke around, and in other ways avoid active contemplation of the stressfulness of the given operational environment.

As was the case in our discussion of the consequences of psychological resources stemming from morale, we argue that social resources should result in a more positive primary appraisal of the stressors encountered during deployments, as well as a more positive secondary appraisal when a threat is perceived. Service members in cohesive units may approach demands with a sense of challenge at being able to accomplish difficult objectives, reflecting an adaptive primary appraisal (Lazarus & Folkman, 1984). In addition, these social resources should enhance the ability of service members to cope with stressors appraised as threats, resulting in more positive secondary appraisals and more effective coping.

Despite the presumed importance of unit cohesion for psychological functioning, no research of which we are aware meets the conditions to show that unit cohesion creates more resilient service members. However, research has examined the role of unit cohesion and the related concept of social support (see Chapter 4, this volume) on the well-being of military personnel. We now review this research and discuss how it could be improved to allow a better test of unit cohesion as a predictor of resilience.

Solomon, Weisenberg, Schwarzwald, and Mikulincer (1987) followed 213 Israeli Defense Forces veterans of the 1982 Lebanon War. The veterans were assessed annually for 3 years post combat. Solomon et al. found that those veterans experiencing higher levels of combat-related stress were more likely to be diagnosed with related psychological disorders. This result showed that combat stress has potentially long-lasting effects that make soldiers emotionally vulnerable. The most common disorder observed was PTSD. They found that 59% of veterans of the 1982 Lebanon War who were diagnosed with combat stress reaction (CSR) had PTSD 1 year after the war. Combat stress reaction is a condition in which soldiers are unable to perform their duty because of extreme situational psychological disturbance.

These results also suggest there were several soldiers who were not unduly affected by their combat experiences. Solomon et al. (1987) considered how cohesion may play the role of a protective mechanism that reduces the negative psychological effects of traumatic events encountered during combat. They defined *troop cohesion* as a feeling of supportiveness within a combat unit that exists among enlisted persons and between these subordinates and their officers. They found that troop cohesion aids soldiers who are exposed to combat, regardless of the perceived intensity of battle. Their results demonstrated that greater troop cohesion was associated with fewer symptoms of loneliness and combat stress reaction. Solomon et al. also examined whether troop cohesion would interact with the intensity of battle to predict the outcome variables. However, they found no interaction, indicating the effects of troop cohesion were not particularly pronounced under high levels of stress. These results are consistent with other analyses of military personnel from Vietnam and the Yom Kippur War, suggesting that units high in group cohesion are more psychologically resistant to the potentially debilitating stressors they confront (e.g., Belenky, 1987; Kellett, 1982).

The effects of social support on psychological well-being are more widely researched than the effects of cohesion itself. Studies have shown that social support aids stress resistance by supplying people with the information that they are loved, are appreciated, and are a part of a network of caring individuals (Caplan, 1974; Cobb, 1976; Häusser, Mojzisch, Niesel, & Schulz-Hardt, 2010). Hobfoll and Walfisch (1984) found that social support aids stress resistance under high-stress life conditions but has little effect under low-stress conditions, and they argued that social support acts as a buffer against psychological stress. With reference to military personnel, Solomon, Mikulincer, and Hobfoll (1986) suggested that the effects of stress on post-traumatic stress symptoms can be compounded if a person under stressful conditions, such as during combat, feels alone and unsupported by friends and fellow officers. This implies that poor cohesion may result in loneliness and that the feeling of loneliness would bring with it a sense of insecurity and isolation. That isolation, compounded with the stress of combat, may lead to long-term psychological breakdown.

Morale and Cohesion as Predictors of Resilience: A Research Agenda

As stated earlier in the chapter, researchers have not used the longitudinal research designs necessary to truly test whether morale and unit cohesion lead to higher levels of resilience among military personnel. In the present chapter, we provide suggestions for such research and argue that testing the model provided in Figure 3.1 is possible, given the recent trend for military research organizations to follow service members over extended periods of time. We also recommend the use of quasi-experimental studies to examine the effects of interventions designed to increase morale and unit cohesion on indexes of resilience.

Longitudinal Research Designs With Multiple Assessment Points

Longitudinal research designs with multiple assessment points are necessary to examine how morale and unit cohesion are related to service member resilience. By definition, models of resilience incorporate a longitudinal component whereby individuals must be assessed prior to stressor exposure and at multiple points following exposure to the stressor. Only then can researchers investigate those factors that predict whether individuals quickly return to baseline psychological functioning after exposure to the stressor. By definition, the importance of longitudinal methods in the field of organizational stress has been repeatedly emphasized (Zapf, Dormann, & Frese, 1996).

Research on resilience in general has not been methodologically sophisticated, and it has failed to take advantage of recent statistical developments such as latent growth curve modeling (Bliese & Ployhart, 2002). Models of resilience, such as that of Bonanno, argue that resilient individuals are those who do not show a large or extended decrease in psychological functioning after exposure to traumatic or highly stressful events (e.g., death of a loved one, exposure to terrorist attacks). However, what specifically qualifies as a "large" or "extended" decrease tends not to be well operationalized. Latent growth curve modeling is suited to examine trajectories of psychological functioning over time and therefore to identify trajectories associated with more resilient functioning (Bonanno & Mancini, 2012). Once these trajectories are better understood, researchers can assess whether trajectories differ by such qualities as morale and unit cohesion.

Recently, military organizations such as the Walter Reed Army Institute of Research in the United States have begun collecting data (including indicators of psychological functioning such as PTSD, depression, and anxiety) from service members before they deploy on combat operations and then at multiple time points after their return from a given deployment (e.g., 3, 6, and 12 months postdeployment; see Hoge et al., 2004). This type of longitudinal design would be ideal for examining whether morale and unit cohesion predict the degree and duration of decreases in psychological functioning as a function of stressors encountered by service members during military operations. Of course, to test the model depicted in Figure 3.1 researchers would also need to assess not only morale and unit cohesion during the deployment but also the hypothesized mediators of the relationships between these constructs and resilience.

Fortunately, established measures exist to measure morale (see Britt & Dickinson, 2006) and cohesion (see Griffith, 1988) within a military context. In addition, established measures of psychological functioning are plentiful. Morale and unit cohesion should ultimately enhance the resilience of military personnel through different mechanisms. However, more work is needed on the development of reliable and valid measures to assess some of the psychological and social resources that are hypothesized to result from morale and unit cohesion, especially in a military context. For example, measures of purpose (Ryff, 1989), perceptions of success (Chen, Gully, & Eden, 2001), and optimism (Carver & Scheier, 2003) exist for the general population, but no military equivalents capture the unique contexts of military personnel. Prior research on frame-of-reference effects in personality assessment has shown that personality variables better predict relevant outcomes when the personality constructs are framed in the specific context in which they are being used (Lievens, De Corte, & Schollaert, 2008). We would make a similar prediction for military-specific measures of morale and cohesion.

Modifications of existing measures are a possibility (Halverson & Bliese, 1996), but additional work is needed to establish whether military-specific morale and cohesion measures would be more useful than standard measures in this area. Similarly, there are established measures of social support in the broader literature (Cobb, 1976), and some of these have been adapted to a military setting (see Solomon et al., 1986). However, we are not aware of measures assessing team orientation during a mission and healthy distractions conferred by team membership.

Quasi-Experimental Designs

Although it is difficult to conduct experiments in operational conditions, quasi-experiments could be used to examine whether programs designed to promote morale and unit cohesion actually do so and whether the programs are also related to increased resilience. Quasi-experiments take into account naturally occurring variations in environmental conditions that may affect outcomes of interest (Cook, Campbell, & Peracchio, 1990). Britt and Dickinson (2006) discussed the importance of examining changes in morale as a result of important mission events. The fact that morale has the capacity to fluctuate over the course of a military operation means that researchers need to assess morale frequently during a given operation. In addition, it would be worthwhile to examine the effects of interventions designed to increase morale and to examine whether these interventions enhance the resilience of service members, perhaps through the effects of the intervention on morale.

For example, prior to the peacekeeping mission in Bosnia, U.S. soldiers were required to participate in predeployment training to prepare them for the mission (see Britt, 2003). One component of the predeployment training involved education on the history of the Bosnian conflict and the purpose that the U.S. soldiers were serving by being involved in the mission. This type of educational intervention would be hypothesized to influence the morale of military personnel as a result of increasing soldiers' perception of the purpose of the military operation and therefore enthusiasm for accomplishing the mission, and it may ultimately enhance the resilience of personnel serving on the mission.

Numerous suggestions have been offered for enhancing unit cohesion among military personnel as well (Manning, 1991; Vaitkus & Griffith, 1990). In one of the largest natural experiments of its type, in 1981 the U.S. Army invoked a policy for some units in which soldiers changed duty stations with their units, in part to enhance the cohesiveness of these military units (Vaitkus & Griffith, 1990). Compared with those in units in which soldiers changed duty stations in a traditional manner (with individual soldiers being reassigned to different locations), the soldiers who moved with their units reported higher unit cohesion and morale. Research examining whether this type of intervention would also enhance the resilience of military personnel to high periods of stress in different military operations remains to be conducted.

CONCLUDING THOUGHTS

In summary, morale and unit cohesion have been argued to be important determinants of resilience among military personnel. Ultimately, morale and unit cohesion should enhance the resilience of military personnel through different mechanisms. However, research designs permitting definitive conclusions on morale and unit cohesions as determinants of resilience have been lacking. The present chapter provided a model for how morale and unit cohesion should influence resilience, reviewed the research that has been conducted on morale and unit cohesion as predictors of psychological functioning, and provided suggestions for future research to better establish morale and cohesion as determinants of resilience.

REFERENCES

Adler, A. B., Bliese, P. B., McGurk, D., Hoge, C. W., & Castro, C. A. (2009). Battlemind debriefing and Battlemind training as early interventions with soldiers returning from Iraq: Randomization by platoon. *Journal of Consulting and Clinical Psychology, 77*, 928–940. doi:10.1037/a0016877

Adler, A. B., Litz, B. T., & Bartone, P. T. (2003). The nature of peacekeeping stressors. In T. W. Britt & A. B. Adler (Eds.), *The psychology of the peacekeeper: Lessons from the field* (pp. 149–167). Westport, CT: Praeger.

Antonovsky, A. (1987). *Unraveling the mystery of health: How people manage stress and stay well.* San Francisco, CA: Jossey-Bass. doi:10.4135/9781446221129.n9

Bandura, A. (2001). Social cognitive theory: An agentic perspective. *Annual Review of Psychology, 52*, 1–26. doi:10.1146/annurev.psych.52.1.1

Bartone, P. T. (1999). Hardiness protects against war-related stress. *Consulting Psychology Journal: Practice and Research, 51,* 72–82. doi:10.1037/1061-4087.51.2.72

Bass, B. M., Avolio, B. J., Jung, D. I., & Berson, Y. (2003). Predicting unit performance by assessing transformational and transactional leadership. *Journal of Applied Psychology, 88,* 207–218. doi:10.1037/0021-9010.88.2.207

Belenky, G. (1987). *Contemporary studies in combat psychiatry: Contributions in military studies.* New York, NY: Greenwood Press.

Blades, J. W. (1986). *Rules for leadership: Improving unit performance.* Washington, DC: National Defense University Press.

Bliese, P. D., & Ployhart, R. E. (2002). Growth modeling using random coefficient models: Model building, testing, and illustration. *Organizational Research Methods, 5,* 362–387. doi:10.1177/109442802237116

Bolton, E., Litz, B. T., Britt, T. W., Adler, A., & Roemer, L. (2001). Reports of prior exposure to potentially traumatic events and PTSD in troops poised for deployment. *Journal of Traumatic Stress, 14,* 249–256. doi:10.1023/A:1007864305207

Bonanno, G. A. (2004). Loss, trauma, and human resilience: Have we underestimated the human capacity to thrive after extremely aversive events? *American Psychologist, 59,* 20–28. doi:10.1037/0003-066X.59.1.20

Bonanno, G. A., & Mancini, A. D. (2012). Beyond resilience and PTSD: Mapping the heterogeneity of responses to potential trauma. *Psychological Trauma: Theory, Research, Practice, and Policy, 4,* 74–83. doi:10.1037/a0017829

Britt, T. W. (1997, October). *What do soldiers think of morale, unit cohesion, and esprit de corps?* Paper presented at the meeting of the Research Committee on Armed Forces and Conflict Resolution, International Sociological Association, Modena, Italy.

Britt, T. W. (2003). Can participation in peacekeeping operations be beneficial? The importance of meaning as a function of attitudes and identity. In T. W. Britt & A. B. Adler (Eds.), *The psychology of the peacekeeper: Lessons from the field* (pp. 71–88). Westport, CT: Praeger.

Britt, T. W., Adler, A. B., & Bartone, P. T. (2001). Deriving benefits from stressful events: The role of engagement in meaningful work and hardiness. *Journal of Occupational Health Psychology, 6,* 53–63. doi:10.1037/1076-8998.6.1.53

Britt, T. W., Adler, A. B., Bliese, P. D., & Moore, D. (2013). Morale as a moderator of the combat exposure–PTSD symptom relationship. *Journal of Traumatic Stress, 26,* 94–101. doi:10.1002/jts.21775

Britt, T. W., & Dickinson, J. M. (2006). Morale during military operations: A positive psychology approach. In T. W. Britt, C. A. Castro, & A. B. Adler (Eds.), *Military life: The psychology of serving in peace and combat. Vol. 1: Military performance* (pp. 157–184). Westport, CT: Praeger Security International.

Britt, T. W., Dickinson, J. M., Moore, D. M., Castro, C. A., & Adler, A. B. (2007). Correlates and consequences of morale versus depression under stressful conditions. *Journal of Occupational Health Psychology, 12,* 34–47. doi:10.1037/1076-8998.12.1.34

Burke, K. L., Joyner, A. B., Czech, D. R., & Wilson, M. J. (2000). An investigation of concurrent validity between two optimism/pessimism questionnaires: The Life Orientation Test–Revised and the Optimism/Pessimism Scale. *Current Psychology*, *19*, 129–136. doi:10.1007/s12144-000-1009-5

Callow, N., Smith, M. J., Hardy, L., Arthur, C. A., & Hardy, J. (2009). Measurement of transformational leadership and its relationship with team cohesion and performance level. *Journal of Applied Sport Psychology*, *21*, 395–412. doi:10.1080/10413200903204754

Caplan, G. (1974). *Support systems and community mental health: Lectures on concept development.* Pasadena, CA: Behavioral Publications.

Carver, C. S., & Scheier, M. (2003). Optimism. In S. J. Lopez & C. R. Snyder (Eds.), *Positive psychological assessment: A handbook of models and measures* (pp. 75–89). Washington, DC: American Psychological Association. doi:10.1037/10612-005

Chen, G., Gully, S. M., & Eden, D. (2001). Validation of a new general self-efficacy scale. *Organizational Research Methods*, *4*, 62–83. doi:10.1177/109442810141004

Cobb, S. (1976). Social support as a moderator of life stress. *Psychosomatic Medicine*, *38*, 300–314.

Cook, T. D., Campbell, D. T., & Peracchio, L. (1990). Quasi experimentation. In M. D. Dunnette & L. M. Hough (Eds.), *Handbook of industrial and organizational psychology* (pp. 491–576). Palo Alto, CA: Consulting Psychologists Press.

Driskell, J. E., Salas, E. S., & Johnston, J. W. (2006). Decision making and performance under stress. In T. W. Britt, C. A. Castro, & A. B. Adler (Eds.), *Military life: The psychology of serving in peace and combat. Vol. 1: Military performance* (pp. 128–154). Westport, CT: Praeger Security International.

Folkman, S., & Moskowitz, J. T. (2000). Positive affect and the other side of coping. *American Psychologist*, *55*, 647–654. doi:10.1037/0003-066X.55.6.647

Frederickson, B. L. (1988). What good are positive emotions? *Review of General Psychology*, *2*, 300–319. doi:10.1037/1089-2680.2.3.300

Frederickson, B. L., & Losada, M. F. (2005). Positive affect and the complex dynamics of human flourishing. *American Psychologist*, *60*, 678–686. doi:10.1037/0003-066X.60.7.678

Gal, R., & Manning, F. J. (1987). Morale and its components: A cross-national comparison. *Journal of Applied Social Psychology*, *17*, 369–391. doi:10.1111/j.1559-1816.1987.tb00319.x

Griffith, J. (1988). Measurement of group cohesion in U.S. Army units. *Basic and Applied Social Psychology*, *9*, 149–171. doi:10.1207/s15324834basp0902_6

Halverson, R. R., & Bliese, P. D. (1996). Determinants of soldier support for Operation Uphold Democracy. *Armed Forces & Society*, *23*, 81–96. doi:10.1177/0095327X9602300104

Häusser, J. A., Mojzisch, A., Niesel, M., & Schulz-Hardt, S. (2010). Ten years on: A review of recent research on the job demand–control (–support) model and psychological well-being. *Work & Stress*, *24*, 1–35. doi:10.1080/02678371003683747

Hobfoll, S. E. (2002). Social and psychological resources and adaptation. *Review of General Psychology, 6,* 307–324. doi:10.1037/1089-2680.6.4.307

Hobfoll, S. E., & Walfisch, S. (1984). Coping with a threat to life: A longitudinal study of self-concept, social support, and psychological distress. *American Journal of Community Psychology, 12,* 87–100. doi:10.1007/BF00896930

Hoge, C. W., Castro, C. A., Messer, S. C., McGurk, D., Cotting, D. I., & Koffman, R. L. (2004). Combat duty in Iraq and Afghanistan, mental health problems, and barriers to care. *The New England Journal of Medicine, 351,* 13–22. doi:10.1056/NEJMoa040603

Jex, S. M., & Bliese, P. T. (1999). Efficacy beliefs as a moderator of the impact of work-related stressors: A multilevel study. *Journal of Applied Psychology, 84,* 349–361. doi:10.1037/0021-9010.84.3.349

Kellett, J. (1982). *Combat motivation: The behavior of soldiers in battle.* Boston, MA: Kluwer.

King, L. A., King, D. W., Fairbank, J. A., Keane, T. M., & Adams, G. A. (1998). Resilience-recovery factors in post-traumatic stress disorder among female and male Vietnam veterans: Hardiness, postwar social support, and additional stressful life events. *Journal of Personality and Social Psychology, 74,* 420–434. doi:10.1037/0022-3514.74.2.420

Lazarus, R. S., & Folkman, S. (1984). *Stress, appraisal, and coping.* New York, NY: Springer.

Lievens, F., De Corte, W., & Schollaert, E. (2008). A closer look at the frame-of-reference effect in personality scale scores and validity. *Journal of Applied Psychology, 93,* 268–279. doi:10.1037/0021-9010.93.2.268

Maguen, S., Suvak, M., & Litz, B. T. (2006). Predictors and prevalence of post-traumatic stress disorders among military veterans. In A. B. Adler, C. A. Castro, & T. W. Britt (Eds.), *Military life: The psychology of serving in peace and combat. Vol. 2: Operational stress* (pp. 141–169). Westport, CT: Praeger Security International.

Manning, F. J. (1991). Morale, unit cohesion, and esprit de corps. In R. Gal & D. Mangelsdorff (Eds.), *Handbook of military psychology* (pp. 453–470). New York, NY: Wiley.

Manning, F. J., & Fullerton, T. D. (1988). Health and well-being in highly cohesive units of the U.S. Army. *Journal of Applied Social Psychology, 18,* 503–519. doi:10.1111/j.1559-1816.1988.tb00032.x

Nolen-Hoeksema, S., Parker, L. E., & Larson, J. (1994). Ruminative coping with depressed mood following loss. *Journal of Personality and Social Psychology, 67,* 92–104. doi:10.1037/0022-3514.67.1.92

Richardson, M. S. (1993). Work in people's lives: A location for counseling psychologists. *Journal of Counseling Psychology, 40,* 425–433. doi:10.1037/0022-0167.40.4.425

Ryff, C. D. (1989). Happiness is everything, or is it? Explorations on the meaning of psychological well-being. *Journal of Personality and Social Psychology, 57,* 1069–1081. doi:10.1037/0022-3514.57.6.1069

Sanders, K., & Schyns, B. (2006). Leadership and solidarity behavior: Consensus in perception of employees within teams. *Personnel Review, 35,* 538–556. doi:10.1108/00483480610682280

Shirom, A. (2010). Feeling energetic at work: On vigor's antecedents. In A. B. Bakker & M. P. Leiter (Eds.), *Work engagement: Recent developments in theory and research* (pp. 69–84). New York, NY: Psychology Press.

Siebold, G. L. (2006). Military group cohesion. In T. W. Britt, C. A. Castro, & A. B. Adler (Eds.), *Military life: The psychology of serving in peace and combat. Vol. 1: Military performance* (pp. 185–201). Westport, CT: Praeger Security International.

Siebold, G. L., & Lindsay, T. J. (1999). The relation between demographic descriptors and soldier-perceived cohesion and motivation. *Military Psychology, 11,* 109–128. doi:10.1207/s15327876mp1101_6

Solomon, Z., Mikulincer, M., & Hobfoll, S. E. (1986). Effects of social support and battle intensity on loneliness and breakdown during combat. *Journal of Personality and Social Psychology, 51,* 1269–1276. doi:10.1037/0022-3514.51.6.1269

Solomon, Z., Weisenberg, M., Schwarzwald, J., & Mikulincer, M. (1987). Posttraumatic stress disorder among soldiers with combat stress reaction: The 1982 Israeli experience. *The American Journal of Psychiatry, 144,* 448–454.

Vaitkus, M., & Griffith, J. (1990). An evaluation of unit replacement on unit cohesion and individual morale in the U.S. Army all-volunteer force. *Military Psychology, 2,* 221–239. doi:10.1207/s15327876mp0204_3

Zapf, D., Dormann, C., & Frese, M. (1996). Longitudinal studies in organizational stress research: A review of the literature with reference to methodological issues. *Journal of Occupational Health Psychology, 1,* 145–169. doi:10.1037/1076-8998.1.2.145

4

SITUATIONAL FACTORS AND RESILIENCE: FACILITATING ADAPTATION TO MILITARY STRESSORS

STEVE M. JEX, JASON KAIN, AND YOUNGAH PARK

Although many military jobs are similar to those in the civilian world, the work environment for military personnel is often drastically different. This is due to many unique stressors associated with combat deployment, such as fellow soldiers' injuries and death, sleep deprivation, and high levels of uncertainty. Military personnel also face many unique postdeployment stressors, such as difficult reunions with spouses and children due to long-term and frequent separations, mental health problems, and injuries (Hoge et al., 2004; Park, 2011). The presence of these unique stressors, coupled with the fact that the modern military has faced more frequent deployments into combat situations than ever before, suggests that the concept of resilience is particularly important. Given the potential importance of resilience, it is important to understand what military organizations need to do in order to increase resilience among soldiers. Military organizations obviously cannot

http://dx.doi.org/10.1037/14190-004
Building Psychological Resilience in Military Personnel: Theory and Practice, R. R. Sinclair and T. W. Britt (Editors)

eliminate stressors related to combat missions and military operations; rather, they must either find highly resilient individuals or identify situations that can facilitate resilience among military personnel.

In reviewing the literature on resilience, one would certainly be justified in concluding that the primary emphasis has been on identifying individual traits that predict resilience, whereas far less attention has been paid to examining how situations contribute to resilience. That is, researchers have looked for individual differences that distinguish those who exhibit resilience in the face of adversity from those who do not (Bonanno, 2004). Studies on individual coping styles, for example, have supported the idea that negative coping styles (e.g., venting negative emotions, denial) interact with acute stressors affecting health outcomes, such as headaches, trouble sleeping, and depressed mood among military personnel (e.g., Day & Livingstone, 2001). Research on gender has shown that the association between deployment length and increased distress (i.e., depression, posttraumatic stress) existed only among male soldiers (e.g., Adler, Huffman, Bliese, & Castro, 2005). The trait of hardiness (Kobasa, Maddi, & Percutti, 1982) has also received considerable support as an individual difference marker of resilience in military research (e.g., Dolan & Adler, 2006). Most recently, an array of positive characteristics, termed *psychological capital*, have been shown to be related to resilience to traumatic exposure among soldiers deployed in combat (Schaubroeck, Riolli, Peng, & Spain, 2011). Readers interested in other positive psychological characteristics are referred to Chapter 2 of this volume.

Given the focus on the individual characteristics described above, one might speculate on the reasons for this emphasis in resilience research. One of the primary reasons for this focus is that in cases where resilience is exhibited (e.g., one individual thrives despite experiencing a traumatic stressor but others are devastated), people tend to attribute the causes of thriving or being devastated to individual characteristics (e.g., optimistic personality) rather than to situational characteristics (e.g., social support available to cope with traumatic events). Social psychologists refer to this phenomenon as the *fundamental attribution error* (Ross, Amabile, & Steinmetz, 1977), which is a general bias in person perception and attribution. In the present context, the term *error* may be a bit strong because in many cases individual characteristics of people probably do facilitate resilience. In addition, studies demonstrating considerable individual differences in developing mental illness after traumatic events (e.g., Bowman, 1997) may reinforce the research emphasis on individual characteristics of resilience. Unfortunately, the relative emphasis of individual differences compared to situations is quite out of balance; in fact, as is shown in this chapter, there are a number of important situational determinants of resilience.

Our purposes in this chapter are, therefore, (a) to isolate and identify organizational factors that bolster resilience among the organization's members and (b) to discuss how these factors apply to the military as an organization. To explore the situational determinants of resilience, we begin with a short discussion of what we mean by *situational* as it relates to resilience. We then shift to a discussion of the major situational determinants of resilience and conclude with a section on future research directions on situational determinants of resilience in military organizations.

SITUATIONAL DETERMINANTS OF RESILIENCE

For the purposes of this chapter, we define *situation* as any conditions, contexts, or resources that can be provided, modified, or controlled by military organizations in order to promote resilience. For example, a training program can be one resource that military organizations can provide to enhance resilience, although the content of training itself may focus on individual states or characteristics conducive to resilience. Military culture can also be a situational factor in that military leaders can attempt to develop or change aspects of the organizational culture in order to enhance resilience.

In considering the major situational determinants of resilience, one could opt for a *developmental* or *biographical* perspective. That is, one could consider the sum total of a person's life experiences and how those experiences contribute to his or her psychological resilience. Research has shown, not surprisingly, that growing up in a stable, supportive family environment contributes to resilience (McFadyen, Kerpelman, & Adler-Baeder, 2005). Despite the considerable merit to such an approach, the military obviously has no control over the family upbringing of its soldiers. Thus, in this chapter, we consider situational factors that the military might be able to exert some control over in order to enhance resilience: *social support, training,* and *military culture*.

Social Support

Social support has a long (and somewhat jaded) history in work-related stress research. According to Beehr (1985), social support represents "the provision of sympathy, evidence of liking, caring, and listening" (p. 183). However, past research has broken this broad definition down into multiple types of social support; two types of social support that have been linked to greater resilience are *structural* and *functional* social support. Structural social support refers to the size of a person's social network, and functional social support refers more to the extent to which the social network provides particular types of support (Cohen & Wills, 1985). Research has shown that both structural and functional support are strongly linked to lower levels of stress (Beehr, 1985), and both are associated with a lower likelihood of developing psychological disorders such as posttraumatic stress disorder (PTSD) among military veterans who have experienced traumatic stressors (King, King, Fairbank, Keane, & Adams, 1998).

Beyond structural and functional forms, social support may come in other forms, including *emotional, instrumental, informational,* and *appraisal.* Emotional social support is defined as communication from others that conveys the message that one is cared for, esteemed, and valued (Beehr, 1985; Cobb, 1976). In a military context, an example of emotional support would be leaders showing that they care about their subordinates' concerns or telling subordinates that they are important to the military and the country and that their efforts are needed to accomplish the group's missions. Instrumental social support is defined as providing resources for other people so they can perform their jobs more effectively (Beehr, 1985; House, 1981). An example of instrumental social support would be leaders ensuring that their subordinates have all the resources (e.g., supplies, information, manpower) needed in order to perform required tasks. Informational social support is defined as providing information to another person during a stressful time period that allows that person to solve problems more efficiently (Beehr, 1985; House, 1981). An example of informational support in a military setting would be one soldier sharing useful strategies for adjusting to a new environment during a deployment with another soldier. Finally, appraisal support is defined as providing information that is relevant to self-evaluation (Beehr, 1985; House, 1981). An example of appraisal support would be a military leader telling subordinates that they executed their job tasks flawlessly.

In general, there are three main situational antecedents that help to increase all types of social support: *social climate, social networks,* and *social embeddedness.* Climate is defined as shared perceptions about the practices and kinds of behaviors that get rewarded in a particular setting (Schneider, 1990). Supportive social climate reflects behavioral norms of respect among people who are working together (Moos & Lemke, 1992). In general, two of the most important norms that create a supportive social climate are helpfulness and protection (Moos & Lemke, 1992). In a military context, this type of climate would be one in which soldiers feel comfortable helping each other learn new skills that will improve their performance. In this type of climate, soldiers would do everything possible to provide the same amount of help for each other that they would want for themselves.

Social networks are defined as the number of people one has access to who can potentially provide social support (Kahn & Antonucci, 1980) or as a set of ties representing some relationship (Brass, 1995). They are the primary mechanism through which social support is provided (Kahn & Antonucci,

1980). In general, when someone knows many people, that person has more people whom he or she potentially can go to for social support (Kahn & Antonucci, 1980). In a military context, soldiers with larger social networks have more people who may be able to provide social support in times of need.

Social embeddedness is defined as the strength of the connections people have to others within a social network (Barrera, 1986). In other words, the stronger people's relationships are within their social network, the more likely they are to receive social support. In the military, soldiers who have stronger relationships with other members in their unit are more likely to receive social support.

In addition, researchers have long made a distinction between different sources of support. The primary sources of support that have been investigated include coworkers, supervisors, and family (usually the spouse). Furthermore, what has often been found is that support is typically more effective if the source of the support matches the stressor one is experiencing (de Jonge & Dormann, 2006). For example, if a soldier is experiencing a stressor during combat, support from a leader or fellow soldiers is likely to be more crucial than support from a spouse.

Because social support from leaders or supervisors has such a strong positive impact on subordinates' ability to handle stressful working conditions, one of the primary ways that soldiers can receive social support is from their immediate leader (Bartone, 2006; Britt, Davidson, Bliese, & Castro, 2004). Past research indicates that leaders who help to clarify roles and reduce group conflict increase the resilience of their subordinates (Britt et al., 2004). Leaders can generally clarify the roles of their subordinates and minimize conflict by defining *goals* for their subordinates, describing the *means* by which their subordinates complete tasks, explaining the *standards* that subordinates will be judged against, and consistently linking *rewards* to good performance and respectful interactions among subordinates (Britt et al., 2004); these elements have been shown to be associated with perceived organizational support among organizational members (Rhoades & Eisenberger, 2002). Additionally, supportive leaders who act as mentors can help their subordinates adjust to new environments and perform better in changing roles (Weiner, 1990). Social support also increases the level of cohesion among group members, which may enhance morale, satisfaction, performance, and well-being (Griffith, 1989; Limbert, 2004).

A unique study by Bliese and Britt (2001) demonstrated a somewhat different approach. These researchers operationalized social support as the level of consensus within a sample of military units regarding the quality of unit leadership. Using a sample of 52 companies that had been deployed to Haiti, Bliese and Britt found that high consensus regarding leadership quality weakened relationships between stressors and both morale and depression.

Though this is admittedly an indirect way of measuring social support, it nevertheless supports the proposition that social support is a key situational resilience factor in military settings (Bliese & Castro, 2000).

A final issue that is frequently debated in social support research and that is quite relevant to the present discussion is the role of social support in the stress process (Cohen & Wills, 1985; Viswesvaran, Sanchez, & Fisher, 1999). Social support has typically been conceived of either as having a main effect on stress reactions (or strains) or as having a buffering effect on the relationship between stressors and strains (Beehr, 1985); note that stressors refer to the causes (e.g., high workload) of strains, which are individuals' reactions to the stressors, such as fatigue (Jex & Britt, 2008). Theories about the main effect of social support on stress reactions indicate that social support can directly mitigate strains or reduce the level of stressors (Beehr, 1985; House, 1981). In other words, people with more social support generally perceive lower levels of stressors and strains than do those with less social support (Beehr, 1985; House, 1981). Viswesvaran et al. (1999) supported the main effect model of social support on stressors and strains in their meta-analysis. However, they acknowledged that because most of the studies in their meta-analysis were cross-sectional, the direction of causality represented by this relationship is unclear. A study on Israeli soldiers' combat stress reactions also showed that lack of emotional and instrumental support from officers was related to greater feelings of loneliness and likelihood of combat stress reactions among soldiers (Solomon, Mikulincer, & Hobfoll, 1986). Although it may be that social support reduces strain, it could also be that individuals experiencing high levels of strain withdraw from others and fail to seek social support.

In contrast, a buffering effect implies that social support influences the strength of the relationship between stressors and strains. For example, relationships between stressors and strains are weakest for people who have high levels of social support (Beehr, 1985; House, 1981; Viswesvaran et al., 1999). As far as why social support buffers the effects of stressors or enhances resilience, the answer lies in the types of social support described above. High levels of social support may make people feel emotionally cared for, provide them with tangible resources that help in coping with stressors, and help them to appraise stressors in a way that is nonthreatening. For example, King, King, Vogt, Knight, and Samper (2006) found that social support during the post-deployment period was a key component of resilience among a large national sample of Gulf War veterans. Evidence of resilience, in this case, was essentially a buffering effect—that is, exposure to deployment-related stressors without showing any adverse effects.

Given the many highly stressful circumstances in the military, such as life-threatening combat situations or separation from family due to prolonged and recurrent deployments, it should not be surprising that social support captures researchers' and practitioners' attention. Furthermore, the weight of the evidence described above suggests that social support can be one of the key situational factors of soldier resilience.

Impact of Social Support for Resilience in the Military

Although there is little debate that social support is an important resilience factor, much less agreement exists regarding ways in which military organizations can enhance social support among their members. Nevertheless, one way to do this is through leadership training. Because leaders have been found to be an important source of social support in the military (Bliese & Castro, 2000; Britt et al., 2004), training leaders to be more supportive would seem to be a logical way to enhance social support.

Alternatively, a study in Great Britain found that military peacekeepers who wanted to talk about their experiences to someone upon return from deployment reported significantly less psychological distress than those who did not wish to do so (Greenberg et al., 2003). Given that many of the soldiers in this study used informal networks of friends, peers, or family members to share those experiences, the study suggests that it is important for military organizations to promote a sense of community and facilitate stable interpersonal relationships. Recent research into promoting *social resilience* in the U.S. Army (Cacioppo, Reis, & Zautra, 2011), defined as an individual and collective group capacity to foster, engage in, and sustain positive relationships and to endure and recover from life stressors and social isolation, is also consistent with this idea.

Training

Research conducted in civilian organizations has shown that employees can be trained to be more resilient. For example, a resilience training program developed by Waite and Richardson (2004) has been shown to be effective. This program teaches participants how to think in a more resilient way about the challenges they face at work through a series of practical experiences. Participants in this program also learn interpersonal skills to help them overcome conflict and create more constructive relationships. The participants are taught how to spot negative thought patterns and change them to thoughts about overcoming challenges and becoming better individuals. As a result of this training program, participants have been shown to improve in areas that positively influence resilience, such as self-esteem, locus of control, purpose in life, and interpersonal reasoning (Waite & Richardson, 2004).

Finally, another line of military-specific research suggests that leaders can enhance resilience through hardiness training (Bartone, 2006). Past research indicates that hardiness can be learned and developed (e.g., Maddi, 1987), and hardiness training has been effective in increasing hardy attitudes among working adults, such as increasing the meaning they find in their work (Maddi, 1987; Maddi, Kahn, & Maddi, 1998). A more indirect way of facilitating hardiness could be accomplished through more general leadership training; that is, training leaders to exhibit hardiness in the presence of their subordinates, which hopefully facilitates resilience in their subordinates. This approach is likely to be viable, as it has been shown that the behavior of leaders can impact hardiness among subordinates (Bartone, 2006).

Training can also facilitate resilience in a more indirect fashion, that is, making sure that military personnel are properly trained to perform their job tasks. Although training of this nature will not directly enhance resilience, it may lead to changes in soldiers that are associated with resilience. For example, one consequence of training that has been shown repeatedly in the training literature (Goldstein & Ford, 2002) is enhanced *self-efficacy*. According to Bandura (1977), self-efficacy represents a person's belief that he or she can successfully carry out some behavior or course of action. By engaging in training, soldiers enhance their self-efficacy regarding the tasks required of them during a deployment. Self-efficacy is important not only for soldiers' task performance but also for their well-being. For example, research has shown that high self-efficacy buffers the relationship between stressors and stress outcomes among U.S. Army soldiers (e.g., Jex & Bliese, 1999; Jex, Bliese, Buzzell, & Primeau, 2001). Eden and Zuk (1995) showed that naval cadets in the Israel Defense Forces received training to enhance their self-efficacy and then, after the training course, were interviewed by a psychologist who made them believe that they had qualifications to overcome seasickness very well. Those who were in the experimental group reported less seasickness and performed better than their counterparts in the control group condition.

Another potential consequence of training that may be related to resilience is enhanced *collective efficacy*. According to Guzzo and Shea (1992), collective efficacy is the group-level analogue to individual-level self-efficacy. Collective efficacy reflects the collective perception among group members that a group can perform successfully or accomplish its goals. Jex and Gudanowski (1992) found that individual perceptions of collective efficacy buffered the relationship between work hours and strains among a sample of university employees, suggesting that this variable may be a resilience factor. Stronger evidence regarding collective efficacy as a resilience factor comes from a later study on U.S. Army soldiers by Jex and Bliese (1999). Consistent with Jex and Gudanowski, collective efficacy was shown to buffer the relationship between stressors and strains. More important, however, in this study collective efficacy was appropriately measured as a *unit-level* variable (the unit of analysis was the company), because it is a shared perception among the members of a group. Furthermore, it is possible that the mechanisms by which group-level variables such as collective efficacy influence resilience may be different than the mechanisms by which individual-level variables (e.g., self-efficacy) influence resilience.

Given the study suggesting that collective efficacy may be associated with resilience, the obvious question is *why*. One answer concerns the effects of individual-level efficacy on collective efficacy. Because many work tasks in the military require a collective or team effort, having a strong sense of collective efficacy makes members of a unit feel confident that they can handle any contingencies and overcome highly stressful situations that may arise. A strong sense of collective efficacy may also enhance resilience for social reasons. Although collective efficacy is clearly not the same as *cohesion*, which is the level of attraction members have toward the group (Forsyth, 1990), it is certainly possible that these two variables are positively related. When the members of a unit feel a strong sense that they can accomplish their collective goals, this may generate positive affect within a unit and ultimately lead to higher levels of cohesion. Another potential by-product of high collective efficacy may be increased social support, which again may further enhance resilience. These points are obviously speculative, however, and should be empirically tested.

Application of Resilience Training in the Military

The U.S. Army and the University of Pennsylvania recently launched a collaborative effort to develop and conduct resilience training through a train-the-trainer model (Reivich, Seligman, & McBride, 2011; see also Chapter 9, this volume). This training model is based on Masten and Reed's (2002) protective factors that contribute to resilience, such as optimism, sense of meaning, strong social relationships, and self-regulation. It is also based on the assumption that there are many aspects of resilience that are trainable (Reivich & Shatté, 2002). Reivich et al. (2011) stated that this military-specific resilience training program focuses mostly on teaching drill and platoon sergeants how to enhance soldiers' ability to handle adversity, prevent psychological distress, and promote well-being and performance. Although evaluation of this training is currently under way, this is still a good example of applying resilience training to a military context. In addition to providing resilience-specific training, military units should make sure that soldiers are well trained in their job tasks to increase self-efficacy as well as collective efficacy.

Military Culture

According to Schein (1992), culture reflects the underlying assumptions and values that guide behavior in organizations. Culture, however, exists at many levels in organizations. According to Janson (1994), there is an organization-wide culture but also many subcultures. The latter are based on the unit one is in or perhaps the geographical location where one lives. Although there has not been a great amount of empirical research on the impact of military-specific cultures or unit cultures on soldier resilience, there is one aspect of military culture that can either enhance resilience or detract from it.

Military cultures are often characterized as hypermasculine because their critical missions often involve combat behaviors, such as bravery, toughness, hardiness, and camaraderie (Dunivin, 1994; Krueger, 2000). In many cases, this combat warrior ethos facilitates the accomplishment of military missions and the successful performance of team-interdependent tasks. On the other hand, it should be recognized that this aspect of military culture can lead to negative stereotypes or stigmas that may actually hinder soldiers' resilience to combat stress. For example, signs of combat stress include trembling, extreme nervousness, inability to make decisions, and uncontrollable crying, to name just a few (Doran, Gaskin, Schumm, & Smith, 2005); none of these symptoms are consistent with stereotypes of what is considered masculine. When these signs of combat stress are not acknowledged and properly addressed, soldiers can develop serious mental health problems that may hinder their ability to perform their job tasks successfully.

Research has shown, however, that soldiers who admit their mental health problems and seek treatment or help are often stigmatized (Greene-Shortridge, Britt, & Castro, 2007). In a survey of soldiers serving in Afghanistan, nearly half reported believing that their unit leaders would treat them differently and that they would have negative career consequences if they sought help for a mental health problem (Mental Health Advisory Team VI, 2009). Although there is no direct empirical link between the stigmatization described above and resilience in troops, it is quite plausible that a culture that discourages soldiers from admitting mental health problems and seeking treatment would not facilitate resilience. This is an issue that obviously requires a cultural change, as has been already recognized within the military (Casey, 2011).

Another aspect of culture worth noting is the extent to which the organization is supportive of its members. In general, organizations that value their members and treat them well have been shown to be more successful than organizations without such values (Kotter & Hesketh, 1992). The reason for such findings may be that such supportive organizational cultures facilitate resilience in organizational members. This type of culture communicates to employees that they are more than just a "pair of hands" to the organization. Such a culture also communicates to organizational members that they will be supported when they face challenges in their work and even in their non-work lives. In a similar vein, *perceived organizational support* refers to individuals' global belief that their organization values their contributions and cares about their well-being (Eisenberger, Huntington, Hutchison, & Sowa, 1986). There is considerable research evidence that perceived organizational support can lead to a variety of positive employee outcomes, such as job satisfaction, positive moods, affective commitment, performance, and less withdrawal (Rhoades & Eisenberger, 2002).

Applications of Culture Change in the Military

As stated in the previous section, resilience may be impacted by the prevailing culture in the military. Furthermore, social support is a part of the contextual environment of organizations rather than just a perception on the part of an individual (Bliese & Jex, 2002). Given this, it would seem that if an organization did not have a very supportive culture, changing it to become more supportive might be a method to enhance resilience. Cultural change, however, is difficult to achieve, as it involves a multitude of long-term efforts from an organization.

With respect to stigmatization of mental health problems and of seeking help in the military, Ruvolo and Bullis's (2003) suggestions for cultural change are worth mentioning, as their suggestions were based on an analysis of failure in cultural change initiatives in the U.S. military. They suggested that military leaders need to communicate the need for cultural change, as well as to develop leader competencies that reflect the goals of their cultural change initiatives. The recent effort of the U.S. Navy in this regard is a good example. The Navy launched the short-term Navy Operational Stress Control (OSC) leader training program (Naval Center for Combat and Operational Stress Control, 2011). This training is designed for Navy officers and chief petty officers to enhance their understanding of the effects of stress, the impact of stigma, and the steps leaders can take to assist their subordinates in getting help for mental health problems. This awareness training may be a good starting point as a cultural change effort to reduce stigmatization, as leaders at all levels can be trained to create a culture in which seeking help for mental health problems is viewed as legitimate (Greene-Shortridge et al., 2007). The British Royal Marines' intervention of solder peer mentoring care and support is another good example of how to increase awareness of mental health issues (Keller et al., 2005).

With respect to promoting a supportive culture, various types of resources may provide a powerful signal regarding the supportiveness of the military as a whole. In the U.S. Army, for example, the primary support groups include the Army Family Team Building Program and Resources for Educating About Deployment and You (known as READY). These programs are designed to help educate families about the military in the hope that this leads to increased support and understanding from the families of soldiers (McFadyen et al., 2005). Soldiers who have participated in these programs have reported better coping abilities and higher morale, commitment, and satisfaction than those who have not participated in them (McFadyen et al., 2005).

There are a number of methods of inducing strategically planned change, but all of those methods come under the general rubric of *organizational change and development*. According to Porras and Robertson (1992), organizational development represents the application of methods and theories from the behavioral sciences in order to foster organizational effectiveness and development of organizational members. One method that could likely have the effect of enhancing supportive culture in the military is *team building*. Team building involves a number of activities aimed at diagnosing and solving barriers to the performance of teams. According to French and Bell (1995), team building may focus on a number of issues, including role clarification, goals of team members, and quality of relationships within a team. Such activities, one might assume, would likely have a direct positive effect on the level of social support within the military. A more indirect impact of organizational change and development activities such as team building is that they have the potential to change the overall culture of an organization.

FUTURE RESEARCH ON RESILIENCE IN MILITARY SETTINGS

In this chapter, we have described organizational factors that can promote resilience in military settings and discussed the potential ways to apply these factors to the military as an organization. In this final section, we offer a number of suggestions for future research.

Interactions Between Situational Factors and Individual Differences

Our purpose in this chapter was to examine situational determinants of resilience; other chapters in this volume examined individual difference predictors. Given this general classification of the determinants of resilience, it is tempting to think of individual differences and situational factors as contributing to resilience in an additive manner. However, it is likely that the relationships between these two categories of predictors of resilience are more complex. It is possible, for example, that the relationship between situational and individual differences may best be described as a *compensatory*. That is, a high level of social support may facilitate resilience in an individual who does not possess traits that have been shown to be indicative of high resilience (e.g., hardiness). Conversely, a person with a set of traits known to be indicative of resilience may be able to thrive and exhibit high levels of resilience even in situations where social support is low. These propositions are both testable hypotheses; yet, to the best of our knowledge, neither has received empirical scrutiny. We also believe that further research examining the interaction between individual differences and situational factors has a great deal of practical value for organizations in their efforts to enhance employee resilience. For example, it may be difficult in some situations for organizations to enhance social support; in such cases, the best approach may be to find individuals who possess traits that are associated with high resilience.

Situational Predictors of Resilience

Although the focus of this chapter has been on social support, training, and military culture, we have not provided a comprehensive list of all situational determinants of resilience. As readers will note, we have provided suggestions in this chapter regarding situational predictors of resilience other than social support (e.g., training, culture), but more work is needed to verify that these situational determinants indeed enhance or inhibit resilience. Determining why situational enablers and inhibitors of resilience influence the development of resilience is equally important. In the case of training, for example, resilience may be enhanced through either increased self-efficacy at an individual level or collective efficacy at a group level, yet little research has specifically examined the role of self-efficacy or collective efficacy in the development of resilience. It is also possible that engaging in training activities facilitates the development of functional anticipatory coping methods that ultimately enhance resilience; again, though, more empirical research is needed to verify this.

Furthermore, linking individual differences that facilitate resilience to situational outcomes is warranted. In other words, situational contexts may mediate the relationship between individual characteristics and resilience outcomes. For example, soldiers with resilience-enhancing characteristics may be more likely to create work contexts (e.g., supportive climate) in which other soldiers' resilience can be facilitated. Another example would be a hardy leader fostering his or her subordinates' hardiness in ways that create situational contexts (e.g., units with high morale) for resilience. This line of research requires longitudinal investigations to examine changes over time in the relationships between individual characteristics and situational factors,

Such research is challenging for researchers, but it can certainly contribute to identifications of processes or mechanisms through which situations develop resilience.

REFERENCES

Adler, A. B., Huffman, A. H., Bliese, P. D., & Castro, C. A. (2005). The impact of deployment length and experience on the well-being of male and female soldiers. *Journal of Occupational Health Psychology, 10,* 121–137. doi:10.1037/1076-8998.10.2.121

Bandura, A. (1977). *Social learning theory.* Englewood Cliffs, NJ: Prentice-Hall.

Barrera, M. (1986). Distinctions between social support concepts, measures, and models. *American Journal of Community Psychology, 14,* 413–445. doi:10.1007/BF00922627

Bartone, P. T. (2006). Resilience under military operational stress: Can leaders influence hardiness? *Military Psychology, 18*(Suppl. 3), S131–S148. doi:10.1207/s15327876mp1803s_10

Beehr, T. A. (1985). *Psychological stress in the workplace.* London, England: Routledge.

Bliese, P. D., & Britt, T. W. (2001). Social support, group consensus and stressor–strain relationships: Social context matters. *Journal of Organizational Behavior, 22,* 425–436. doi:10.1002/job.95

Bliese, P. D., & Castro, C. A. (2000). Role clarity, work overload and organizational support: Multilevel evidence of the importance of support. *Work & Stress, 14,* 65–73. doi:10.1080/026783700417230

Bliese, P. D., & Jex, S. M. (2002). Incorporating a multilevel perspective into occupational stress and research: Theoretical, methodological, and practical implications. *Journal of Occupational Health Psychology, 7,* 265–276. doi:10.1037/1076-8998.7.3.265

Bonanno, G. A. (2004). Loss, trauma, and human resilience: Have we underestimated the human capacity to thrive after extremely aversive events? *American Psychologist, 59,* 20–28. doi:10.1037/0003-066X.59.1.20

Bowman, M. L. (1997). *Individual differences in posttraumatic response: Problems with the adversity–distress connection.* Mahwah, NJ: Erlbaum.

Brass, D. J. (1995). A social network perspective on human resources management. In G. R. Ferris (Ed.), *Research in personnel and human resources management* (Vol. 13, pp. 39–79). Greenwich, CT: JAI Press.

Britt, T. W., Davidson, J., Bliese, P. D., & Castro, C. A. (2004). How leaders can influence the impact that stressors have on soldiers. *Military Medicine, 169,* 541–545.

Cacioppo, J. T., Reis, H. T., & Zautra, A. J. (2011). Social resilience: The value of social fitness with an application to the military. *American Psychologist, 66,* 43–51. doi:10.1037/a0021419

Casey, G. W., Jr. (2011). Comprehensive soldier fitness: A vision for psychological resilience in the U.S. Army. *American Psychologist, 66*, 1–3. doi:10.1037/a0021930

Cobb, S. (1976). Social support as a moderator of life success. *Psychosomatic Medicine, 38*, 300–314.

Cohen, S., & Wills, T. A. (1985). Stress, social support, and the buffering hypothesis. *Psychological Bulletin, 98*, 310–357. doi:10.1037/0033-2909.98.2.310

Day, A. L., & Livingstone, H. A. (2001). Chronic and acute stressors among military personnel: Do coping styles buffer their negative impact on health? *Journal of Occupational Health Psychology, 6*, 348–360. doi:10.1037/1076-8998.6.4.348

de Jonge, J., & Dormann, C. (2006). Stressors, resources, and strain at work: A longitudinal test of the triple-match principle. *Journal of Applied Psychology, 91*, 1359–1374. doi:10.1037/0021-9010.91.5.1359

Dolan, C. A., & Adler, A. B. (2006). Military hardiness as a buffer of psychological health on return from deployment. *Military Medicine, 171*, 93–98.

Doran, A., Gaskin, T., Schumm, W., & Smith, J. E. (2005). Dealing with combat and operational stress. Retrieved from http://www.nmcphc.med.navy.mil/healthy_living/psychological_health/stress_management/operandcombatstress.aspx

Dunivin, K. O. (1994). Military culture: Change and continuity. *Armed Forces and Society, 20*, 531–547. doi:10.1177/0095327X9402000403

Eden, D., & Zuk, Y. (1995). Seasickness as a self-fulfilling prophecy: Raising self-efficacy to boost performance at sea. *Journal of Applied Psychology, 80*, 628–635. doi:10.1037/0021-9010.80.5.628

Eisenberger, R., Huntington, R., Hutchison, S., & Sowa, D. (1986). Perceived organizational support. *Journal of Applied Psychology, 71*, 500–507. doi:10.1037/0021-9010.71.3.500

Forsyth, D. R. (1990). *Group dynamics* (2nd ed.). Pacific Grove, CA: Brooks/Cole.

French, W. L., & Bell, C. H. (1995). *Organization development: Behavioral science interventions for organization improvement* (5th ed.). Englewood Cliffs, NJ: Prentice-Hall.

Goldstein, I. L., & Ford, J. K. (2002). *Training in organizations: Needs assessment, development, and evaluation* (4th ed.). Belmont, CA: Wadsworth.

Greenberg, N., Thomas, S. L., Iversen, A., Unwin, C., Hull, L., & Wessely, S. (2003). Do military peacekeepers want to talk about their experiences? Perceived psychosocial support of UK military peacekeepers on return from deployment. *Journal of Mental Health, 12*, 565–573. doi:10.1080/09638230310001627928

Greene-Shortridge, T. M., Britt, T. W., & Castro, C. A. (2007). The stigma of mental health problems in the military. *Military Medicine, 172*, 157–161.

Griffith, J. (1989). The Army's new unit personnel replacement and its relationship to unit cohesion and social support. *Military Psychology, 1*, 17–34. doi:10.1207/s15327876mp0101_2

Guzzo, R. A., & Shea, G. P. (1992). Group performance and intergroup relations in organizations. In M. D. Dunnette & L. M. Hough (Eds.), *Handbook of industrial and organizational psychology* (pp. 269–313). Palo Alto, CA: Consulting Psychologists Press.

Hoge, C. W., Castro, C. A., Messer, S. C., McGurk, D., Cotting, D. I., & Koffman, R. L. (2004). Combat duty in Iraq and Afghanistan, mental health problems, and barriers to care. *The New England Journal of Medicine, 351*, 13–22. doi:10.1056/NEJMoa040603

House, J. S. (1981). *Work stress and social support*. Reading, MA: Addison-Wesley.

Janson, N. (1994). *Safety culture: A study of permanent way staff at British Rail*. Amsterdam, the Netherlands: Vrije University.

Jex, S. M., & Bliese, P. D. (1999). Efficacy beliefs as a moderator of the impact of work-related stressors: A multilevel study. *Journal of Applied Psychology, 84*, 349–361. doi:10.1037/0021-9010.84.3.349

Jex, S. M., Bliese, P. D., Buzzell, S., & Primeau, J. (2001). The impact of self-efficacy on stressor–strain relations: Coping style as an explanatory mechanism. *Journal of Applied Psychology, 86*, 401–409. doi:10.1037/0021-9010.86.3.401

Jex, S. M., & Britt, T. W. (2008). *Organizational psychology: A scientist-practitioner approach* (2nd ed.). Hoboken, NJ: Wiley.

Jex, S. M., & Gudanowski, D. M. (1992). Efficacy beliefs and work stress: An exploratory study. *Journal of Organizational Behavior, 13*, 509–517. doi:10.1002/job.4030130506

Kahn, R. L., & Antonucci, T. C. (1980). Convoys over the life course: Attachment, roles, and social support. In P. B. Baltes & O. Brim (Eds.), *Aging from birth to death: Interdisciplinary perspectives* (pp. 253–286). New York, NY: Academic Press.

Keller, R. T., Greenberg, N., Bobo, W. V., Roberts, P., Jones, N., & Orman, D. T. (2005). Soldier peer mentoring care and support: Bringing psychological awareness to the front. *Military Medicine, 170*, 355–361.

King, L. A., King, D. W., Fairbank, J. A., Keane, T. M., & Adams, G. A. (1998). Resilience–recovery factors in post-traumatic stress disorder among female and male Vietnam veterans: Hardiness, postwar social support, and additional stressful life events. *Journal of Personality and Social Psychology, 74*, 420–434. doi:10.1037/0022-3514.74.2.420

King, L. A., King, D. W., Vogt, D. S., Knight, J., & Samper, R. E. (2006). Deployment Risk and Resilience Inventory: A collection of measures for studying deployment-related experiences of military personnel and veterans. *Military Psychology, 18*, 89–120. doi:10.1207/s15327876mp1802_1

Kobasa, S. C., Maddi, S. R., & Percutti, M. C. (1982). Personality and exercise as buffers in the stress–illness relationship. *Journal of Behavioral Medicine, 5*, 391–404. doi:10.1007/BF00845369

Kotter, J. P., & Hesketh, J. L. (1992). *Corporate culture and performance*. New York, NY: Free Press.

Krueger, G. P. (2000). Military culture. In A. E. Kazdin (Ed.), *Encyclopedia of psychology* (Vol. 5, pp. 251–259). Washington, DC: American Psychological Association.

Limbert, C. (2004). Psychological well-being and job satisfaction amongst military personnel on unaccompanied tours: The impact of perceived social support and coping strategies. *Military Psychology, 16,* 37–51. doi:10.1207/s15327876mp1601_3

Maddi, S. R. (1987). Hardiness training at Illinois Bell Telephone. In J. P. Opatz (Ed.), *Health promotion evaluation* (pp. 101–105). Stevens Point, WI: National Wellness Institute.

Maddi, S. R., Kahn, S., & Maddi, K. L. (1998). The effectiveness of hardiness training. *Consulting Psychology Journal: Practice and Research, 50,* 78–86. doi:10.1037/1061-4087.50.2.78

Masten, A. S., & Reed, M. G. J. (2002). Resilience in development. In C. R. Snyder & S. J. Lopez (Eds.), *Handbook of positive psychology* (pp. 74–88). New York, NY: Oxford University Press.

McFadyen, J. M., Kerpelman, J. L., & Adler-Baeder, F. (2005). Examining the impact of workplace supports: Work–family fit and satisfaction in the U.S. military. *Family Relations, 54,* 131–144. doi:10.1111/j.0197-6664.2005.00011.x

Mental Health Advisory Team VI. (2009). Mental Health Advisory Team (MHAT) VI Operation Enduring Freedom 2009 Afghanistan. Retrieved from http://www.armymedicine.army.mil/reports/mhat/mhat_vi/MHAT_VI-OEF_Redacted.pdf

Moos, R., & Lemke, S. (1992). *Sheltered Care Environment Scale manual.* Palo Alto, CA: Department of Veterans Affairs and Stanford University Medical Center.

Naval Center for Combat and Operational Stress Control. (2011). *The Naval Center for Combat & Operational Stress Control.* Retrieved from http://www.med.navy.mil/sites/nmcsd/nccosc/coscconferencev2/2012/pre-conferenceworkshops/Pages/default.aspx#navyOSCLeader

Park, N. (2011). Military children and families: Strengths and challenges during peace and war. *American Psychologist, 66,* 65–72. doi:10.1037/a0021249

Porras, J. I., & Robertson, P. J. (1992). Organizational development: Theory, practice, and research. In M. D. Dunnette & L. Hough (Eds.), *Handbook of industrial and organizational psychology* (Vol. 2, pp. 719–822). Palo Alto, CA: Consulting Psychologists Press.

Reivich, K. J., Seligman, M. E. P., & McBride, S. (2011). Master resilience training in the U.S. Army. *American Psychologist, 66,* 25–34. doi:10.1037/a0021897

Reivich, K. J., & Shatté, A. (2002). *The resilience factor: Seven essential skills for overcoming life's inevitable obstacles.* New York, NY: Broadway Books.

Rhoades, L., & Eisenberger, R. (2002). Perceived organizational support: A review of the literature. *Journal of Applied Psychology, 87,* 698–714. doi:10.1037/0021-9010.87.4.698

Ross, L., Amabile, T. M., & Steinmetz, J. L. (1977). Social roles, social control, and biases in social-perception processes. *Journal of Personality and Social Psychology, 35*, 485–494. doi:10.1037/0022-3514.35.7.485

Ruvolo, C. M., & Bullis, R. C. (2003). Essentials of cultural change: Lessons learned the hard way. *Consulting Psychology Journal: Practice and Research, 55*, 155–168. doi:10.1037/1061-4087.55.3.155

Schaubroeck, J. M., Riolli, L. T., Peng, A. C., & Spain, E. S. (2011). Resilience to traumatic exposure among soldiers developed in combat. *Journal of Occupational Health Psychology, 16*, 18–37. doi:10.1037/a0021006

Schein, E. H. (1992). *Organizational culture and leadership: A dynamic view* (2nd ed.). San Francisco, CA: Jossey-Bass.

Schneider, B. (1990). The climate for service: An application of the climate construct. In B. Schneider (Ed.), *Organizational climate and culture* (pp. 383–412). San Francisco, CA: Jossey-Bass.

Solomon, Z., Mikulincer, M., & Hobfoll, S. E. (1986). Effects of social support and battle intensity on loneliness and breakdown during combat. *Journal of Personality and Social Psychology, 51*, 1269–1276. doi:10.1037/0022-3514.51.6.1269

Viswesvaran, C., Sanchez, J. I., & Fisher, J. (1999). The role of social support in the process of work stress: A meta-analysis. *Journal of Vocational Behavior, 54*, 314–334. doi:10.1006/jvbe.1998.1661

Waite, P. J., & Richardson, G. E. (2004). Determining the efficacy of resiliency training in the work site. *Journal of Allied Health, 33*, 178–183.

Weiner, H. R. (1990). Group-level and individual-level mediators of the relationship between soldier satisfaction with social support and performance motivation. *Military Psychology, 2*, 21–32. doi:10.1207/s15327876mp0201_2

5

THE ROLE OF TRANSFORMATIONAL AND ETHICAL LEADERSHIP IN BUILDING AND MAINTAINING RESILIENCE

ALLISTER MacINTYRE, DANIELLE CHARBONNEAU, AND DAMIAN O'KEEFE

As discussed in more detail by other authors in this volume, *resilience* is often defined as the ability to adapt to or bounce back from threatening situations and refrain from engaging in maladaptive behavior. According to van Breda (2011), resilience, "along with assets, strengths, and solutions, has become an increasingly mainstream concept in recent years" (p. 33). If we accept that stressors can have extremely adverse consequences and understand that resilience provides people with the capacity to deal effectively with life and work stress, then it is easy to appreciate why resilience should be so important for military leaders. After all, leaders should always be interested in the well-being of their subordinates. Furthermore, leaders cannot exist without followers, and issues associated with mental health can be every bit as devastating as physical health problems. Military leaders who fail to let subordinates know that their physical and emotional well-being

http://dx.doi.org/10.1037/14190-005
Building Psychological Resilience in Military Personnel: Theory and Practice, R. R. Sinclair and T. W. Britt (Editors)

are important will have difficulty instilling any sense of loyalty and intrinsic motivation toward work. With these issues in mind, our objective in this chapter is to provide some tools or tips for leaders so that they will be better able to (a) minimize stressors in the workplace, (b) buffer the impact of unavoidable stressors, and (c) increase the resilience of their subordinates.

CHAPTER OVERVIEW

The model that we propose argues that, in most situations, transformational leadership, contingent rewards, and ethical leadership are sufficient to minimize work stress and assure that followers are coping. Although this may be a useful approach for most situations, the focus of this volume is associated with military leadership. Military leaders do not always have the luxury to exercise their leadership skills in ideal settings. They often find themselves in situations that are fraught with excessive hardships, intense conflict, and the ever-present awareness not only that their own mortality is at risk but also that their decisions could lead to serious injuries and death in their followers. For example, Castro and Hoge (2005) acknowledged that "nearly 90% of soldiers deployed to Iraq reported that they were attacked or ambushed, with over 60% reporting that they were in a threatening situation where they were unable to respond due to rules of engagement" (p. 13-2).

In recognition of this unique aspect of military performance, researchers coined the term *in extremis leadership* to refer to circumstances in which "leadership is defined as giving purpose, motivation, and direction to people when there is imminent physical danger and where followers believe that leader behavior will influence their physical well-being or survival" (Kolditz, 2006, p. 657). During these particularly stressful or extreme situations, we suggest, two leader attributes are highly desirable: adaptability and hardiness. The adaptability aspect of leadership was highlighted by Castro, Adler, McGurk, and Thomas (2006), who contended that leaders who are flexible and pragmatic will be much more successful at building resilience in followers than are leaders who take a rigid institutional approach. Even with such attributes as adaptability and hardiness, it is insufficient for leaders to lead by example; they must actively develop similar attributes in their followers. Finally, we describe recent findings in the leadership literature and propose a model that incorporates concepts such as authentic leadership and psychological capital. Authentic leaders, in addition to being transformational and ethical, are aware of their strengths and weaknesses as well as their thinking patterns. Psychological capital (PsyCap) is a recently developed second-order construct that incorporates not only resilience but also optimism, self-efficacy, and hope (Chen & Lim, 2012; Luthans, Luthans,

& Luthans, 2004). In simple terms, a second-order construct is one that is determined or influenced by one or more first-level constructs, such as resilience, optimism, self-efficacy, and hope (see Chapter 2, this volume, for further discussion of PsyCap). In the future, military leaders may wish to expand their focus on developing their followers' PsyCap.

LEADERSHIP

Although military leaders often know much about leadership from personal experience, leadership academics, theorists, and scholars continue to debate the nature of leadership. For example, Bass (1997a) argued that there "are almost as many definitions of leadership as there are persons who have attempted to define the concept" (p. 17). More recently, Hackman and Wageman (2007) acknowledged that even though scholars agree that leadership is extremely important, "there are no generally accepted definitions of what leadership is, no dominant paradigms for studying it, and little agreement about the best strategies for developing and exercising it" (p. 43). It seems there is only one common thread of agreement. Leaders do things that come to be recognized as evidence of leadership by followers and observers. As compellingly noted by Bennis (2007), "psychologists have not sorted out which traits define leaders or whether leadership exists outside of specific situations, and yet we know with absolute certainty that a handful of people have changed millions of lives and reshaped the world" (p. 3).

Leadership Approaches

Most of the leadership theories and associated research can be grouped into three primary categories: trait, behavioral, and contingency theories (Hellriegel, Slocum, & Woodman, 1989; Schermerhorn, Hunt, & Osborn, 1982). In brief, the trait approaches focus on the personal qualities held by leaders, the behavioral approaches emphasize a leader's actions, and the contingency approaches consider situational factors to be of the highest significance. Other theorists adopt much broader definitions of leadership and maintain that effective leadership may be dependent on the leader, the follower, the situation, or a combination of these factors. Without a doubt, there are additional factors that do not fit neatly into any of these categories, but this is simply part of the challenge of understanding leadership.

Countless approaches toward understanding leadership have been developed. Regardless of the terminology used to describe leadership behaviors, most of the typologies postulate that leadership can be categorized as operating along two primary dimensions. One of these dimensions concentrates on how people and relationship oriented a leader tends to be, and the other dimension depicts leaders as being more focused on tasks and productivity. For example, Kurfi (2009) argued that a leader's "relative concerns for human relationships or task orientation tend to reflect . . . leadership style" (p. 75).

Transactional and Transformational Leadership

Keeping the two leadership dimensions of people and task in mind, one must also understand that some theories enjoy greater prominence among researchers and are more extensively endorsed than others. Currently, two of the most widely accepted ways to categorize leadership behaviors are transactional or transformational in nature (G. A. Yukl, 1998). The decision to focus on the transactional–transformational leadership approach was deliberate, for four main reasons: (a) its considerable empirical support on its psychometric properties and its positive impact on several work outcomes; (b) its application in a wide variety of settings; (c) its demonstrated capacity to be taught and learned; and (d) its adaptability to various situational demands.

First, the transactional–transformational approach has garnered considerable support in the literature, with several meta-analytical studies demonstrating its effectiveness as a leadership style (e.g., Judge & Piccolo, 2004; Lowe, Kroeck, & Sivasubramaniam, 1996). Other meta-analytic studies have examined links between transformational leadership and constructs like emotional intelligence (Harms & Credé, 2010) and personality (Bono & Judge, 2004). In military samples, transformational leaders have been shown to have a positive impact on several work outcomes, such as followers' perceptions of fairness (Tremblay, 2010) and motivation (Masi & Cooke, 2000); climate strength (Zohar & Tenne-Gazit, 2008); affective/cognitive processes and team effectiveness (Boies & Howell, 2009); performance (Lim & Ployhart, 2004); situational awareness and interpersonal influence (Eid et al., 2004); unit performance, potency, and cohesion (Bass, Avolio, Jung, & Berson, 2003); job satisfaction and commitment (Yang, Wu, Chang, & Chien, 2011); and subordinates' extra effort (Stadelmann, 2010).

Second, the effectiveness of transformational leadership in generating superior performance has been demonstrated not only in the military population but also in civilian organizations (e.g., Barling, Weber, & Kelloway, 1996; Geyery & Steyrer, 1998). Bass (2000) contended that the effectiveness of transformational leadership cuts across organizational boundaries and predicted that future leaders will have to become more transformational in nature. Similarly, Wong, Bliese, and McGurk (2003) acknowledged that transformational leadership "is clearly applicable to organizations other than the military" (p. 658).

The third factor guiding our decision was that transformational leadership can be taught and developed. For example, Dvir, Eden, Avolio, and Shamir (2002) randomly assigned military squads to undergo an experimental workshop (Transformational Leadership Training) or a control workshop (Eclectic Leadership Training). They demonstrated that those who underwent the transformational leadership training had a greater impact on follower development and performance. In answering the question of whether transformational leadership can be taught, Kelloway and Barling (2000) stated that they "believe that the answer to this question is an unequivocal yes! There is now consistent evidence that transformational leadership can be taught" (p. 356).

Last, although this fact is sometimes misunderstood or ignored, the transformational and transactional leadership model takes into consideration the situational demands, such as the nature of the task, organizational constraints, time restrictions, available resources, and experience levels among followers. This model is based more on the impact leaders have on their followers than on the specific behaviors of the leaders. That is, transactional and transformational leaders can adopt either a directive or a participative approach (Bass, 1998). For example, one can be participative ("Let's reexamine your assumptions together") or more directive ("You need to reexamine your assumptions"). The selection of a specific behavior depends not only on the followers' characteristics but also on the demands of the situation. Having explained why this chapter focuses primarily on the transactional–transformational leadership paradigm, we now turn to a brief description of the various dimensions of this leadership model.

Transactional Leadership

Transactional leadership involves an exchange that takes place between leaders and followers; hence, as its name suggests, it is transactional in nature. Four types of leadership behaviors are associated with transactional leadership: contingent rewards, active management by exception, passive management by exception, and laissez-faire leadership (Bass, 1998). Leaders who adopt a contingent reward approach tend to clarify the performance standards required to receive a reward and to use incentives and contingent rewards to motivate followers. Conversely, some leaders can be described as using a passive management by exception approach. These leaders are less likely to monitor followers closely, but they react adversely (using contingent punishments and corrective actions) when a follower's performance is judged as being unacceptable. When using active management by exception, leaders will closely monitor performance and take corrective action as soon as a problem occurs. Laissez-faire leadership, although normally included as part of the transactional leadership style, is more appropriately viewed as an absence of leadership and is often described as nonleadership. These leaders show a lack of concern for tasks and for followers. They fail to monitor activities, take corrective action, or do anything to ensure the well-being of followers (Bass, 1998). In effect, they abdicate their leadership responsibilities.

Because of its emphasis on establishing performance standards and applying contingent rewards and punishments to manage behavior, transactional leadership is often strongly associated with stereotypes of military leadership. After all, the perception held by many people about those in uniform is that they are highly disciplined, obedient, task focused, inflexible, and rule oriented. These Hollywood-driven stereotypes might lead one to view a transactional style of leadership as an appropriate choice for mission success. However, personnel serving in modern Western militaries tend to be well educated, innovative, flexible in their thinking, and capable of thinking outside the box. Transactional leadership may be an appropriate choice for some operational situations, but it does not represent the ideal leadership style sought by the military for all situations.

Transformational Leadership

Research into selecting the ideal military officer has centered on constructs described in the literature on transformational leadership. Transformational leadership has been adopted as a label for a style of leadership that results in some fundamental changes in followers; thus, in a manner of speaking, subordinates are transformed. The essence of transformational leadership, as articulated by Burns (1978), is to transform followers into leaders. According to Bass (1997b), transformational leadership takes place "when leaders broaden and elevate the interests of their employees, when they generate awareness and acceptance of the purposes and mission of the group, and when they stir their employees to look beyond their own self-interest for the good of the group" (p. 320). Unlike transactional leadership, transformational leadership is not viewed as including an exchange between leader and follower. However, like transactional leadership, the concept includes four types of leadership behaviors: idealized influence, individualized consideration, inspirational motivation, and intellectual stimulation (Bass, 1998).

Through idealized influence, leaders stimulate enhanced feelings of wanting to belong, and followers come to identify with the leader. Leaders who use individualized consideration encourage followers, are supportive of them and concerned for their well-being. Such leaders respect differences between people and will effectively coach them to bring out their best. When leaders go beyond simply having a vision by inspiring followers to be committed to the vision, they are exhibiting one of the critical aspects of inspirational motivation. They create this sense of a shared vision by communicating effectively (using symbols and emotional appeals) and through modeling appropriate behaviors. Through intellectual stimulation, leaders increase the awareness of problems, encourage followers to view these dilemmas from a new perspective, and challenge them to become creative and innovative in their attempts to resolve the difficulties.

Because transformational leadership includes aspects that can transform followers by inspiring, stimulating, motivating, and supporting them, one could quickly surmise that transformational leadership stands among the best approaches for leaders in any given situation, with transactional leadership being focused more on motivating followers to achieve task completion than on developing followers to achieve above expectation. This is not far from the perspective taken by Burns (1978), who viewed transactional and transformational leadership as being on opposite ends of a continuum. In contrast, Bass (1990) argued that transformational leadership can serve to augment transactional leadership. He also stated that even though these two approaches are "conceptually distinct, transformational and transactional leadership are likely to be displayed by the same individuals in different amounts and intensities" (Bass, 1985, p. 26). Indeed, Bass (1999) described the optimal leadership profile as one where effective leaders will display aspects of both transactional and transformational leadership to some degree. In fact, G. Yukl (1999) claimed that "providing praise and recognition is usually more personal and may involve transformational leadership as well as transactional leadership" (p. 289).

Research has shown that transformational factors have been more highly correlated than transactional leadership with outcomes of effectiveness (Bass, 1999). In their meta-analytical study, Judge and Piccolo (2004) found that the contingent reward aspect of transactional leadership "appeared to have validity levels comparable with those of transformational leadership" (p. 763). In fact, contingent reward is often included in studies investigating the effects of transformational leadership and has positive effects on work outcomes, albeit weaker than those generated by the transformational dimensions (e.g., Harland, Harrison, Jones, & Reiter-Palmon, 2005; McMurray, Pirola-Merlo, Sarros, & Islam, 2010). Hence, although a transaction, contingent reward "has been found to be reasonably effective" (Bass, 1998, p. 6), at least in part because performance goals and standards are usually clarified with followers at the time of the exchange.

Ethical Leadership

In the mid to late 1990s, some theorists argued that the understanding of leadership would remain incomplete unless ethical and moral values were considered explicitly (e.g., Kanungo & Mendonca, 1998). For instance, given that transformational leaders change their followers in a fundamental way, one would hope that these changes are guided by moral values and occur for the greater good. Bass and Steidlmeier (1999) coined the term *authentic transformational leadership* to designate leadership that is ethical, but they admitted to the existence of pseudo-transformational leaders who are manipulative and deceptive. Others have discussed ethical leadership more generally, without necessarily associating it with transformational leadership (Kanungo & Mendonca, 1998). Taking a behavioral approach, Brown, Trevino, and Harrison (2005) defined *ethical leadership* as the demonstration of normatively appropriate conduct through personal actions and interpersonal relationships, as well as the promotion of such conduct through two-way communication, reinforcement, and decision making.

Empirical research on the ethical dimension of leadership has begun relatively recently. In particular, two aspects of interest have been investigated: the positive impact that ethical leaders have on followers and a proposed mechanism to explain this influence. O'Keefe (2009) reported that Canadian Army personnel who perceived their immediate supervisor to be more ethical had more confidence in their leader's ability, had more affective commitment to the organization, and reported engaging in less unethical behavior in the past. Other studies have shown that ethical leadership is related to job task significance, autonomy, and organizational citizenship behavior (Piccolo, Greenbaum, Den Hartog, & Folger, 2010); self-efficacy and job performance (Walumbwa, Mayer, et al., 2011); workplace deviance (Avey, Palanski, & Walumbwa, 2011); ethical climate and employee misconduct (Mayer, Kuenzi, & Greenbaum, 2010); job-related affective well-being (Kalshoven & Boon, 2012); and organizational commitment (Walumbwa, Avolio, Gardner, Wernsing, & Peterson, 2008).

Furthermore, ethical leadership has been shown to predict trust in the leader, interactional justice (i.e., being treated with dignity and respect), perceived effectiveness of leaders, and followers' job satisfaction and dedication (Brown et al., 2005). These relationships were over and above the outcomes accounted for by transformational leadership, suggesting that the construct of ethical leadership is indeed different from that of transformational leadership.

With respect to a mechanism by which ethical leaders influence their followers, O'Keefe (2006) found that the perception of the ethicality of Canadian Forces leaders was influential in modeling ethical norms among subordinates by behaving with honesty and integrity, as well as treating others fairly. Using the social learning perspective, Brown et al. (2005) proposed that leaders influence the ethical conduct of followers via modeling. They argued that leaders are models for ethical conduct and, as such, become the targets for emulation for followers, influence ethics-related outcomes, and engage in and reinforce ethical behavior. Dickson, Smith, Grojean, and Ehrhart (2001) contended that a critical determinant in the climate of an organization is the leader's ethical behavior.

Given that ethical leaders will be committed to maintaining high ethical standards, one could also surmise that there would be a concomitant reduction in the number and severity of stressors experienced by followers. After all, leaders who behave ethically will always be on guard to protect the well-being of followers and will have the courage to take a stand on critical issues. In effect, they will shelter their followers from enduring inappropriate workloads or unfair situations as well as take steps to minimize work conflicts. However, at the time of writing, these proposed links remained to be empirically tested.

There are as yet very few extensive models of ethical leadership as it relates to organizational outcomes. Kaptein, Huberts, Avelino, and Lasthuizen (2005) postulated that a strong ethical leadership within organizations would promote the development of ethics programs and a strong ethical climate. Such development would result in less unethical conduct (e.g., discrimination, violation of health and safety orders, and a hostile work environment), thus leading to greater trust in and commitment to the organization.

Toor and Ofori (2009) found that ethical leadership not only influenced perceptions of leader effectiveness and employee commitment but was also positively related to transformational culture (a supportive context for ethical practices) and negatively related to transactional culture (the promotion of productivity as an overarching goal and less healthy organizational context). Moreover, they found that ethical leadership mediated the relationship between organizational culture and employee outcomes, such that organizational culture in concert with ethical leadership leads to perceptions of leader effectiveness and extra effort by employees. In sum, because of its potential to impact climate and followers, the ethical aspect of leadership can no longer be ignored and should be included in all serious discussions on leadership.

PROPOSED MODEL OF LEADERSHIP AND RESILIENCE

Our proposed basic model (see Figure 5.1) of how military leaders can increase and maintain the resilience of their followers advocates the use of transformational leadership and ethical leadership. Many fans of transformational leadership and contingent reward regard this approach as a preferable means of influencing followers in all circumstances, albeit in some circumstances more than others. We consider this model basic because it focuses on constructs and relations between these constructs that have, for the most part, received extensive empirical support. For instance, serving as a foundation is the concept that stressors (aspects of life that we find challenging, disturbing, or unsettling) will lead to a perception and experience of stress (body and mind response to stressors), and this stress will, in turn, lead to

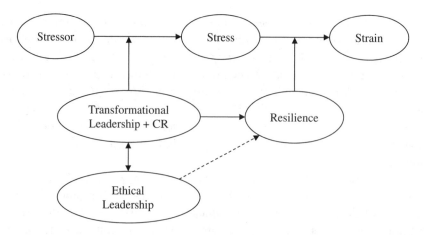

Figure 5.1. Proposed basic model linking leadership and resilience. The dashed arrow line represents a suspected link that remains to be empirically verified. CR = contingent reward.

some sort of undesirable consequence (strain; e.g., anxiety, elevated blood pressure, burnout, posttraumatic stress disorder). The stressors can range from daily hassles (e.g., flat tire, arguments, broken shoelace) to acute stressors (e.g., car accident, injury, brief illness) and chronic stressors such as financial problems and unpleasant work conditions (Pratt & Barling, 1988).

Transformational leaders and those using contingent reward contribute to reducing the stressors for their followers, but it is reasonable to expect them also to have a positive effect on the resilience levels of their followers. This notion is supported by negative first-order correlations between transactional and transformational leadership and symptoms of stress/burnout (Bass, 1990). Bass (1990) also reported that "transformational leadership contributes to effective leadership under stress. . . . Charismatic transformational leaders tend to keep their 'cool' when faced with threats to their lives" (p. 652).

Through the use of intellectual stimulation, leaders will encourage followers to be more innovative and analytical when confronting stress. They will seek solutions rather than simply be overwhelmed. When leaders show individualized consideration, they are contributing to a sense of self-worth and self-esteem and providing some of the tools necessary to deal with stressors. In other words, they are offering some individualized support to their followers. When leaders lead by example (idealized influence), they are providing an emotional reference point and contributing to the optimism that is so important for resilience. Finally, through the use of inspirational motivation, leaders will galvanize followers to take an active rather than a passive role when confronted by stressful situations.

There is empirical evidence that transformational leadership serves as a stress buffer. For example, Lyons and Schneider (2009) demonstrated that when study participants received directions from a leader exhibiting transformational characteristics, they viewed a forthcoming stressor as less threatening than they did when a transactional leadership approach was used. In view of the fact that Lyons and Schneider used an impending stressor, their findings lend credence to the notion that a transformational leadership style would contribute to follower resilience. In their study of Australian Army personnel on deployment, Murphy and Fogarty (2009) demonstrated that effective leadership can contribute to resilience in followers and serve as a buffer in the stress–strain relationship.

One proposed mechanism for this buffering effect of transformational leaders is that they can turn crises into developmental opportunities and promote adaptive and creative solutions through intellectual stimulation (Bass, 1990). Harland et al. (2005) asked participants to recall a challenging work situation and asked them what helped them deal with this situation. In addition to intellectual stimulation, individualized consideration and idealized influence were found to contribute. Harland et al. proposed that an employee who is made to feel competent and valued by leaders would be more confident about his or her capacity to meet a challenge. Furthermore, they argued that focusing on a higher purpose and on the common good would likely lead to the use of adaptive coping responses. The fourth transformational dimension, inspirational motivation, failed to be significantly associated with resilience after controlling for optimism, but contingent reward was significantly associated with it. Harland et al. explained that by focusing their followers' attention on the positive benefits of resolving a challenge, leaders steer their subordinates toward an adaptive coping approach.

Given the nature of resilience, it is unlikely that a transactional leadership style, with the exception of contingent reward, would contribute to the development or maintenance of resilience. Transactional leaders generate extrinsic motivation, and their reactions will be averse if performance is below par. And laissez-faire leadership, being best described as nonleadership, will not enhance resilience. After all, these laissez-faire leaders show a lack of concern for followers and do not do anything to ensure the well-being of subordinates.

It is noteworthy that in this model, ethical leaders do not directly reduce the stressors. Rather, we propose, their influence on the reduction of stressors goes through transformational leadership. However, we propose that ethical leaders may have a direct impact on resilience, although that link remains to be empirically tested. As discussed earlier, the leader's ethical behavior can be critical in instilling a vision that aims at the common good and in encouraging subordinates not to engage in maladaptive behavior. Brown et al.'s (2005) proposal that leaders influence the ethical conduct of followers via modeling is similar to what Bass (1998) called *idealized influence*, thereby suggesting a link between ethical leadership and subordinates' resilience.

Several external factors, not shown in the model, may affect leaders' ability to influence followers' resilience. Let us just mention, for instance, group factors such as the cohesiveness of the unit and the intragroup communication. Although we recognize that leaders have an impact at the group level, we have chosen to limit the focus of this chapter to the individual level.

LEADERSHIP AND RESILIENCE IN CRISES OR EXTREME SITUATIONS

In crises or extreme situations, leaders must be directive to be effective, while asserting their transformational and ethical influence. In such situations, leaders play a critical role in maintaining and/or increasing their followers' resilience to withstand adversities associated with extreme and dangerous working conditions. For example, military leaders will need to function under conditions of in extremis leadership and thus give purpose, motivation, and direction to followers when there is imminent physical danger.

Keeping in mind that resilience is a necessary ingredient to help people spring back from the consequences of stress, we cannot ignore that a leader's ethical behavior can be critical in encouraging subordinates to refrain from engaging in maladaptive behavior in the first place. In their study of resilience among Australian soldiers deployed in East Timor, Murphy and Fogarty (2009) concluded that effective leadership was able to ameliorate the experience of strain by moderating the consequence of stressors and by contributing to levels of morale and cohesiveness. They concluded that the results of their study "suggest that important ingredients of psychological resilience during operational deployment are effective leadership at all levels in the military unit, a sense of purpose or meaning, and strong cohesion and morale" (p. 100).

When a group encounters a hostile environment, subordinates expect leaders to be more assertive, directive, and decisive in crisis situations rather than participative. In a study conducted on leadership in crisis versus non-crisis situations, Mulder, de Jong, Koppelaar, and Verhage (1986) reported that in crisis situations, effective leaders (as rated by subordinates) displayed more forceful leadership approaches, such as expert power (e.g., knowledge based), formal power (e.g., position based), upward influence (e.g., ability to influence superiors), and less open consultation (e.g., soliciting feedback from subordinates). While taking such a more directive approach, leaders can remain transformational (Bass, 1998) by providing a short-term vision of success and instilling hope in their followers. Furthermore, transformational leaders are more trusted by their subordinates (Arnold, Barling, & Kelloway, 2001; Burke, Sims, Lazzara, & Salas, 2007); hence, they are more likely to be listened to during a crisis.

So far, we have focused on the impact of leaders on subordinates in crisis situations. Others have focused on the impact of leaders at the team level rather than at the individual level. For instance, Kozlowski, Watola, Jensen, Kim, and Botero (2009) investigated how leaders develop a team's adaptive capability. Although it is important to consider, the impact of leaders at the team level lies outside the scope of this chapter.

The Case of Extreme Situations

As noted earlier, military leaders and followers function in situations that can be incredibly intense in terms of significant danger and high risk. For example, in their overview of the duties that military medical personnel may have to endure, Maguen et al. (2008) included "providing direct, sometimes intensive, medical care to combat casualties in a hostile area . . . clearing human remains from combat zones under life-threatening conditions, being assigned to graves registration, and assisting with body handling and identification" (p. 1). Similarly, those soldiers engaged in frontline fighting will be in almost constant threat of being injured or killed. The challenges faced by military leaders to make meaningful decisions and motivate followers during these adverse conditions go well beyond anything that might confront leaders in the civilian sector or even military leaders in garrison settings.

In Extremis Leaders

Recent research highlighting the importance of strong leadership in adverse situations postulated the concept of *in extremis leadership*, which is defined as giving purpose, motivation, and direction to followers when there is imminent physical danger and when followers believe that leader behavior will influence their physical well-being or survival (Kolditz, 2005). Kolditz (2005) described the in extremis leadership pattern as being characterized by inherent motivation (i.e., the danger of the situation energizes those who are in it), learning orientation (i.e., the potential hostility of the situation places a premium on leaders scanning the environment and learning very rapidly), shared risk (i.e., willingness to share the same or more risk than followers), and common lifestyle (i.e., accepting and embracing a lifestyle that is common to their followers as an expression of values, which becomes part of the credibility of the leaders). According to Kolditz, when operating in extremis, transactional leaders are ineffective; instead, a value-based form of transformational leadership emerges and becomes part of the operating style in this situation. Indeed, even though crisis situations may require the leader to take immediate and directive action, it is transformational leadership behavior (e.g., enabling followers' collective interpretations of volatile situations and encouraging creative problem solving) that could help followers make sense of an ambiguous and dangerous environment and thus help to build resilience (Baran & Scott, 2010).

Through his or her actions, the leader can instill higher levels of motivation in followers and ensure that they remain optimistic about their ability to have an effect on outcomes. For example, Goleman, Boyatzis, and McKee (2002) discussed how leaders can sway emotions through their behaviors:

> Simply, in any human group, the leader has maximal power to sway everyone's emotions. If people's emotions are pushed toward the range of enthusiasm, performance can soar; if people are driven toward rancor and anxiety, they will be thrown off stride. (p. 5)

They described the effect as being like a contagion where followers look to a leader's emotional reaction as the most valid response, particularly if the situation is ambiguous. Leaders consequently must be aware that their reactions can be either motivating or demoralizing.

The perception of leader competence is crucial in crisis situations and is the building block for leader–follower trust relationships (Fisher, Hutchings, & Sarros, 2010; Kolditz, 2005). Indeed, Fisher et al. (2010) argued that trust is the most salient component of in extremis leadership, because followers need to feel confident that their leader has the competence to keep them alive in a crisis situation. It is this trust that helps builds resilience.

Adaptive Leaders

Cronshaw and O'Keefe (2006) argued that any attempt to identify a leadership taxonomy to cover all possible circumstances, even when limited to in extremis situations, is doomed to failure. Rather, a critical skill set required of leaders is the ability to adapt to a changing environment. This ability to adapt to change, on which all other skill sets are based, is the cornerstone of resilience, the ability to quickly recover from change or misfortune.

In their description of the adaptive skills model (ASM), Fine and Cronshaw (1999) declared that adaptive skills are those competencies that enable the individual to manage the self in relation to conformity and change and to accept and adjust to the physical, interpersonal, and organizational arrangements present in the work environment. From this perspective, a highly adaptive leader is crucial in building and maintaining resilience in subordinates.

The ASM does not ask leaders to choose between transformational and transactional styles of leadership. Either may be appropriate, depending on the circumstances facing the leader and followers. Even coercive leadership (which is strongly discouraged by many transformational leadership advocates) may be appropriate under some circumstances. The ASM stresses that leader adaptability requires that the fullest possible range of constructively assertive responses be available to the leader as behavioral repertoires across the full possible range of contexts. To stereotype a leader as being transformational or transactional, or as having a particular personality, is not a useful strategy in trying to determine the relationship between leadership and resilience. What matters is whether a leader can lead and take the necessary actions when circumstances of a given kind (and many different kinds) arise and, ipso facto, help build and maintain not only his or her own resilience but that of subordinates (Cronshaw, 2003; Cronshaw & O'Keefe, 2006).

Hardy Leaders

Resilience has also been linked to individual characteristics such as hardiness, in that hardy people are viewed as being more resilient (Bartone, 2006). This should not come as a surprise, given that hardy people

> have a high sense of life and work commitment, a greater feeling of control, and are more open to change and challenges in life. They tend to interpret stressful and painful experiences as a normal aspect of existence, part of life that is overall interesting and worthwhile. (Bartone, 2006, p. S137)

In their study of Norwegian Navy officer cadets in a simulated prisoner of war camp, Eid and Morgan (2006) found that subjects high in hardiness exhibited lower levels of peritraumatic dissociation. Similarly, Bartone (1999) demonstrated that hardiness was able to protect against war-related stress, and this was especially true for those in high- and multiple stress conditions. In subsequent research, Bartone (2006) determined that leaders can have an influence on the levels of hardiness exhibited by followers in a military context and thus have a mediating effect on resilience (i.e., strong leadership leading to increased hardiness and thus to an increase in resilience). Bartone (2006) argued that leaders can influence levels of hardiness in followers in a number of ways. When leaders are hardy, their behaviors "influence subordinates to think and behave in more hardy or resilient ways" (Bartone, 2006, p. S139). Leaders who contribute to cohesion will influence hardiness, because research has shown that hardiness is associated with higher cohesion levels. Finally, the inspirational motivation component of transformational leadership is thought to influence enthusiasm, commitment, challenge, and a sense of meaning in subordinates. This, in turn, can have an influence on hardiness (Bartone, 2006).

Additionally, Vogt, Rizvi, Shipherd, and Resick (2008) demonstrated a reciprocal relationship between hardiness and stress reactions. In short, although hardiness may protect us from stress reactions, the actual experience of stress may make us less hardy. Consequently, the role played by leaders may be viewed as being multifaceted. Effective leaders not only will have to focus on increasing the levels of hardiness in their followers but will need to buffer the impact of stressors themselves. By doing so, they will protect the existing levels of hardiness from deterioration.

From the foregoing, it is highly evident that military leaders must carry out their responsibilities while experiencing situational demands that can be fraught with danger, ambiguity, and chaos. Plus, leaders must rise to the challenge while instilling a sense of confidence and trust in followers that will contribute to their survival and well-being. In essence, leaders need to enhance levels of resilience in their followers. They achieve this by becoming hardy, behaving ethically, creating a fair environment, and maximizing the flexibility required to adapt to ever-changing environments. But, is this enough to ensure the successful development of resilience? Could other aspects of leadership play a meaningful role?

THE ROAD AHEAD: PSYCHOLOGICAL CAPITAL AND AUTHENTIC LEADERSHIP

So far, we have proposed a model that is mostly empirically based, in which transformational and ethical leaders positively influence their followers' resilience. In this last section, we speculate about a more complex model (see Figure 5.2) that incorporates two nascent constructs that are receiving increasing attention in the industrial/organizational literature: psychological capital (PsyCap) and authentic leadership. These constructs were derived from the field of positive psychology, which itself is a relatively young field. In this model, resilience is grouped with the three related dimensions of hope, self-efficacy, and optimism to form the construct PsyCap, thereby being incorporated into a more comprehensive construct. Authentic leadership refers to knowing oneself. That is, leaders' awareness about themselves may influence their followers' PsyCap level. Other differences between the two models presented in this chapter include the addition of appraisal of situations and situational demands in Model 2. Finally, the second model focuses on general work outcomes rather than on the stressor–stress–strain sequence.

The model illustrates how three types of leadership style may contribute to resilience and its associated dimensions (e.g., PsyCap), which in turn may influence the appraisal of situations, which finally may impact on work outcomes, such as performance and organizational outcomes. Furthermore, situ-

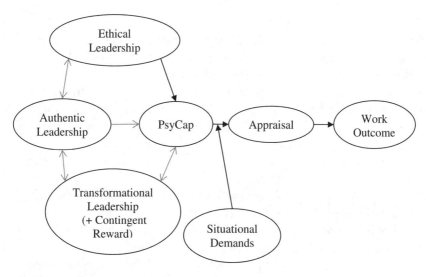

Figure 5.2. A more speculative model involving two nascent constructs. PsyCap represents psychological capital.

ational demands are postulated to moderate the relation between PsyCap and appraisal. The model is highly hypothetical because it is based on very limited empirical findings, which are described next. The model is included nonetheless because of its novelty, interest, and potential to influence future research.

Psychological Capital

In the past decade, resilience has been incorporated into a higher order construct that has been labeled as PsyCap by some (e.g., Luthans, Avey, & Patera, 2008) or as core confidence by Stajkovic (2006). Stajkovic noted that

> core confidence influences four manifestations that portray a person who figures out what is to be done and how to do it (hope), develops a belief that he or she can do specific tasks (self-efficacy), forms a positive outcome outlook on the entire undertaking (optimism), and works on the belief that he or she can bounce back if things go awry (resilience). (p. 1209)

These four dimensions are thought to be distinct, although they are highly correlated. Because of this overlap, they have been grouped into a higher order construct named core confidence or PsyCap. In the future, researchers may prefer to investigate how leaders may influence their followers' PsyCap dimensions rather than to focus on resilience alone.

Although the proponents of PsyCap originally intended this construct to represent a positive psychological state, which is malleable and open to development (e.g., Luthans et al., 2008), Stajkovic (2006) argued that core confidence could be construed either as a statelike belief or as a personality trait that is more stable. According to Stajkovic, core confidence will be statelike when it is applied to a specific domain of activity and traitlike when it represents a more general statement about the self. In other words, individuals have a baseline core confidence that can be modified for specific contexts or activities. For example, Luthans et al. (2008) showed that PsyCap could be increased after 2 hours of web-based training.

Some studies have revealed the existence of a link between PsyCap and transformational leadership. For instance, Peterson, Walumbwa, Byron, and Myrowitz (2009) found that leaders who scored higher on the three PsyCap dimensions included in the study (hope, optimism, and resilience) were perceived as being more transformational by their followers; this perception in turn related to firm performance. This is reminiscent of the concept of the hardy leader (Bartone, 2006) previously discussed. But can transformational leaders influence their followers' PsyCap?

At least two studies suggest that this is possible. First, results from an exploratory study showed strong positive correlations between subordinates' perceptions of their superior's transformational leadership on one hand and subordinates' own PsyCap and well-being on the other hand (McMurray et al., 2010). That is, followers who perceived their leader as being more transformational reported higher levels of PsyCap and well-being. In the McMurray et al. study, contingent reward, a transactional leadership dimension, presented a pattern of correlation with PsyCap and well-being that was similar to that of the transformational dimensions. These results suggest that contingent reward may also be related to followers' PsyCap. In the second study (Gooty, Gavin, Johnson, Frazier, & Snow, 2009), carried out with a university marching band that had a newly appointed leader, PsyCap mediated the relationship between followers' perceptions of their leader's transformational leadership and work outcomes such as in-role performance and organizational citizenship behaviors, which are discretionary behaviors willingly performed above the call of duty. Hence, there is evidence for PsyCap as a mediator between transformational leadership and desirable work outcomes.

To our knowledge, the mechanism by which PsyCap may facilitate performance remains unknown. However, Schaubroeck, Riolli, Peng, and Spain (2011) showed that optimism, hope, and ego resilience, taken collectively, were protective of undesirable health outcomes in high-stress situations experienced by American soldiers stationed in Iraq. In their study, PsyCap was measured as a personality trait. The cognitive appraisal of stressors as a loss, a threat, and/or a challenge was found to partially mediate the relationship between the soldiers' PsyCap on one hand and anxiety, somatic complaints, and depression on the other hand. The PsyCap trait advantage was minimal in low-stress situations. Its buffering effect became more apparent with higher reports of combat-related exposures. Hence, situational demands were included as moderating the relationship between PsyCap and appraisal in the proposed model (see Figure 5.2).

Authentic Leadership

The term *authentic leadership* is relatively new (e.g., Bass & Steidlmeier, 1999). Authentic leadership has been used to explain the processes that underlie positive leadership, such as transformational and ethical leadership, among others (Avolio & Gardner, 2005). The theoretical foundation of authentic leadership resides in a heightened self-awareness and self-regulation, which facilitate the finding of meaning and connection at work. It is a dynamic leadership style in which leaders contribute to increasing their followers' self-awareness and followers increase their leaders' self-awareness (Avolio & Gardner, 2005). The Authentic Leadership Questionnaire, a newly developed measure for authentic leadership, has been shown to have acceptable psychometric properties (Walumbwa et al., 2008). This measure comprises four subscales—self-awareness, relational transparency, internalized moral perspective, and balanced processing—but Walumbwa et al. noted that only a subset of authentic behaviors was included in this measure. Nevertheless, using this measure, they demonstrated that authentic leadership contributed over and above transformational leadership and ethical leadership to positive work-related attitudes, such as job satisfaction, organizational citizenship behaviors, organizational commitment, and satisfaction with the superior. This finding explains the inclusion of both transformational and ethical leadership proposed in Figure 5.2, although we are unaware of any studies that empirically link ethical leadership with PsyCap.

Finally, using the Authentic Leadership Questionnaire developed by Walumbwa et al. (2008), Walumbwa, Luthans, Avey, and Oke (2011) investigated the link between authentic leadership and collective PsyCap and trust with groups from a financial institution. Results showed that collective PsyCap mediated the relationship between authentic leadership and group performance and group citizenship behaviors and did this after removal of the effects of transformational leadership. Hence, we included a link between authentic leadership and PsyCap in the second model.

Overall, the model proposed in Figure 5.2 is highly speculative because it rests on nascent constructs that, although promising, require further investigation to strengthen their existence. Should they be confirmed, these constructs would impact our recommendations to leaders who want to increase their followers' resilience. First, PsyCap implies that there would be some benefit to extending the resilience training to incorporate hope, efficacy, and optimism. Second, it would be essential for leaders to get to know themselves better to maximize positive leadership. Finally, the benefits of PsyCap would be more apparent in highly stressful situations.

In fact, the U.S. Army has developed a resilience training program (Reivich, Seligman, & McBride, 2011) that incorporates elements of authentic and transformational leadership as well as elements of PsyCap. Indeed, the initial portion of the course focuses on six core competencies associated with resilience: self-awareness, self-regulation, optimism, mental agility, character strengths, and the development of strong relationships (Reivich et al., 2011). Hence, at the time of writing, the training of soldiers in the U.S. Army incorporates several elements presented in Model 2.

CONCLUSION

In this chapter, we presented a model in which an appropriate set of leadership behaviors could ameliorate the impact of stressful events on followers by encouraging the development of resilience in followers. We proposed that leaders who use an ethical transformational style will be effective at helping their followers develop and maintain resilience. This does not mean that leaders can disregard task and situational demands, but building resilience requires the consistency, respect, and stimulation generated by an ethical leader who adopts a transformational leadership style. Transformational leaders adjust their behavior according to the situation by being either participative or directive. The four dimensions of transformational leadership—idealized influence, inspirational motivation, individualized consideration, and intellectual stimulation—may all contribute to the process of developing and maintaining resilience in followers, provided that the leaders' values are strongly grounded in a moral/ethical foundation.

In the context of extremely stressful situations, the most effective military leaders must be directive and adaptive, with the capability to adjust their communication style to the demands of the situation. Indeed, highly adaptive leaders are crucial in building and maintaining resilience in subordinates. In turn, this ability to adapt to change provides one of the primary aspects of resilience, the ability to recover quickly from change or misfortune.

Not only must leaders be directive and adaptive, they should also be hardy. Much of the essence of hardiness resides in the way a person perceives and thinks about a situation. With dedication and effort, it is possible to change perceptions and thoughts. One method, known as cognitive restructuring or cognitive therapy, is described in a practical manner in several self-help books, such as those written by Beck (1976), Ellis (2001), and Greenberger and Padesky (1995).

On a final note, we discussed a possible avenue for future research by introducing the nascent constructs of psychological capital and authentic leadership. The second model presented is based on very limited empirical evidence. Should this model be supported, this would imply that leaders need to know themselves and to be without a facade with their subordinates. Furthermore, it would imply that resilience should be studied along with hope, efficacy, and optimism.

REFERENCES

Arnold, K. A., Barling, J., & Kelloway, E. K. (2001). Transformational leadership or the iron cage: Which predicts trust, commitment and team efficacy? *Leadership & Organization Development Journal, 22*, 315–320. doi:10.1108/EUM0000000006162

Avey, J. B., Palanski, M. E., & Walumbwa, F. O. (2011). When leadership goes unnoticed: The moderating role of follower self-esteem on the relationship between ethical leadership and follower behavior. *Journal of Business Ethics, 98*, 573–582. doi:10.1007/s10551-010-0610-2

Avolio, B. J., & Gardner, W. L. (2005). Authentic leadership development: Getting to the root of positive forms of leadership. *The Leadership Quarterly, 16*, 315–338. doi:10.1016/j.leaqua.2005.03.001

Baran, B. E., & Scott, C. W. (2010). Organizing ambiguity: A grounded theory of leadership and sensemaking within dangerous contexts. *Military Psychology, 22*(Suppl. 1), S42–S69. doi:10.1080/08995601003644262

Barling, J., Weber, T., & Kelloway, E. K. (1996). Effects of transformational leadership training on attitudinal and financial outcomes: A field experiment. *Journal of Applied Psychology, 81*, 827–832. doi:10.1037/0021-9010.81.6.827

Bartone, P. T. (1999). Hardiness protects against war-related stress in Army Reserve Forces. *Consulting Psychology Journal: Practice and Research, 51*, 72–82. doi:10.1037/1061-4087.51.2.72

Bartone, P. T. (2006). Resilience under military operational stress: Can leaders influence hardiness? *Military Psychology, 18*(Suppl. 3), S131–S148. doi:10.1207/s15327876mp1803s_10

Bass, B. M. (1985). *Leadership and performance beyond expectations*. New York, NY: Free Press.

Bass, B. M. (1990). *Bass and Stogdill's handbook of leadership: Theory, research, and managerial applications* (3rd ed.). New York, NY: Free Press.

Bass, B. M. (1997a). Concepts of leadership. In R. P. Vecchio (Ed.), *Leadership: Understanding the dynamics of power and influence in organizations* (pp. 3–23). Notre Dame, IN: University of Notre Dame Press.

Bass, B. M. (1997b). From transactional to transformational leadership: Learning to share the vision. In R. P. Vecchio (Ed.), *Leadership: Understanding the dynamics of power and influence in organizations* (pp. 318–333). Notre Dame, IN: University of Notre Dame Press. doi:10.1016/0090-2616(90)90061-S

Bass, B. M. (1998). *Transformational leadership: Industrial, military, and educational impact*. Mahwah, NJ: Erlbaum.

Bass, B. M. (1999). Two decades of research and development in transformational leadership. *European Journal of Work and Organizational Psychology, 8*, 9–32. doi:10.1080/135943299398410

Bass, B. M. (2000). The future of leadership in learning organizations. *Journal of Leadership Studies, 7*(3), 18–40. doi:10.1177/107179190000700302

Bass, B. M., Avolio, B. J., Jung, D. I., & Berson, Y. (2003). Predicting unit performance by assessing transformational and transactional leadership. *Journal of Applied Psychology, 88*, 207–218. doi:10.1037/0021-9010.88.2.207

Bass, B. M., & Steidlmeier, P. (1999). Ethics, character, and authentic transformational leadership behavior. *The Leadership Quarterly, 10*, 181–217. doi:10.1016/S1048-9843(99)00016-8

Beck, A. T. (1976). *Cognitive therapy and the emotional disorders*. New York, NY: Meridian.

Bennis, W. (2007). The challenges of leadership in the modern world: Introduction to the special issue. *American Psychologist, 62*, 2–5. doi:10.1037/0003-066X.62.1.2

Boies, K., & Howell, J. M. (2009). Leading military teams to think and feel: Exploring the relations between leadership, soldiers' cognitive and affective processes, and team effectiveness. *Military Psychology, 21*, 216–232. doi:10.1080/08995600902768743

Bono, J. E., & Judge, T. A. (2004). Personality and transformational and transactional leadership: A meta-analysis. *Journal of Applied Psychology, 89*, 901–910. doi:10.1037/0021-9010.89.5.901

Brown, M. E., Trevino, L. K., & Harrison, D. A. (2005). Ethical leadership: A social learning perspective for construct development and testing. *Organizational Behavior and Human Decision Processes, 97*, 117–134. doi:10.1016/j.obhdp.2005.03.002

Burke, C. S., Sims, D. E., Lazzara, E. H., & Salas, E. (2007). Trust in leadership: A multi-level review and integration. *The Leadership Quarterly, 18*, 606–632. doi:10.1016/j.leaqua.2007.09.006

Burns, J. M. (1978). *Leadership*. New York, NY: Harper & Row.

Castro, C. A., Adler, A. B., McGurk, D., & Thomas, J. L. (2006). Leader actions to enhance soldier resiliency in combat. In *Human dimensions in military operations—Military leaders' strategies for addressing stress and psychological support* (pp. 3-1–3-14). Retrieved from http://www.cso.nato.int/abstracts.asp

Castro, C. A., & Hoge, C. W. (2005). Building psychological resiliency and mitigating the risks of combat and deployment stressors faced by soldiers. Retrieved from ftp://host.70.200.23.62.rev.coltfrance.com/PubFullText/RTO/MP/RTO-MP-HFM-124/MP-HFM-124-13.pdf

Chen, D. J. Q., & Lim, V. K. G. (2012). Strength in adversity: The influence of psychological capital on job search. *Journal of Organizational Behavior, 33*, 811–839. doi:10.1002/job.1814

Cronshaw, S. F. (2003). Development of leadership as the pre-eminent people skill. In J. P. Boyer (Ed.), *Leading in an upside-down world: New Canadian perspectives on leadership* (pp. 101–112). Toronto, Ontario, Canada: Dundurn Press.

Cronshaw, S. F., & O'Keefe, D. F. (2006). Adaptive skills as a basis for leadership success in the Canadian military with an emphasis on special operations. In A. MacIntyre & K. D. Davis (Eds.), *From the Canadian Forces Leadership Institute's research files: Dimensions of military leadership* (pp. 81–110). Kingston, Ontario, Canada: Canadian Defence Academy Press.

Dickson, M. W., Smith, D. B., Grojean, M. W., & Ehrhart, M. (2001). An organizational climate regarding ethics: The outcome of leader values and the practices that reflect them. *The Leadership Quarterly, 12*, 197–217. doi:10.1016/S1048-9843(01)00069-8

Dvir, T., Eden, D., Avolio, B. J., & Shamir, B. (2002). Impact of transformational leadership on follower development and performance: A field experiment. *Academy of Management Journal, 45*, 735–744. doi:10.2307/3069307

Eid, J., Johnson, B. H., Brun, W., Laberg, J. C., Nyhus, J. K., & Larsson, G. (2004). Situational awareness and transformational leadership in senior military leaders: An exploratory study. *Military Psychology, 16*, 203–209. doi:10.1207/s15327876mp1603_4

Eid, J., & Morgan, C. A., III. (2006). Dissociation, hardiness, and performance in military cadets participating in survival training. *Military Medicine, 171*, 436–442.

Ellis, A. (2001). *Feeling better, getting better, staying better: Profound self-help therapy for your emotions.* Atascadero, CA: Impact.

Fine, S., & Cronshaw, S. F. (1999). *Functional job analysis: A foundation for human resources management.* Mahwah, NJ: Erlbaum.

Fisher, K., Hutchings, K., & Sarros, J. (2010). The bright and shadow aspects of in extremis leadership. *Military Psychology, 22*(Suppl. 1), S89–S116. doi:10.1080/08995601003644346

Geyery, A. L. J., & Steyrer, J. M. (1998). Transformational leadership and objective performance in banks. *Applied Psychology, 47*, 397–420. doi:10.1111/j.1464-0597.1998.tb00035.x

Goleman, D., Boyatzis, R., & McKee, A. (2002). *Primal leadership: Realizing the power of emotional intelligence.* Boston, MA: Harvard Business School Press.

Gooty, J., Gavin, M., Johnson, P. D., Frazier, M. L., & Snow, D. B. (2009). In the eyes of the beholder: Transformational leadership, positive psychological capital, and performance. *Journal of Leadership & Organizational Studies, 15*, 353–367. doi:10.1177/1548051809332021

Greenberger, D., & Padesky, C. A. (1995). *Mind over mood: Change how you feel by changing the way you think.* New York, NY: Guilford Press.

Hackman, J. R., & Wageman, R. (2007). Asking the right questions about leadership: Discussion and conclusions. *American Psychologist, 62*, 43–47. doi:10.1037/0003-066X.62.1.43

Harland, L., Harrison, W., Jones, J. R., & Reiter-Palmon, R. (2005). Leadership behaviors and subordinate resilience. *Journal of Leadership & Organizational Studies, 11*(2), 2–14. doi:10.1177/107179190501100202

Harms, P. D., & Credé, M. (2010). Emotional intelligence and transformational and transactional leadership: A meta-analysis. *Journal of Leadership & Organizational Studies, 17*, 5–17. doi:10.1177/1548051809350894

Hellriegel, D., Slocum, J. W., Jr., & Woodman, R. W. (1989). *Organizational behavior* (5th ed.). New York, NY: West.

Judge, T. A., & Piccolo, R. F. (2004). Transformational and transactional leadership: A meta-analytic test of their relative validity. *Journal of Applied Psychology, 89*, 755–768. doi:10.1037/0021-9010.89.5.755

Kalshoven, K., & Boon, C. T. (2012). Ethical leadership, employee well-being, and helping: The moderating role of human resource management. *Journal of Personnel Psychology, 11*, 60–68. doi:10.1027/1866-5888/a000056

Kanungo, R. N., & Mendonca, M. (1998). Ethical leadership in three dimensions. *Journal of Human Values, 4*, 133–148. doi:10.1177/097168589800400202

Kaptein, M., Huberts, L., Avelino, S., & Lasthuizen, K. (2005). Demonstrating ethical leadership by measuring ethics: A survey of U.S. public servants. *Public Integrity, 7*, 299–311.

Kelloway, K., & Barling, J. (2000). What have we learned about developing transformational leaders. *Leadership & Organization Development Journal, 21*, 355–362. doi:10.1108/01437730010377908

Kolditz, T. A. (2005). The in extremis leader. *Leader to Leader, 38*(Suppl. 1), 6–18. doi:10.1002/ltl.370

Kolditz, T. A. (2006). Research in *in extremis* settings: Examining the critique of "Why they fight." *Armed Forces & Society, 32*, 655–658. doi:10.1177/0095327X05283853

Kozlowski, S. W. J., Watola, D. J., Jensen, J. M., Kim, B. H., & Botero, I. C. (2009). Developing adaptive teams: A theory of dynamic team leadership. In E. Salas, G. F. Goodwin, & C. S. Burke (Eds.), *Team effectiveness in complex organizations: Cross-disciplinary perspectives and approaches* (pp. 113–155). New York, NY: Routledge.

Kurfi, A. K. (2009). Leadership styles: The managerial challenges in emerging economies. *International Bulletin of Business Administration, 6*, 73–81. Retrieved from http://www.eurojournals.com

Lim, B. C., & Ployhart, R. E. (2004). Transformational leadership: Relations to the five-factor model and team performance in typical and maximum contexts. *Journal of Applied Psychology, 89*, 610–621. doi:10.1037/0021-9010.89.4.610

Lowe, K. B., Kroeck, K. G., & Sivasubramaniam, N. (1996). Effectiveness correlates of transformational and transactional leadership: A meta-analytic review of the literature. *The Leadership Quarterly, 7*, 385–425. doi:10.1016/S1048-9843(96)90027-2

Luthans, F., Avey, J. B., & Patera, J. L. (2008). Experimental analyses of a Web-based training intervention to develop positive psychological capital. *Academy of Management Learning & Education, 7*, 209–221. doi:10.5465/AMLE.2008.32712618

Luthans, F., Luthans, K. W., & Luthans, B. C. (2004). Positive psychological capital: Beyond human and social capital. *Business Horizons, 47*(1), 45–50. doi:10.1016/j.bushor.2003.11.007

Lyons, J. B., & Schneider, T. R. (2009). The effects of leadership style on stress outcomes. *The Leadership Quarterly, 20*, 737–748. doi:10.1016/j.leaqua.2009.06.010

Maguen, S., Turcotte, D. M., Peterson, A. L., Dremsa, T. L., Garb, H. N., McNally, R. J., & Litz, B. T. (2008). Description of risk and resilience factors among military medical personnel before deployment to Iraq. *Military Medicine, 173*, 1–9.

Masi, R. J., & Cooke, R. A. (2000). Effects of transformational leadership on subordinate motivation, empowering norms, and organizational productivity. *International Journal of Organizational Analysis, 8*, 16–47. doi:10.1108/eb028909

Mayer, D. M., Kuenzi, M., & Greenbaum, R. L. (2010). Examining the link between ethical leadership and employee misconduct: The mediating role of ethical climate. *Journal of Business Ethics, 95*, 7–16. doi:10.1007/s10551-011-0794-0

McMurray, J. J., Pirola-Merlo, A., Sarros, J. C., & Islam, M. M. (2010). Leadership, climate, psychological capital, commitment, and wellbeing in a non-profit organization. *Leadership & Organization Development Journal, 31*, 436–457. doi:10.1108/01437731011056452

Mulder, M., de Jong, R. D., Koppelaar, L., & Verhage, J. (1986). Power, situation, and leaders' effectiveness: An organizational field study. *Journal of Applied Psychology, 71*, 566–570. doi:10.1037/0021-9010.71.4.566

Murphy, P. J., & Fogarty, G. J. (2009). Leadership: The key to meaning and resilience on deployment? In P. J. Murphy (Ed.), *Focus on human performance in land operations* (Vol. 1, pp. 92–101). Canberra, Australia: Australian Defence Force Psychology Organisation.

O'Keefe, D. F. (2006). *Assessing the moderating effects of ethical climate on the relations between social dominance orientation/right-wing authoritarianism and self-reported unethical behaviour* (Unpublished doctoral dissertation). University of Guelph, Guelph, Ontario, Canada.

O'Keefe, D. F. (2009). Ethical climate and leadership: Can leaders really make a difference? In E. Spencer & D. Lagacé-Roy (Eds.), *Ethical decision-making in the new security environment: Proceedings from the Canadian Conference on Ethical Leadership* (Vol. 2, pp. 107–120). Kingston, Ontario, Canada: Canadian Defence Academy Press.

Peterson, S. J., Walumbwa, F. O., Byron, K., & Myrowitz, J. (2009). CEO positive psychological traits, transformational leadership, and firm performance in high-technology start-up and established firms. *Journal of Management, 35*, 348–368. doi:10.1177/0149206307312512

Piccolo, R. F., Greenbaum, R., Den Hartog, D. N., & Folger, R. (2010). The relationship between ethical leadership and core job characteristics. *Journal of Organizational Behavior, 31*, 259–278. doi:10.1002/job.627

Pratt, L., & Barling, J. (1988). Differentiating daily hassles, acute and chronic stressors: A framework and its implications. In J. R. Hurrell, L. R. Murphy, S. L. Sauter, & C. L. Cooper (Eds.), *Occupational stress: Issues and developments in research* (pp. 41–53). London, England: Taylor & Francis.

Reivich, K. J., Seligman, M. E. P., & McBride, S. (2011). Master resilience training in the U.S. Army. *American Psychologist, 66*, 25–34. doi:10.1037/a0021897

Schaubroeck, J. M., Riolli, L. T., Peng, A. C., & Spain, E. S. (2011). Resilience to traumatic exposure among soldiers deployed in combat. *Journal of Occupational Health Psychology, 16*, 18–37. doi:10.1037/a0021006

Schermerhorn, J. R., Hunt, J. G., & Osborn, R. (1982). *Managing organizational behavior*. New York, NY: Wiley.

Stadelmann, C. (2010). Swiss Armed Forces militia system: Effect of transformational leadership on subordinates' extra effort and the moderating role of command structure. *Swiss Journal of Psychology, 69*, 83–93. doi:10.1024/1421-0185/a000010

Stajkovic, A. D. (2006). Development of a core confidence–higher order construct. *Journal of Applied Psychology, 91*, 1208–1224. doi:10.1037/0021-9010.91.6.1208

Toor, S., & Ofori, G. (2009). Ethical leadership: Examining the relationships with full range leadership model, employee outcomes, and organizational culture. *Journal of Business Ethics, 90*, 533–547. doi:10.1007/s10551-009-0059-3

Tremblay, M. A. (2010). Fairness perceptions and trust as mediators on the relationship between leadership style, unit commitment, and turnover intentions of Canadian Forces personnel. *Military Psychology, 22*, 510–523. doi:10.1080/08995605.2010.513271

van Breda, A. D. (2011). Resilient workplaces: An initial conceptualization. *Families in Society, 92*, 33–40. doi:10.1606/1044-3894.4059

Vogt, D. S., Rizvi, S. L., Shipherd, J. C., & Resick, P. A. (2008). Longitudinal investigation of reciprocal relationship between stress reactions and hardiness. *Personality and Social Psychology Bulletin, 34*, 61–73. doi:10.1177/0146167207309197

Walumbwa, F. O., Avolio, B. J., Gardner, W. L., Wernsing, T. S., & Peterson, S. J. (2008). Authentic leadership: Development and validation of a theory-based measure. *Journal of Management, 34*, 89–126. doi:10.1177/0149206307308913

Walumbwa, F. O., Luthans, F., Avey, J. B., & Oke, A. (2011). Authentically leading groups: The mediating role of collective psychological capital and trust. *Journal of Organizational Behavior, 32*, 4–24. doi:10.1002/job.653

Walumbwa, F. O., Mayer, D. M., Wang, P., Wang, H., Workman, K., & Christensen, A. L. (2011). Linking ethical leadership to employee performance: The roles of leader–member exchange, self-efficacy, and organizational identification. *Organizational Behavior and Human Decision Processes, 115*, 204–213. doi:10.1016/j.obhdp.2010.11.002

Wong, L., Bliese, P., & McGurk, D. (2003). Military leadership: A context specific review. *Leadership Quarterly, 14,* 657–692. doi:10.1016/j.leaqua.2003.08.001

Yang, F. H., Wu, M., Chang, C. C., & Chien, Y. (2011). Elucidating the relationships among transformational leadership, job satisfaction, commitment foci and commitment bases in the public sector. *Public Personnel Management, 40,* 265–278.

Yukl, G. (1999). An evaluation of conceptual weaknesses in transformational and charismatic leadership theories: Charisma and the founders of Mothers Against Drunk Driving. *Leadership Quarterly, 10,* 285–305. doi:10.1016/S1048-9843(99)00013-2

Yukl, G. A. (1998). *Leadership in organizations* (4th ed.). Upper Saddle River, NJ: Prentice Hall.

Zohar, D., & Tenne-Gazit, O. (2008). Transformational leadership and group interaction as climate antecedents: A social network analysis. *Journal of Applied Psychology, 93,* 744–757. doi:10.1037/0021-9010.93.4.744

II

BUILDING RESILIENCE: MODELS AND PROGRAMS

6

COGNITIVE BEHAVIORAL METHODS FOR BUILDING RESILIENCE

JULIA M. WHEALIN, JOSEF I. RUZEK, AND EDWARD M. VEGA

Today's military missions are extraordinarily demanding, physically, psychologically, and interpersonally. Military operations in the early 21st century have been considered to be more unpredictable than previous military contexts (Petraeus, 2006), and the scope of military missions has expanded (Hotopf et al., 2003), calling for more and more sophisticated training methods. For example, combat rehearsal exercises in the past were more likely to include a somewhat conventional template for how the enemy was going to attack, where the long-range reconnaissance was, and where the enemy's forward echelon was (Petraeus, 2006). Also, combat rehearsal exercises traditionally have used learning tactics focused on task repetition (Driskell & Salas, 1991). To adapt to ever-evolving mission demands, training centers must, more than ever, understand the individual and group mechanisms that can promote personnel resilient to continuously dangerous and complex environments.

This chapter was coauthored by employees of the U.S. Department of Veterans Affairs as part of official duty and is considered to be in the public domain. Any views expressed herein do not necessarily represent the views of the United States government, and the authors' participation is not meant to serve as an official endorsement.
http://dx.doi.org/10.1037/14190-006
Building Psychological Resilience in Military Personnel: Theory and Practice, R. R. Sinclair and T. W. Britt (Editors)

Resilience is a multidimensional construct, consisting of numerous characteristics. It involves the capacity of individuals or groups to put in place early and effective adjustment processes to help reduce the strain that comes from exposure to chronic or severe stressors (Layne, Warren, Watson, & Shalev, 2007). Increasingly sophisticated research with military personnel and other groups has shown that resilience in the face of highly stressful events, within limits, is not purely a random phenomenon (Ozer, Best, Lipsey, & Weiss, 2003). Specific physiological, emotional, and cognitive factors are emerging that identify those who are better able to rebound from severe stress and those who are likely to experience problems (e.g., Morgan et al., 2004; Whealin, Ruzek, & Southwick, 2008). Similarly, empirical research with military personnel has begun to identify factors that correlate with resilience to chronic disorders following operational stressors. For example, specific attitudes and coping styles, measured prior to combat, have been shown to be associated with those who are more resilient to posttraumatic stress disorder (PTSD; Ginzburg, Solomon, Dekel, & Neria, 2003). Some research, as well as a good deal of accumulated knowledge of experienced trainers, suggests that such attitudes and behaviors can be altered through training (e.g., Bandura, Reese, & Adams, 1982; Seligman et al., 1988).

Many of the traditional military training methods that have been used for centuries to improve human performance and well-being, from physical fitness training to specialized mission preparation, use techniques that are supported by current empirical research and theory. Further, recent advances in the field of resilience increasingly enable military organizations to incorporate new research findings to fine-tune training methods or add new techniques that may amplify and/or streamline the effectiveness of training programs. Much of this research centers on regulation of physical, mental, and emotional stress.

PHYSICAL, MENTAL, AND EMOTIONAL STRESS REGULATION

Stress arousal is a physical, mental, and/or emotional response to a perceived stressor or stressors. The relationship between stress arousal and performance is frequently depicted as following an inverted or upside-down U shape, where initially performance improves with increasing arousal—to a point. As arousal levels continue to increase to very high levels, performance begins to degrade, and the optimal level of arousal varies based on the difficulty of the task (Yerkes & Dodson, 1908). Although valid challenges have been levied against the methodology of the original Yerkes and Dodson (1908) study and simple conceptualizations of arousal (e.g., Hancock, Ganey, & Szalma, 2002; Neiss, 1988), various areas of research continue to support the idea that low to moderate levels of stress can have a beneficial effect on performance (e.g., by increasing arousal and attention; Alexander, Hillier, Smith, Tivarus, & Beversdorf, 2007).

Once the demands of a stressor (or stressors) exceed the resources individuals perceive are available to cope with them, stress responses become detrimental. Research shows that under high and/or chronic stress levels, functioning is impaired in several domains. For instance, high stress results in increased cortisol release that is correlated with impairment of memory for facts, knowledge, and learning (Newcomer et al., 1999). Other physiological changes, such as heightened functioning of the locus ceruleus–norepinephrine system, seem to impair the ability to make decisions, manage multifaceted tasks, and negotiate complex environments (Alexander et al., 2007). During stressful combat-simulation training, deficits range from simple cognitive functions, such as reaction time and vigilance, to complex functions including memory and logical reasoning. These cognitive deficits degrade operational effectiveness considerably and are likely to be even more severe during actual combat (Alexander et al., 2007). Given the complexity of decision making in modern military contexts, as well as obvious high levels of stress sustained by individuals serving in these positions, it is necessary to find ways to reduce physical, mental, and emotional responses to severe stressors.

Some of the most compelling research on resilience suggests that individual differences in the ability to regulate responses to severe stressors are among the most important determinants of both short- and long-term adaptation to those stressors. For example, the ability to modulate physiological and emotional reactions, measured prior to training, can discriminate Special Forces troops who successfully tolerate and recover from stress related to the demanding Survival, Evasion, Resistance, and Escape (SERE) training from those who are slower to return to baseline (McNeil & Morgan, 2010; Morgan et al., 2004). Additionally, research indicates that intensity of physiological and emotional reactions, including the degree of dissociation (i.e., involuntary/ automatic disruption of normal consciousness) experienced during a stressor, is integral to the etiology of PTSD (Brewin, Andrews, & Rose, 2000; Galea et al., 2002; Jones & Barlow, 1990; Ozer et al., 2003; Pitman, 1989). In a recent meta-analysis of 68 studies, dissociation around the time of a highly stressful event was the strongest predictor of PTSD, with a moderate estimated effect size of .35 (adjusted for sample size; Ozer et al., 2003). Emotional responses around the time of the event had an estimated effect size of .26 (adjusted for sample size).

In summary, whereas low to moderate stress levels facilitate cognitive functioning, chronic and/or extreme stress levels can impair several domains of cognition necessary for military missions (McNeil & Morgan, 2010). In addition, excessive physiological and emotional stress responses appear to have an important causative role in chronic disorders such as PTSD. The ability to attenuate or recover from physiological and emotional arousal following exposure to extreme stressors is associated with immediate gains in performance as well as long-term resilience to both acute and chronic stressors (McNeil & Morgan, 2010). Therefore, it makes sense, both empirically and theoretically, to identify and evaluate techniques that can assist service members in regulating physiological and emotional stress responses during demanding operational situations.

BUILDING PSYCHOLOGICAL RESILIENCE

In the remainder of this chapter, we explore military training techniques proposed to influence stress regulation and stress-related cognitive appraisals. Because it is beyond the scope of this chapter to describe all of the interventions currently used by the military, we identify six approaches that, from a theoretical and empirical research perspective, are likely to promote the specialized skills and attitudes necessary to minimize the impact of operational stressors and maximize troop well-being and readiness for military missions. These approaches include stress management training, preparatory education, cognitive appraisals, role modeling, exposure/mission rehearsal exercises, and exposure to internal stimuli.

Stress Management Training

Both theory and empirical research suggest a strong need for skills that personnel can use prior to and during potentially overwhelming situations to regulate stress arousal and enable them to accomplish their tasks effectively. As described earlier, excessive anxiety is associated with decreased performance on cognitive and physical tasks. Recent focus on concepts such as operational-demand-related cognitive decline (McNeil & Morgan, 2010) highlights the need to accommodate the reality that combat-related stress produces significant decrements in many domains of cognitive functioning (e.g., Lieberman et al., 2005), and it also suggests that increasing the ability of military personnel to regulate arousal would be reflected in improved performance during stressful conditions. Therefore, interventions have been developed in which techniques that focus on reduction of anxious arousal, using a range of behavioral and cognitive techniques, are employed.

One such approach is Stress Inoculation Training (SIT; Meichenbaum, 2007; Meichenbaum & Deffenbacher, 1988), which uses relaxation as well as a broad variety of cognitive techniques (e.g., cognitive restructuring of negative self-statements and guided self-dialogue). SIT involves three phases.

In the first phase, education is provided to help participants understand how the intervention works. The second phase, skills acquisition and rehearsal, involves learning and practicing coping skills tailored to the specific situation. Cognitive approaches such as cognitive restructuring, task-oriented self-dialogue, and relaxation skills are used to maximize the application of the relaxation skills. The third phase, application and follow-through, involves application of skills in real-life environments. During this stage, individuals practice implementing a series of personalized statements to help them manage fear and remain focused on the task during realistic training experiences.

Training in SIT techniques aims to increase understanding of responses to stress and improve coping skills used in stressful environments, thereby desensitizing or inoculating the individual to upcoming situations. A meta-analysis of 37 studies supports the role of SIT in decreasing anxiety and increasing performance in stressful occupations (Driskell & Johnston, 1998; Saunders, Driskell, Johnston, & Salas, 1996). However, research indicates that the impact of stress management training upon performance and individual well-being varies depending upon a variety of factors, including the length of training (Saunders et al., 1996). Unfortunately, studies have not confirmed the effectiveness of stress management techniques as a preventive measure for future stressful situations. One examination of a single-session pre-deployment stress briefing given to 4,046 military personnel showed no positive or negative impact postdeployment (Sharpley, Fear, Greenberg, Jones, & Wessely, 2008). However, because research also indicates that length of treatment is correlated with likelihood of positive change and that in many cases interventions may not last long enough to produce the desired or expected positive changes (Hansen, Lambert, & Forman, 2002), most recent trainings using longer interventions (i.e., higher treatment "dose") can be anticipated to produce stronger outcomes (Sharpley et al., 2008).

A more recent approach to stress management involves mindfulness meditation (MM). MM involves training one's attention to focus completely on the present moment, without judgment. MM stress reduction training has been adapted for those who have physical and mental health problems (e.g., Grossman, Niemann, Schmidt, & Walach, 2004) and, more recently, has been adapted as a preventive tool (e.g., Ma & Teasdale, 2004). Jha, Stanley, Kiyonaga, Wong, and Gelfand (2010) examined its role as a prophylactic intervention to prevent decline in cognitive capacity in marines undergoing stressful deployment preparation. MM training was given to a convenience sample of 29 U.S. Marine reservists who volunteered for the training in MM; they were compared with marine reservists drawn from the same unit and preparing for the same deployment to and mission in Iraq. The training consisted of 24 hours of practical education and practice over an 8-week period. Marines who received the training did not have the decrease in cognitive capacity that the group who did not receive the training showed. Also, those marines who practiced MM the most showed less cognitive degradation over time. Jha et al. concluded that MM training may decrease the likelihood of cognitive failures during deployment. More research is needed to see if this promising resilience-building technique can result in changes over time.

When traditional stress management training programs (e.g., SIT) are applied to the training of military personnel, various challenges arise that may limit their effectiveness. Many of these challenges involve adapting mental health techniques to the cultural and logistical needs of the personnel being trained. Thompson and McCreary (2006) identified several specific issues that should be addressed when implementing stress training programs among military personnel. For example, personnel may be resistant to mental health information and/or its provision by mental health professionals due to factors such as stigma or simply because they do not believe that mental health problems are a personal concern for them (Hoge et al., 2004; Thompson & McCreary, 2006). Additionally, some military personnel may not relate to the academic lecture format typically used to deliver the stress management training, and thus they may infer that the technique is irrelevant (Thompson & McCreary, 2006). One resilience-building program developed by the 732nd Combat Stress Control Clinic ("One Shot, One Kill," in Mallisham, 2007) is designed to overcome these barriers by utilizing popular movie clips, analogies, athletics, small groups, and animation to demonstrate concepts and skills. However, evaluation data are not available for this program.

Another approach that is becoming more prevalent is embedding stress management training as part of traditional military training programs that are provided by military instructors with operational credibility. For example, several U.S. Army convoy courses now embed mental health clinicians in every step of the training. Clinicians initially educate command, instructors, and personnel about combat stress, stress management, and referral procedures. Then, during the exercises, personnel receive training from their instructors on how to monitor themselves and each other for overwhelming stress reactions. When a potentially risky reaction occurs, participants obtain immediate support from clinicians for "combat stress" reactions. Using nonclinical nomenclature further decreases stigma and promotes prompt use of services aimed to decrease arousal, improve thinking, and enable personnel to accomplish their tasks effectively. Battlemind training, described in the next section, is also a good example of utilizing training at multiple levels of personnel to increase the operational credibility of the training provided.

It is likely that a successful and comprehensive integration of stress management techniques into preexisting trainings (e.g., the exposure techniques described later in this chapter), using methods that are culturally relevant to the personnel, will improve performance. For example, Thompson and McCreary (2006) recommended that stress management principles be integrated into traditional training programs as a "mental readiness" model, similar to the military model of physical and technical operational readiness. However, it remains to be seen whether training applications will be effective in improving performance and reducing negative outcomes from the highly demanding and unpredictable tasks related to military operations.

Preparatory Education

The emotional and physiological reactions of individuals during a mission are influenced by their thoughts about how prepared they are for the mission and how closely the actual scenario matches what they anticipate (Inzana, Driskell, Salas, & Johnston, 1996). Preparatory education is information provided to individuals and groups that helps them guide their appraisal of and better cope with an event. Research has shown that preparatory education can decrease the intensity of emotional responses to subsequent fear-producing events (e.g., Blount, Davis, Powers, & Roberts, 1991; Inzana et al., 1996). Additionally, some research suggests that giving individuals preparatory information about potentially feared events or objects is helpful in preventing long-term disorders (Gardenswartz & Craske, 2001).

Military trainers have long known that providing information about what may happen during upcoming events helps promote adaptation to stress (e.g., Ahrenfeldt, 1958, cited in Marks, 1987). Briefings traditionally include very detailed and concrete information about the conditions that personnel will encounter during the mission. As our understanding of cognitions and stress arousal becomes more sophisticated, training programs are increasingly including education about the human stress response as a strategy to prevent poor outcomes related to stress. For example, new combat stress courses have been developed to provide training in the stress-response system, including possible responses to severe stress. Programs that provide education about the biological response to fear, as well as how stress affects body, mind, emotions, and behavior/functioning, help to prepare individuals to cope with their own or others' stress reactions. This information is thought to help normalize routine stress reactions, so as to reduce negative thoughts individuals may have when they experience fear or other normal reactions.

One of the largest U.S. military psychological resilience programs is the Battlemind predeployment training. The concept of Battlemind has been defined as "a soldier's inner strength to face adversity, fear, and hardship during combat with confidence and resolution" (Castro, Hoge, & Cox, 2006, p. 42-2). Standard training for all U.S. Army soldiers and leaders deploying to Iraq or Afghanistan, Battlemind is a resilience program designed to increase psychological resilience and overall self-efficacy by creating more realistic expectations and by targeting specific actions that soldiers and leaders can engage in to meet the challenges of combat (McGurk, Castro, Thomas, & Hoge, 2007). Unprecedented in its application, the Battlemind training is designed to be culturally relevant to the soldier population. The training draws from the military model of aiding fellow soldiers who are physically wounded in combat. In Battlemind, soldiers are trained to respond in a similar fashion to cues of psychological distress in their peers. The training is led by senior soldiers who served in those conflicts and thus are seen as credible sources of information. Additionally, instead of taking a strictly didactic approach, the training provides vignettes of other soldiers' experiences and encourages discussion among attendees.

Battlemind training seeks to promote resilience through its comprehensive and thorough approach. By including specific modules for soldiers, National Guard/Reservists, and leaders, it seeks to address specific needs of multiple populations in the U.S. Army environment. Also, the training addresses numerous specific thoughts or expectations that are important for successful adjustment to deployment to and return from combat. For example, the leader training focuses on "10 tough facts" including "fear is a common response. . . . Unit members will be injured or killed. . . . Combat impacts every member both physically and mentally. . . . Soldiers are afraid to admit that they have mental health problems. . . . Soldiers frequently perceive failures in leadership." Similarly, soldier training addresses "tough facts about combat," such as "the combat environment is harsh and demanding," "fear in combat is not a sign of weakness," and "soldiers are afraid to admit that they have a mental health problem" (Castro et al., 2006, p. 42-3). Further, additional trainings immediately postdeployment and 3 to 6 months later focus on defining re-transition issues and recognizing problems needing additional intervention (Castro et al., 2006). It is anticipated that creating realistic expectations of the combat environment and individuals' reactions to it attenuates the negative impact, reduces stigma, and facilitates appropriate help seeking thereafter.

Preliminary research showed that Battlemind training delivered post-deployment is seen as a practical and stigma-free training (Adler, Bliese, McGurk, Hoge, & Castro, 2009; McGurk et al., 2007). Surveys distributed to soldiers indicate that, following the training, they feel able to look for and respond to cues of distress from their fellow soldiers (McGurk et al., 2007). A study evaluated post-deployment Battlemind provided in small groups and large groups (i.e., approximately 100 participants) compared with a stress education intervention provided in large groups upon return from a yearlong deployment to Iraq (Adler et al., 2009). Among those who experienced heavy combat in Iraq prior to training, results showed, soldiers reported lower posttraumatic stress symptoms if they received Battlemind training provided in either small and large groups. Also, regardless of combat exposure, Battlemind provided in small and large groups was associated with fewer depressive symptoms (Adler et al., 2009).

Other innovative programs have used preparatory education during specialized task role training. For example, body handling is an occupational role considered to be highly stressful. Research that has examined military body handlers has identified a number of areas associated with increased stress and postdeployment trauma symptoms, such as fear and discomfort with mutilation and the grotesque (e.g., McCarroll, Ursano, Fullerton, & Lundy, 1995). During U.S. Marine Corps Mortuary Affairs Division training, education on a variety of specialized topics related to body-handling tasks is embedded in training, such as detailed information about the dying process, the natural function of bodily death, and adaptive ways to deal with grief (C. Ikes, personal communication, February 23, 2007). Although no evaluative data are available at this time, this program aims to increase self-efficacy and decrease arousal related to future novel and/or unexpected stressors.

Stress-Related Cognitive Appraisals

Another important major focus for preparatory intervention is related to the types of thoughts about or cognitive appraisals associated with stressful deployment experiences. Many new training interventions designed to promote resilience use techniques that are consistent with cognitive behavioral theory and research (e.g., A. T. Beck, 1976; J. S. Beck, 1995; Lewisohn, Muñoz, Youngren, & Zeiss, 1992; Tomaka, Blascovich, Kelsey, & Leitten, 1993), which articulates a close relationship among cognitions, feelings, and behaviors. For example, research has demonstrated that cognitions predictably affect feelings and behaviors (e.g., Seligman et al., 1988). Such early work has been adapted, originally for successful prevention interventions with children (e.g., Gillham et al., 2007) and more recently for training of large military groups (e.g., Reivich, Seligman, & McBride, 2011). When individuals focus on the successful or positive aspects of an event, they are more likely to experience positive emotions and vice versa (Folkman & Moskowitz, 2000).

Individuals vary in the degree to which they tend to appraise events as positive or negative, which can influence their physical and emotional reactions to stressors. Individuals who tend to appraise stressful events positively experience more positive emotions during those events and are able to recover more quickly from negative events and emotional arousal (Tugade & Fredrickson, 2004). For example, a service member who tends to appraise difficult missions as successful is more likely to overcome negative feelings related to difficult circumstances surrounding the mission. Conversely, a service member who tends to make negative appraisals about events (e.g., viewing a mission as a failure) is more likely to generate anxiety, guilt, and anger—emotional reactions that are strongly associated with chronic PTSD (e.g., Riggs, Cahill, & Foa, 2006).

One type of appraisal, self-efficacy (referring to people's evaluation of their own capability to manage events), is of particular importance to the promotion of resilience. Self-efficacy greatly impacts how individuals respond during stressful situations, both behaviorally and emotionally (e.g., Bandura, 1989). To respond effectively, service members must realistically believe that they are capable of success. Perceiving that one is able to cope during stressful experiences is correlated with lower distress and less physiological arousal during those experiences (Bandura et al., 1982), such as lower secretion of adrenaline, than found among those who report lower self-efficacy (Bandura, Taylor, Williams, Mefford, & Barchas, 1985). In training settings, one study indicated that cadets who appraised stressful events as a "challenge" (vs. appraising situations as difficult or overwhelming) were less likely to experience dissociation in response to a highly stressful prisoner-of-war exercise (Eid & Morgan, 2006). Alternatively, when self-efficacy is threatened, distress and physiological arousal increase (Novaco, Cook, & Sarason, 1983, cited in Thompson & McCreary, 2006).

In addition to reducing personnel effectiveness and increasing physiological arousal, negative cognitive appraisals regarding deployment are associated with vulnerability to long-term problems (e.g., Lubow, 1998) including PTSD (Bliese & Castro, 2003; Ginzburg et al., 2003; King, King, Foy, Keane, & Fairbank, 1999). Alternatively, service members who positively appraise deployment events are more resilient to negative outcomes (King et al., 1999; Litz, King, King, Orsillo, & Friedman, 1997; Sharkansky et al., 2000; Southwick, Vythilingam, & Charney, 2005). In a longitudinal study, higher levels of self-efficacy in Israeli war veterans measured prior to combat were correlated with lower incidence of PTSD following combat (Ginzburg et al., 2003). Perceived self-efficacy is also a key factor in the personality construct of hardiness (Kobasa, 1979), which is correlated with resilience to PTSD (e.g., Bartone, 1999; King et al., 1999). A cross-sectional study of veterans of Operation Enduring Freedom/Operation Iraqi Freedom found that several factors of resilience, including personal competence, tolerance of negative affect, and acceptance of changes, were associated with lower rates of PTSD postdeployment (Pietrzak, Johnson, Goldstein, Malley, & Southwick, 2009). The strongest association, however, was with personal control (including feeling in control of one's life and having a strong sense of purpose). Overall, the strength of the association between traumatic stress symptoms and resilience was equivalent to that of traumatic stress symptoms and severity of combat exposure (Pietrzak et al., 2009).

Cognitive appraisals are among a variety of mechanisms targeted by the U.S. Army's Master Resilience Trainer course. This 10-day resilience-building program targeting noncommissioned officers (NCOs) incorporates many of the basic principles of cognitive therapy (e.g., J. S. Beck, 1995; Seligman et al., 1988) but adapts them so they are culturally meaningful for a military population (see Reivich et al., 2011). The first 5 days of the program entail large-group plenary sessions interspersed with small-group breakouts that apply the skills learned. The comprehensive program includes training such as (a) identifying thoughts and the consequences of those thoughts; (b) exploring explanatory styles, such as the tendency to overgeneralize facts based on a single experience, that can hinder (or help) resilience; (c) countering negative thoughts in real time; and (d) attending to positive events and actions and consciously acknowledging them via a gratitude or "three blessings" journal.

The subsequent 3 days focus on training the NCOs how to teach these skills to other soldiers. Two final days reinforce skills learned and introduce skills from sports psychology (e.g., Krane & William, 2006). During the last day, training identifies the relationship among thoughts, emotions, physical states, and performance to help participants build confidence, set goals, control attention, use imagery, and optimize energy. The Master Resilience Trainer course is currently being evaluated longitudinally.

Role Modeling

Although straightforward provision of educational information may be helpful in preparing military personnel, the use of role models to deliver that education and demonstrate adaptive responding may increase the impact of training experiences. A role model is a person who serves as an example and whose behavior is emulated by others. As defined by social learning theory, role modeling is viewed as a fairly straightforward imitation–change process based on vicarious learning (Bandura, 1977). Research has suggested that modeling affects the cognitive processes of acquiring, developing, and altering internalized rules about appropriate behaviors, thereby causing the observer to act like the role model in a similar, future situation (e.g., Gioia & Manz, 1985).

Role modeling, particularly by sources with operational credibility, such as peers and/or leaders who have undergone similar stressful events, is used consistently as a training technique in military settings. Military leaders, for instance, are encouraged to "lead by example" by facilitating open communication about planning and demonstrating to their subordinates how they correct and learn from mistakes. Role modeling techniques are thought to be particularly helpful in encouraging cognitive strategies that enhance coping resources in the face of otherwise discouraging and/or stressful adverse events (Affleck & Tennen, 1996; Himelein & McElrath, 1996).

An example of an expanding use of role modeling can be seen in marines' body-handling training (C. Ikes, personal communication, February 23, 2007). A vital component of the training is the role modeling that experienced body handlers provide to the new trainees. The "old hands" provide critical advice to help promote healthy ways of thinking, feeling, and behaving at several points during the training. Once marines enroll in the training program, experienced marines discuss any concerns or problems that might take place during their training duties and give advice about what trainees can do to avoid problems. Throughout, the experienced marines challenge traditional methods of coping and role model flexible, healthy coping, such as the ability to experience and openly discuss a range of emotional reactions.

Research has shown that visual depictions via computer or other technology are effective role modeling tools that can impact personnel appraisals of events. In one study, U.S. Marines were filmed during their basic training (Novaco et al., 1983). Marines in the film described the types of thoughts they had during basic training, how they felt, and how they coped with stressors, thus modeling adaptive coping attitudes and behaviors. By sharing their stories of stressful events and how they coped with them, the marines in the film helped to normalize common and minor stress reactions, thus helping recruits to understand and better cope with some of their own reactions. Increased use of technology has allowed military training programs to use a variety of modalities to provide visual (and auditory) role modeling depictions.

Role modeling is often used in conjunction with verbal preparatory education to influence positive thinking and behavior about upcoming events. For instance, during the body-handling training mentioned above, the importance of the mission and the value of the body-handling role within the mission are discussed by trainers who have experience in the field as part of the classroom training, thus influencing students to appraise their role positively (C. Ikes, personal communication, February 23, 2007). Role modeling and verbal preparation aim to enable personnel to understand the broader significance of the task by teaching them that they are providing an honorable service that may be of comfort to families, which may enable them to tolerate the emotional stress of the work. However, more research is needed to evaluate whether these applications will be effective in improving performance and reducing negative outcomes.

Exposure/Mission Rehearsal Exercises

Military personnel who are new to stressful tasks anticipate higher levels of stress during their jobs and seem to be more vulnerable to overwhelming stress reactions than those who have experience with the task (McCarroll, Ursano, & Fullerton, 1995; McCarroll, Ursano, Fullerton, & Lundy, 1995). For centuries, military organizations have used realistic rehearsal training to prepare individuals for highly stressful military operations. Such rehearsal programs traditionally identified overlearning of behavior (e.g., through use of repeated drills during which personnel practice the same tasks over and over) as the effective mechanism for training (Driskell & Salas, 1991).

In the past, rehearsal training rarely paid attention to the role of cognitions and emotions in learning (Thompson & McCreary, 2006). However, such factors play a vital role in stress adaptation. For instance, personnel vary in their abilities to learn new tasks and tolerate emotional arousal. Individuals who have difficulty acquiring skills may be less effective and may undermine operations (Thompson & McCreary, 2006). Moreover, personnel may experience failure rather than mastery during training, making them even more vulnerable to operational stress injuries. Today, military organizations increasingly supplement traditional strategies with interventions that target cognitions and emotions, thereby decreasing arousal while increasing sense of self-efficacy (e.g., Morgan, Southwick, Hazlett, & Steffian, 2007). For example, relaxation techniques can be used to develop mastery over arousal reactions during realistic exposure exercises (Goldfried & Davison, 1994), including virtual reality computer-simulated environments (Rothbaum et al., 1995). Research suggests that these methods reduce adverse reactions by helping individuals to exert control over physical and psychological arousal levels.

Although research has shown that therapeutic exposure to feared memories or situations following stressful events effectively ameliorates anxiety disorders (e.g., Foa & Jaycox, 1999), research has yet to fully examine its impact as a preventative intervention. However, theory suggests that exposure principles and stress management techniques used proactively should decrease stress arousal during future real-life situations (e.g., Feldner, Monson, & Friedman, 2007; Whealin et al., 2008; Wilson, 1967), and such techniques increasingly are implemented in the field.

The previously mentioned mortuary affairs training program, for example, employs exposure to stressful situations in a graduated fashion. Following the role modeling and educational components discussed earlier, participants are exposed to increasingly distressing stimuli and are trained in skills to manage their own physiological and emotional reactions at each level of exposure. Initially, participants conduct body-handling tasks with mannequins, acquiring the techniques and procedures of the position with minimal unpleasant stimuli. Then, participants conduct body-handling tasks with bodies at a civilian morgue, which exposes them to the sights, smells, sounds, and tactile stimuli of dead bodies. Once participants are able to tolerate the stress of the civilian morgue stimuli, they begin conducting their tasks with bodies of military personnel at military facilities, again habituating to and mastering stressors at increasingly intense levels of exposure. Other programs (i.e., Simulation-Based Training; Lai, Entin, Dierks, Raemer, & Simon, 2004) use computer-based simulated environments to develop these skills.

Exposure/rehearsal exercises aim to develop functional and practical skills that help personnel to survive in challenging environments and accomplish mission-oriented goals, as well as to develop cognitive and emotional skills that help them cope with highly stressful stimuli. Although empirical evidence is needed to evaluate these techniques, theory suggests that combining realistic training with methods for regulating stress should result in performance superior to "training as usual."

Exposure to Internal Stimuli

New military personnel often have little experience with the intense bodily states that can be triggered during highly stressful and/or dangerous events. These intense bodily reactions, if unexpected, may be more likely to trigger overwhelming reactions such as panic or disorientation. Overwhelming reactions compromise functioning and contribute to a perception of psychological chaos, placing individuals at risk for chronic problems (e.g., Ginzburg et al., 2003).

Internal emotional and physical stress reactions have been duplicated during in vivo training to promote resilience during a mission. For example, training has included exposure to stimuli found in high altitudes, polar regions, deserts, and underground or isolated environments. Such exposure purposefully provokes uncontrollable and aversive stress reactions such as panic, dissociation, or overwhelming emotions, which are likely to be activated during actual deployments. With exposure to such reactions, personnel become familiar with these bodily sensations, understand how long such reactions are expected to last, recognize in what types of situations they may occur, and experience how they diminish over time. Personnel also come to understand that these reactions are normal, rather than signs of weakness or pathology.

Several of the courses conducted by the U.S. military Special Forces include stress resistance training for extraordinarily demanding settings or situations. These programs are designed to prevent decrements in cognitive performance or decision making resulting from the pressure and stressors characteristic of dangerous or extreme environments (McNeil & Morgan, 2010). For example, the Terrorism Counteraction Department SERE training is a 3-week course designed to help military personnel avoid capture by the enemy or, if captured, to resist interrogation or exploitation and plan their escape. The training elicits many of the potentially disorienting internal physiological stress responses that take place during real-life capture and torture. Personnel are "captured," hooded, and roped together for a resistance-training laboratory phase that simulates the environment of a prisoner-of-war compound. Participants are exposed to harsh bodily stressors, such as sleep deprivation and food deprivation. The stressors are severe enough that, during intensive training, symptoms of dissociation are reported by 96% of participants (Morgan et al., 2001).

The intended goal of the training is to overwhelm physical and psychological coping resources. Training inundates or "floods" personnel with stressors all at once to purposely overwhelm coping resources (Moulds & Nixon, 2006) in a controlled setting. The aim of such training is to teach personnel principles needed to manage both the external environment and their own intense internal emotional reactions, producing increased self-efficacy, efficiency, and resilience. Many experienced trainers believe that when personnel surpass their physical stress threshold while performing their work role in a controlled environment, they learn principles in a profound way (G. Hoyt, personal communication, January 6, 2007). Whereas flooding and other forms of exposure have been shown to be effective treatments for trauma reactions such as PTSD, there are no data yet regarding the effectiveness of such training as a preparation for stressful experiences.

Military programs have also incorporated mental health clinicians within the training to help personnel learn to master internal stimuli. During high-intensity combat training courses, some personnel experience internal reactions such as dissociative reactions or panic attacks, which interfere with training success. Additionally, some personnel may suffer severe psychological reactions, resulting in suicide attempts, psychotic breaks, or other manifestations of mental illness. Historically, such individuals were removed from the training exercises and, at times, dismissed from service. These risks are now being addressed by including, as part of the training team, clinicians who provide intense on-site psychological support services on an as-needed basis. Although evaluation data are not available for such programs, leaders aim to promote mastery of internal reactions so that personnel can perform effectively and remain qualified for duty status.

SUMMARY AND FUTURE DIRECTIONS

Specific physiological, emotional, and cognitive factors are emerging that help identify personnel who are better able to rebound from severe stress and those who are likely to experience problems (e.g., Whealin et al., 2008). Evolving research, as well as a good deal of accumulated knowledge, suggests that personnel can learn some of the specific behaviors and attitudes associated with resilience to postdeployment problems (e.g., Bandura et al., 1982; Seligman et al., 1988). To date, little empirical research is available that clearly identifies mechanisms that causally influence successful adaption to high stress (Layne et al., 2007). However, some compelling research suggests a variety of possible candidates to better regulate physical, mental, and emotional stress consequences. Emerging trainings have increasingly focused on these areas. Further, recent military training models, such as the U.S. Army's Battlemind training targeting all deploying soldiers and leaders and the Master Resilience Training targeting all NCOs, have been implemented on a national level. New models have also included means for ongoing assessments of training effectiveness and outcomes (e.g., the U.S. Army's Soldier Fitness Tracker and the Global Assessment Tool) designed to assess all U.S. Army soldiers on an ongoing basis (Fravell, Nasser, & Cornum, 2011).

This chapter drew from data examining these purported mechanisms of resilience, as well as from military expertise, theory, and existing outcome data, to identify six training techniques: stress management skills training, preparatory education, cognitive appraisals, role modeling, realistic exposure to stressful external stimuli, and exposure to stress-related internal stimuli. Empirical research will continue to clarify specific mechanisms and scientifically validate training techniques purported to causally influence outcome. Additionally, research will continue to establish the best ways of implementing prevention interventions among specific military populations and specific military environments.

REFERENCES

Adler, A. B., Bliese, P. D., McGurk, D., Hoge, C. W., & Castro, C. A. (2009). Battlemind debriefing and Battlemind training as early interventions with soldiers returning from Iraq: Randomization by platoon. *Journal of Consulting and Clinical Psychology, 77,* 928–940. doi:10.1037/a0016877

Affleck, G., & Tennen, H. (1996). Construing benefits from adversity: Adaptational significance and dispositional underpinnings. *Journal of Personality, 64,* 899–922. doi:10.1111/j.1467-6494.1996.tb00948.x

Ahrenfeldt, R. H. (1958). *Psychiatry in the British Army in the Second World War.* Oxford, England: Columbia University Press.

Alexander, J. K., Hillier, A., Smith, R. M., Tivarus, M. E., & Beversdorf, D. Q. (2007). Beta-adrenergic modulation of cognitive flexibility during stress. *Journal of Cognitive Neuroscience, 19,* 468–478. doi:10.1162/jocn.2007.19.3.468

Bandura, A. (1977). *Social learning theory.* Englewood Cliffs, NJ: Prentice Hall.

Bandura, A. (1989). Human agency in social cognitive theory. *American Psychologist, 44*, 1175–1184. doi:10.1037/0003-066X.44.9.1175

Bandura, A., Reese, L., & Adams, N. E. (1982). Microanalysis of action and fear arousal as a function of differential levels of perceived self-efficacy. *Journal of Personality and Social Psychology, 43*, 5–21. doi:10.1037/0022-3514.43.1.5

Bandura, A., Taylor, C. B., Williams, S. L., Mefford, I. M., & Barchas, J. D. (1985). Catecholamine secretion as a function of perceived coping self-efficacy. *Journal of Consulting and Clinical Psychology, 53*, 406–414. doi:10.1037/0022-006X.53.3.406

Bartone, P. (1999). Hardiness protects against war-related stress in Army Reserve Forces. *Consulting Psychology Journal: Practice and Research, 51*, 72–82. doi:10.1037/1061-4087.51.2.72

Beck, A. T. (1976). *Cognitive therapy and the emotional disorders.* New York, NY: International Universities Press.

Beck, J. S. (1995). *Cognitive therapy: Basics and beyond.* New York, NY: Guilford Press.

Bliese, P. D., & Castro, C. A. (2003). The soldier adaptation model (SAM): Applications to peacekeeping research. In T. W. Britt & A. B. Adler (Eds.), *The psychology of the peacekeeper: Lessons from the field* (pp. 185–203). Westport, CT: Praeger.

Blount, R. L., Davis, N., Powers, S. W., & Roberts, M. C. (1991). The influence of environmental factors and coping style on children's coping and distress. *Clinical Psychology Review, 11*, 93–116. doi:10.1016/0272-7358(91)90139-L

Brewin, C. R., Andrews, B., & Rose, S. (2000). Fear, helplessness, and horror in post-traumatic stress disorder: Investigating DSM–IV criterion A2 in victims of violent crime. *Journal of Traumatic Stress, 13*, 499–509. doi:10.1023/A:1007741526169

Castro, C. A., Hoge, C. W., & Cox, A. L. (2006). *Battlemind training: Building soldier resiliency.* Retrieved from http://www.dtic.mil/dtic/tr/fulltext/u2/a472734.pdf

Driskell, J. E., & Johnston, J. H. (1998). Stress exposure training. In J. A. Cannon-Bowers & E. Salas (Eds.), *Making decisions under stress: Implications for individual and team decision making* (pp. 191–217). Washington, DC: American Psychological Association. doi:10.1037/10278-007

Driskell, J. E., & Salas, E. (1991). Overcoming the effects of stress of military performance: Human factors, training, and selection strategies. In R. Gal & A. D. Mangelsdorff (Eds.), *Handbook of military psychology* (pp. 183–193). New York, NY: Wiley.

Eid, J., & Morgan, C. A. (2006). Dissociation, hardiness, and performance in military cadets participating in survival training. *Military Medicine, 171*, 436–442.

Feldner, M. T., Monson, C. M., & Friedman, M. J. (2007). A critical analysis of approaches to targeted PTSD prevention: Current status and theoretically derived future directions. *Behavior Modification, 31*, 80–116. doi:10.1177/0145445506295057

Foa, E. B., & Jaycox, L. H. (1999). Cognitive-behavioral theory and treatment of post-traumatic stress disorder. In D. Spiegel (Ed.), *Efficacy and cost-effectiveness of psychotherapy* (pp. 23–61). Washington, DC: American Psychiatric Press.

Folkman, S., & Moskowitz, J. T. (2000). Positive affect and the other side of coping. *American Psychologist, 55,* 647–654. doi:10.1037/0003-066X.55.6.647

Fravell, M., Nasser, K., & Cornum, R. (2011). The Soldier Fitness Tracker: Global delivery of Comprehensive Soldier Fitness. *American Psychologist, 66,* 73–76. doi:10.1037/a0021632

Galea, S., Ahern, J., Resnick, H., Kilpatrick, D., Bucuvalas, M., Gold, J., & Vlahov, D. (2002). Psychological sequelae of the September 11 terrorist attacks in New York City. *New England Journal of Medicine, 346,* 982–987. doi:10.1056/NEJMsa013404

Gardenswartz, C. A., & Craske, M. G. (2001). Prevention of panic disorder. *Behavior Therapy, 32,* 725–737. doi:10.1016/S0005-7894(01)80017-4

Gillham, J. E., Reivich, K. J., Freres, D. R., Chaplin, T. M., Shatté, A. J., Samuels, B., . . . Seligman, M. E. P. (2007). School-based prevention of depressive symptoms: A randomized controlled study of the effectiveness and specificity of the Penn Resiliency Program. *Journal of Consulting and Clinical Psychology, 75,* 9–19. doi:10.1037/0022-006X.75.1.9

Ginzburg, K., Solomon, Z., Dekel, R., & Neria, Y. (2003). Battlefield functioning and chronic PTSD: Associations with perceived self-efficacy and causal attribution. *Personality and Individual Differences, 34,* 463–476. doi:10.1016/S0191-8869(02)00066-1

Gioia, D. A., & Manz, C. C. (1985). Linking cognition and behavior: A script processing interpretation of vicarious learning. *Academy of Management Review, 10,* 527–539.

Goldfried, M. R., & Davison, G. C. (1994). *Clinical behavior therapy.* New York, NY: Wiley.

Grossman, P., Niemann, L., Schmidt, S., & Walach, H. (2004). Mindfulness-based stress reduction and health benefits: A meta-analysis. *Journal of Psychosomatic Research, 57,* 35–43. doi:10.1016/S0022-3999(03)00573-7

Hancock, P. A., Ganey, H. C. N., & Szalma, J. L. (2002, December). *Performance under stress: A re-evaluation of a foundational law of psychology.* Paper presented at the Army Science Conference, Orlando, FL.

Hansen, N. B., Lambert, M. J., & Forman, E. M. (2002). The psychotherapy dose–response effect and its implications for treatment delivery services. *Clinical Psychology: Science and Practice, 9,* 329–343. doi:10.1093/clipsy.9.3.329

Himelein, M. J., & McElrath, J. V. (1996). Resilient child sexual abuse survivors: Cognitive coping and illusion. *Child Abuse & Neglect, 20,* 747–758. doi:10.1016/0145-2134(96)00062-2

Hoge, C. W., Castro, C. A., Messer, S. C., McGurk, D., Cotting, D. I., & Koffman, R. L. (2004). Combat duty in Iraq and Afghanistan, mental health problems, and barriers to care. *New England Journal of Medicine, 351,* 13–22. doi:10.1056/NEJMoa040603

Hotopf, M., David, A. S., Hull, L., Palmer, I. I., Unwin, D., & Wellsley, S. (2003). The health effects of peace-keeping in the UK armed forces: Bosnia 1992–1996. *Psychological Medicine, 33*, 155–162. doi:10.1017/S0033291702006840

Inzana, C. M., Driskell, J. E., Salas, E., & Johnston, J. H. (1996). Effects of preparatory information on enhancing performance under stress. *Journal of Applied Psychology, 81*, 429–435. doi:10.1037/0021-9010.81.4.429

Jha, A. P., Stanley, E. A., Kiyonaga, A., Wong, L., & Gelfand, L. (2010). Examining the protective effects of mindfulness training on working memory capacity and affective experience. *Emotion, 10*, 54–64. doi:10.1037/a0018438

Jones, J. C., & Barlow, D. H. (1990). The etiology of PTSD. *Clinical Psychology Review, 10*, 299–328. doi:10.1016/0272-7358(90)90064-H

King, D. W., King, L. A., Foy, D. W., Keane, T. M., & Fairbank, J. A. (1999). Posttraumatic stress disorder in a national sample of female and male Vietnam veterans: Risk factors, war-zone stressors, and resilience–recovery variables. *Journal of Abnormal Psychology, 108*, 164–170. doi:10.1037/0021-843X.108.1.164

Kobasa, S. C. (1979). Stressful life events, personality, and health: An inquiry into hardiness. *Journal of Personality and Social Psychology, 37*, 1–11. doi:10.1037/0022-3514.37.1.1

Krane, V., & William, J. M. (2006). Psychological characteristics of peak performance. In J. M. Williams (Ed.), *Applied sport psychology: Personal growth to peak performance* (5th ed., pp. 207–227). New York, NY: McGraw-Hill.

Lai, F., Entin, E., Dierks, M., Raemer, D., & Simon, R. (2004). Designing simulation-based training scenarios for emergency medical first responders. *Proceedings of the Human Factors and Ergonomics Society Annual Meeting, 48*, 1670–1674. doi:10.1177/154193120404801509

Layne, C. M., Warren, J. S., Watson, P. J., & Shalev, A. (2007). Risk, vulnerability, resistance, and resilience: Toward an integrative model of posttraumatic adaptation. In M. J. Friedman, T. M. Kean, & P. A. Resick (Eds.), *Handbook of PTSD: Science and practice* (pp. 497–520). New York, NY: Guilford Press.

Lewisohn, P. M., Muñoz, R. F., Youngren, M. A., & Zeiss, A. M. (1992). *Control your depression: Revised and updated.* New York, NY: Simon & Schuster.

Lieberman, H. R., Bathalon, G. P., Falco, C. M., Morgan, C. A., III, Niro, P. J., & Tharion, W. J. (2005). The fog of war: Decrements in cognitive performance and mood associated with combat-like stress. *Aviation, Space, and Environmental Medicine, 76*(7), C7–C14.

Litz, B. T., King, L. A., King, D. W., Orsillo, S. M., & Friedman, M. J. (1997). Warriors as peacekeepers: Features of the Somalia experience and PTSD. *Journal of Consulting and Clinical Psychology, 65*, 1001–1010. doi:10.1037/0022-006X.65.6.1001

Lubow, R. E. (1998). Latent inhibition and behavior pathology: Prophylactic and other possible effects of stimulus preexposure. In W. T. O'Donohue (Ed.), *Learning and behavior therapy* (pp. 107–121). Needham Heights, MA: Allyn & Bacon.

Ma, S. H., & Teasdale, J. D. (2004). Mindfulness-based cognitive therapy for depression: Replication and exploration of differential relapse prevention effects. *Journal of Consulting and Clinical Psychology, 72,* 31–40. doi:10.1037/0022-006X.72.1.31

Mallisham, C. P. T. (2007, January). One shot, one kill. *The Medicine Warrior Tribune, 1*(2), 5–13.

Marks, I. M. (1987). *Fears, phobias, and rituals: Panic, anxiety, and their disorders.* Oxford, England: Oxford University Press.

McCarroll, J. E., Ursano, R. J., & Fullerton, C. S. (1995). Symptoms of PTSD following recovery of war dead: 13–15-month follow-up. *American Journal of Psychiatry, 152,* 939–941.

McCarroll, J. E., Ursano, R. J., Fullerton, C. S., & Lundy, A. (1995). Anticipatory stress of handling human remains from the Persian Gulf War: Predictors of intrusion and avoidance. *Journal of Nervous and Mental Disease, 183,* 698–703. doi:10.1097/00005053-199511000-00005

McGurk, D., Castro, C. A., Thomas, J. L., & Hoge, C. W. (2007, August). *Predeployment Battlemind training: Mentally preparing soldiers for combat.* Paper presented at the meeting of the American Psychological Association, San Francisco, CA.

McNeil, J. A., & Morgan, C. A., III. (2010). Cognition and decision making in extreme environments. In C. H. Kennedy & J. L. Moore (Eds.), *Military neuropsychology* (pp. 361–382). New York, NY: Springer.

Meichenbaum, D. H. (2007). Stress inoculation training: A preventative and treatment approach. In P. M. Lehrer, R. L. Woolfolk, & W. E. Sime (Eds.), *Principles and practice of stress management* (3rd ed., pp. 497–516). New York, NY: Guilford Press.

Meichenbaum, D. H., & Deffenbacher, J. L. (1988). Stress inoculation training. *Counseling Psychologist, 16,* 69–90. doi:10.1177/0011000088161005

Morgan, C. A., III, Hazlett, G., Wang, S., Richardson, E. G., Schnurr, P., & Southwick, S. (2001). Symptoms of dissociation in humans experiencing acute, uncontrollable stress: A prospective investigation. *American Journal of Psychiatry, 158,* 1239–1247. doi:10.1176/appi.ajp.158.8.1239

Morgan, C. A., III, Southwick, S., Hazlett, G., Rasmusson, A., Hoyt, G., Zimolo, Z., & Charney, D. (2004). Relationships among plasma dehydroepiandrosterone sulfate and cortisol levels, symptoms of dissociation, and objective performance in humans exposed to acute stress. *Archives of General Psychiatry, 61,* 819–825. doi:10.1001/archpsyc.61.8.819

Morgan, C. A., III, Southwick, S. M., Hazlett, G., & Steffian, G. (2007). Symptoms of dissociation in healthy military populations: Why and how do war fighters differ in responses to intense stress? In E. Vermetten, M. Dorahy, & D. Spiegel (Eds.), *Traumatic dissociation: Neurobiology and treatment* (pp. 157–179). Washington, DC: American Psychiatric Publishing.

Moulds, M. L., & Nixon, R. D. V. (2006). In vivo flooding for anxiety disorders: Proposing its utility in the treatment posttraumatic stress disorder. *Journal of Anxiety Disorders, 20,* 498–509. doi:10.1016/j.janxdis.2005.05.005

Neiss, R. (1988). Reconceptualizing arousal: Psychobiological states in motor performance. *Psychological Bulletin, 103,* 345–366. doi:10.1037/0033-2909.103.3.345

Newcomer, J. W., Selke, G., Melson, A. K., Hershey, T., Craft, S., Richards, K., & Alderson, A. L. (1999). Decreased memory performance in healthy humans induced by stress-level cortisol treatment. *Archives of General Psychiatry, 56,* 527–533. doi:10.1001/archpsyc.56.6.527

Novaco, R. W., Cook, T. M., & Sarason, I. G. (1983). Military recruit training: An area for coping skills training. In D. Meichenbaum & M. E. Jaremko (Eds.), *Stress reduction and prevention* (pp. 377–418). New York, NY: Plenum Press.

Ozer, E. J., Best, S. R., Lipsey, T. L., & Weiss, D. S. (2003). Predictors of posttraumatic stress disorder and symptoms in adults: A meta-analysis. *Psychological Bulletin, 129,* 52–73. doi:10.1037/0033-2909.129.1.52

Petraeus, D. H. (2006). *Transforming military training: Using the lessons of the past to build the Army of the future.* Washington, DC: Brookings Institution.

Pietrzak, R. H., Johnson, D. C., Goldstein, M. B., Malley, J. C., & Southwick, S. M. (2009). Psychological resilience and postdeployment social support protect against traumatic stress and depressive symptoms in soldiers returning from Operations Enduring Freedom and Iraqi Freedom. *Depression and Anxiety, 26,* 745–751. doi:10.1002/da.20558

Pitman, R. K. (1989). Post-traumatic stress disorder, hormones, and memory. *Biological Psychiatry, 26,* 221–223. doi:10.1016/0006-3223(89)90033-4

Reivich, K. J., Seligman, M. E. P., & McBride, S. (2011). Master resilience training in the U.S. Army. *American Psychologist, 66,* 25–34. doi:10.1037/a0021897

Riggs, D. S., Cahill, S. P., & Foa, E. B. (2006). Prolonged exposure treatment of posttraumatic stress disorder. In V. F. Follette & J. I. Ruzek (Eds.), *Cognitive-behavioral therapies for trauma* (2nd ed., pp. 65–95). New York, NY: Guilford Press.

Rothbaum, B. O., Hodges, L. F., Kooper, R., Opdyke, D., Williford, J. S., & North, M. (1995). Effectiveness of computer-generated (virtual reality) graded exposure in the treatment of acrophobia. *American Journal of Psychiatry, 152,* 626–628.

Saunders, T., Driskell, J. E., Johnston, J. H., & Salas, E. (1996). The effect of stress inoculation training on anxiety and performance. *Journal of Occupational Health Psychology, 1,* 170–186. doi:10.1037/1076-8998.1.2.170

Seligman, M. E. P., Castellon, C., Cacciola, J., Schulman, P., Luborsky, L., Ollove, M., & Downing, R. (1988). Explanatory style change during cognitive therapy for unipolar depression. *Journal of Abnormal Psychology, 97,* 13–18. doi:10.1037/0021-843X.97.1.13

Sharkansky, E. J., King, D. W., King, L. A., Wolfe, J., Erickson, D. J., & Stokes, L. R. (2000). Coping with Gulf War combat stress: Mediating and moderating effects. *Journal of Abnormal Psychology, 109,* 188–197. doi:10.1037/0021-843X. 109.2.188

Sharpley, J. G., Fear, N. T., Greenberg, N., Jones, M., & Wessely, S. (2008). Predeployment stress briefing: Does it have an effect? *Occupational Medicine, 58,* 30–34. doi:10.1093/occmed/kqm118

Southwick, S. M., Vythilingam, M., & Charney, D. S. (2005). The psychobiology of depression and resilience to stress: Implications for prevention and treatment. *Annual Review of Clinical Psychology, 1,* 255–291. doi:10.1146/annurev. clinpsy.1.102803.143948

Thompson, M. M., & McCreary, D. R. (2006). Enhancing mental readiness in military personnel. In A. Adler, C. A. Castro, & T. W. Britt (Eds.), *Military life: The psychology of serving in peace and combat: Vol. 2. Operational stress* (pp. 54–79). New York, NY: Praeger.

Tomaka, J., Blascovich, J., Kelsey, R. M., & Leitten, C. L. (1993). Subjective, physiological, and behavioral effects of threat and challenge appraisal. *Journal of Personality and Social Psychology, 65,* 248–260. doi:10.1037/0022-3514.65.2.248

Tugade, M. M., & Fredrickson, B. L. (2004). Resilient individuals use positive emotions to bounce back from negative emotional experiences. *Journal of Personality and Social Psychology, 86,* 320–333. doi:10.1037/0022-3514.86.2.320

Whealin, J. M., Ruzek, J., & Southwick, S. (2008). Cognitive behavioral theory and preparation for professionals at risk for trauma exposure. *Trauma, Violence, & Abuse, 9,* 100–113. doi:10.1177/1524838008315869

Wilson, G. D. (1967). Efficacy of "flooding" procedures in desensitization of fear: A theoretical note. *Behaviour Research and Therapy, 5,* 138–139. doi:10.1016/ 0005-7967(67)90010-1

Yerkes, R. M., & Dodson, J. D. (1908). The relation of strength of stimulus to rapidity of habit-formation. *Journal of Comparative Neurology and Psychology, 18,* 459–482. doi:10.1002/cne.920180503

7

FOSTERING RESILIENCE ACROSS THE DEPLOYMENT CYCLE

NEIL GREENBERG

The previous chapter in this volume focused on building resilience before one encounters extraordinary demands of deployment, and earlier chapters address the importance of cohesion, morale, and leadership in fostering resilience. This chapter reviews additional opportunities to build resilience across the deployment cycle while acknowledging a number of important gaps in the available empirical evidence. Focusing attention on building resilience around the deployment cycle has intuitive advantages: First, it could provide "just in time" training prior to deployment, where it will be needed most. If the effects of resilience training are in part transient (Seligman & Fowler, 2011), offering such training close to when it will be needed may be most effective. Predeployment training and exercises also provide an opportunity to immediately apply and reinforce resilience through practice of what is learned in resilience training (Reivich, Seligman, & McBride, 2011). Finally,

The composition of this chapter would not have been possible without the expert advice and guidance from Dr. Mark Zamorski, whose input is highly appreciated.

http://dx.doi.org/10.1037/14190-007
Building Psychological Resilience in Military Personnel: Theory and Practice, R. R. Sinclair and T. W. Britt (Editors)

resource-intensive interventions could be provided only to those who are actually likely to deploy in the near future, as opposed to the larger military population.

THE PREDEPLOYMENT PERIOD

The predeployment period provides a number of potential opportunities to foster resilience. This section concentrates on two possible mechanisms: predeployment mental health screening and predeployment mental health briefings.

Predeployment Psychological Screening

Although predeployment psychological screening does not promote resilience per se, it aims to achieve the same end (i.e., limiting the psychological impact of deployment). Because there are measurable psychological factors associated with resilience, "screening in" personnel who report more of those factors might lead to a more resilient deployed force. Specific military groups, such as snipers (Girard & Scholtz, 2005) and Special Forces (Burwell, 1999), already use this approach, and advocates of screening might argue that if screening works for these groups, it should work for the general military population. However, this view may be too simplistic.

Predeployment psychological screening could theoretically serve two distinct purposes. First, it could ensure adequate performance while deployed by weeding out those who will be unable to respond to the demands of deployment. Second, it could ensure long-term mental health after return by preventing nonresilient individuals from deploying.

While both purposes are valuable aims, they often get conflated. Some authors have argued that assuring performance while deployed will optimize favorable long-term mental health (Grossman & Christensen, 2004). Although an important minority of service members will succumb to mental health problems as a result of their deployment (Institute of Medicine, 2000), most of these individuals apparently performed adequately while deployed, as evidenced by the low rates of repatriation (Ritchie, 2007; Rundell, 2006). Good operational performance is thus not sufficient to ensure good long-term mental health.

World War II–era data are often cited as evidence that screening for psychological vulnerability is ineffective (E. Jones, Hyams, & Wessely, 2003). However, the applicability of this finding to current times is limited because of scientific advances in many relevant areas over the past 60 years. Moreover, that (and other) research has focused exclusively on short-term performance as an outcome, and psychological screening to predict military performance is likely always to be weak relative to other screening and selection mechanisms such as routine supervision and evaluation during realistic training.

The potential value of screening to predict long-term mental health is harder to dismiss out of hand. In research settings (where confidentiality and freedom from consequences of disclosure are ensured), predeployment impaired well-being is a modest predictor of postdeployment well-being (Leardmann, Smith, Smith, Wells, & Ryan, 2009; Rona et al., 2006; Sandweiss et al., 2011). Practical experience with predeployment screening for the prevention of deployment-related mental health problems has, however, been largely disappointing. For example, evaluation of an intensive predeployment screening process examined more than 5,000 Canadian personnel preparing for a peacekeeping deployment to Kabul, Afghanistan (Zamorski, Galvin, & Humeniuk, 2007). Less than 1% of those screened were deferred from deployment because very few reported problems; estimated predeployment prevalence rates of mental health problems were unrealistically low (Zamorski, Uppal, Boddam, & Gendron, 2006). Data from a recent U.K. study (Hacker Hughes et al., 2005) also showed that very few members reported problems during predeployment screening, and a recent U.S. study showed that there was substantial underreporting of recent mental health care use on predeployment screening forms (Nevin, 2009).

In a U.S. screening trial, a higher proportion (21%) reported problems during predeployment screening (Wright et al., 2005). However, after a more detailed clinical evaluation, very few of those with positive screening tests were judged to have a problem serious enough to require deferral of deployment. This observation invites three possible explanations. The screening instruments might have been overly sensitive, but this seems unlikely because the tests used were reasonably specific. It is also possible that the screening tests accurately identified those with mental health problems, but these problems were not severe enough to have precluded deployment. Finally, it is possible that the operational imperative made it difficult to make the right decision with respect to deployment. This hypothesis is supported by the finding that many of those who initially screened positive were deemed to have "misunderstood" the question after further questioning.

Although the available data do not indicate which of these explanations is correct, it is clear that in some contexts service members are willing to disclose psychological symptoms during predeployment screening. This refutes the criticism that screening cannot work simply because no one will disclose (Rona, Hyams, & Wessely, 2005). It does not, however, address the question as to whether the "right" people will disclose: Some of those who disclose might be healthy people who are simply unmotivated, and some of those who fail to disclose might be ill people who are motivated to deploy.

Three factors conspire to make screening for psychological vulnerabilities ineffective in real-world circumstances:

- The association between self-reported premorbid psychological factors and long-term mental health is modest (Brewin, 2005; Brewin, Andrews, & Valentine, 2000; Rona et al., 2006; Vogt, Proctor, King, King, & Vasterling, 2008).
- Routinely used screening tests are transparent and hence subject to reporting bias. These tests may thus better reflect motivation to deploy than fitness to deploy and might also be influenced by stigma-related concerns.
- Finally, the prevalence of adverse mental health outcomes is, in most cases, modest. Researchers are trying to identify that small fraction of people in the general military population who might become ill as a direct result of their deployment and go on to have long-term disability; this prevalence rate will be well below the 15% to 20% of combat troops who disclose symptoms shortly after their return (Hoge et al., 2004). Epidemiological longitudinal data from the United States showed that only 4% of service members deployed to Afghanistan or Iraq had new-onset post-traumatic stress disorder (PTSD; Smith et al., 2008); many of these individuals will go on to recover more or less fully.

In a time of high operational tempo, commanders will be understandably intolerant of false positives and will reasonably demand that burdensome screening prevent a significant fraction of postdeployment mental health problems. The inescapable trade-off between sensitivity and specificity makes these competing goals: Highly sensitive screening tests correctly identify a large fraction of nonresilient individuals, but they result in large numbers of false positives (i.e., resilient individuals being identified as nonresilient). Highly specific tests correctly identify almost all resilient individuals, but they result in large numbers of false negatives (i.e., nonresilient individuals being misidentified as resilient). False positives are particularly problematic when the prevalence of the outcome (nonresilience) is low. A screening process with 80% sensitivity (a sensitive test is able to detect all real cases) and 80% specificity (a completely specific test does not have to provide any false positives) implies an odds ratio of 16, which is huge in epidemiological terms. Such a process would prevent 80% of cases. However, at an outcome prevalence rate of 5% it would also preclude the deployment of 23% of the cohort, and five out of six of those excluded would be false positives. Faking would worsen this performance.

These concerns notwithstanding, one recent study comparing an intensive predeployment screening process in one Army division with a conventional approach in a similar division preparing for a similar deployment showed that though only 0.7% were precluded from deployment and only 0.9% deployed with "additional requirements," those screened more intensively had dramatically more favorable mental health outcomes (Warner, Appenzeller, Parker, Warner, & Hoge, 2011). For example, they received care for psychiatric disorders while deployed at far lower rates (2.9% vs. 13.2%). The mismatch between the low deferral rate and the substantial apparent impacts on mental health could reflect ancillary benefits of the screening (and subsequent targeted care) or significant underlying differences between the two divisions. Although encouraging enough to warrant further investigation, this evidence is not strong enough to drive systematic changes in screening policy.

Predeployment Briefings

Deploying troops are often briefed about psychological matters, with the intention of helping to maintain their psychological health. These briefings presumably include education about the nature of traumatic stress, mechanisms for coping with separation from family and dealing with culture shock, and education about how to seek care if needed and related topics. The evaluation of the effectiveness of these briefings is very limited: In the United Kingdom, an opportunistic, nonrandomized study found no evidence that predeployment mental health briefings had any effect on long-term subsequent mental health status (Sharpley, Fear, Greenberg, Jones, & Wessely, 2008). However, studies that have examined the impact of such briefings while troops are deployed show a somewhat different picture. A study of U.S. soldiers who received a specific predeployment briefing package called Battlemind felt significantly more prepared for dealing with combat stress and were also much less likely to report mental health symptoms while deployed (U.S. Office of the Surgeon General, 2008). A U.K. study found similarly that troops who had received predeployment briefing were less likely to report mental health problems while deployed than troops who had not. However, in both studies, assignment to the predeployment briefing condition was not random, and the apparent benefit may be due to factors other than the training itself.

DURING DEPLOYMENT

As alluded to in Chapter 4 of this volume, the tools of morale, cohesion, good leadership, and effective training work their magic during deployment to mitigate distress and enhance performance. Given that most service members appear to manage their distress well enough to perform adequately while deployed, these tools appear to be largely working as they should and are all that are needed for the majority of service members. This crucial aspect of operational stress management should not be medicalized: Military leaders need to be squarely in charge of helping those under their command perform under the extreme but foreseeable demands of deployment; this requires that leaders find ways of preventing, recognizing, and managing distress in their subordinates (Britt, Davison, Bliese, & Castro, 2004). But there will always be an important minority for whom these important tools will not be enough.

Mental Health Problems During Deployment

Symptoms of mental health problems are common in personnel deployed on combat operations. The richest data come from the U.S. Army Mental Health Advisory Team (MHAT) reports and the U.K. Operational Mental Health Needs Evaluation (OMHNE). Over the past 5 years, between 13% and 19% of U.S. personnel surveyed during deployment have reported symptoms of anxiety, depression, or acute traumatic stress (U.S. Office of the Surgeon General, 2008); similar figures have been found in deployed populations of U.K. troops (Mulligan et al., 2010).

Not surprisingly, mental health problems influence performance while deployed. Substantial fractions of frontline combat troops reported that stress or emotional problems limited their ability to do their job (15%), made them work less carefully (23%), or made their supervisor concerned (13%; U.S. Office of the Surgeon General, 2008). Those who reported mental health symptoms were also substantially more likely to report having committed unethical behavior while deployed (U.S. Office of the Surgeon General, 2006).

Barriers to Mental Health Care on Deployed Operations

Service members commonly report barriers to accessing mental health care while deployed, due to attitudinal, geographic, and logistical factors. These include stigma, fear of career impact, unsupportive leadership, lack of trust in mental health providers, geographical isolation, difficulty getting time off work, and difficulty getting appointments. As a result, only 40% of respondents who reported problems had actually sought care (U.S. Office of the Surgeon General, 2006).

Building Resilience During Deployment by Facilitating Mental Health Care and Support

One strategy to build resilience (or more properly to restore it) involves overcoming the barriers to mental health care while deployed. To this end, the United States (Ritchie, 2007; U.S. Office of the Surgeon General, 2008), Canada, and the United Kingdom (McAllister, Blair, & Philpott, 2004) all deploy mental health clinicians on major operations. The ratio of providers to deployed personnel varies: Estimates include 1:2,500–4,000 in the United Kingdom (Fertout et al., 2011), 1:700 in the United States (U.S. Office of the Surgeon General, 2008), and 1:500–600 in Canada (Lt. Col. R. Jetly, personal communication, November 26, 2008). The United States has modestly increased the number of deployed mental health providers over the past few years (U.S. Office of the Surgeon General, 2003, 2006), and this has been associated with significant increase (29% vs. 40%) in the fraction of those with symptoms who had sought care in theater (U.S. Office of the Surgeon General, 2003, 2006). This favorable trend cannot be reliably attributed to an increase in the number of providers, because other system-level changes (e.g., greater emphasis on mental health training) occurred at the same time.

But it would be wrong to assume that the responsibility for the mental health of personnel lies with mental health professionals. Rather, it is better to conceptualize an individual's resilience to withstand the operational environment as coming from a number of sources, including the unit in which he or she serves. Within the U.K. Armed Forces, for instance, the psychological welfare of troops is, doctrinally, a chain of command responsibility (Greenberg, Jones, Jones, Fear, & Wessely, 2011). The role of clinicians is to support the unit imperative to maintain personnel's health.

Peers are another potential source of nonprofessional support. Service members are much more likely to turn to a peer for help than to a mental health provider or chaplain, both on deployment (U.S. Office of the Surgeon General, 2003) and afterward (Greenberg et al., 2003). The U.K. Royal Marines have attempted to leverage this through their Trauma Risk Management (TRiM) program, which trains nonmedical personnel in psychological risk assessment and referral (Greenberg, Cawkill, & Sharpley, 2005). Although one aim of the TRiM program is to reduce stigma, the randomized evaluation study did not confirm widespread stigma change 12 to 18 months after TRiM training (Gould, Greenberg, & Hetherton, 2007); nor did it influence the primary outcome of psychological well-being. It was, however, well accepted and appeared to show some benefits in terms of organizational functioning (Greenberg & Langston, 2007). It may be that the study did not continue for long enough or that the personnel surveyed (sailors aboard ship) had too little trauma exposure to see any benefits (Greenberg & Langston, 2007).

Although some enthusiasm about the potential of nonprofessionals to extend and complement the care of professionals is appropriate, this approach has potential risks; if service members are encouraged to seek such help, military organizations must ensure that the nonprofessional guidance given is sound. The preference for service members to turn to peers for help with psychosocial problems should be taken with a grain of salt; just because they might prefer nonprofessional care does not mean that this is what they need. The limited social distance between peers is both an asset and a potential liability here; it might be hard for a peer to do the right thing and tell his buddy that he or she needs some professional help. If those with potentially serious problems are inappropriately reassured, genuine harm may occur.

Because of their stronger confidentiality protections and their direct integration into military units, military chaplains are presumed to bridge the void between the desires for help of distressed service members and their concerns about what might happen if they sought it out. A similar role can be played by a number of other military personnel, such as welfare officers, trusted leaders, and indeed medical staff, though confidentiality protection may not be as strong as it is with chaplains.

Critical Incident Stress Debriefing

Critical Incident Stress Debriefing (CISD) was initially a group-level intervention designed to meet psychological needs in the aftermath of a "critical incident," such as a serious automobile accident, a fire, or a natural disaster. CISD can be provided by trained laypersons or by mental health professionals and is intended to follow a rigid, seven-step process over 2 to 3 hours (Mitchell & Everly, 2001). CISD was implemented widely in some military organizations; until recently, the Canadian military required that CISD occur after each and every "critical incident" (Department of National Defence, 1994).

Formal evaluation of CISD shows that although it is well received by nearly all participants (Mitchell & Everly, 2001), there is no beneficial effect on PTSD or depression, and some studies have suggested the potential for harm (McNally, Bryant, & Ehlers, 2003; Rose, Bisson, & Wessely, 2003; van Emmerik, Kamphuis, Hulsbosch, & Emmelkamp, 2002). But these studies have been criticized by CISD proponents, who have pointed out that the protocol used, the target population, the context, and the outcomes measured differed from those intended by its developers (Bisson, Brayne, Ochberg, & Everly, 2007).

Randomized trials of psychological debriefing in military populations have been recently reported. In U.S. peacekeepers with limited trauma exposure, CISD did not promote (or retard) recovery compared with a conventional stress education lecture; soldiers did evaluate CISD more favorably (Adler et al., 2008). Subsequent work with U.S. personnel returning from a demanding combat deployment showed that in comparison with a conventional stress lecture, a modified form of group CISD facilitated recovery in a number of domains (Adler, Bliese, McGurk, Hoge, & Castro, 2009); benefits were seen only in those who had more exposure to traumatic events while deployed. These results are encouraging, but additional validation is needed before CISD is widely implemented as standard practice for service members during or after deployment.

Cognitive Behavioral Therapy

In traumatized civilians with acute stress disorder or acute PTSD, short-term, trauma-focused cognitive behavioral therapy (CBT) dramatically hastens recovery and (far less dramatically) decreases the fraction afflicted with PTSD 1 year later compared with supportive psychotherapy (Ehlers & Clark, 2003; McNally et al., 2003; National Collaborating Centre for Mental Health, 2005). Short-term CBT should be applied only to those who have significant posttrauma symptoms lasting more than a few weeks (McNally et al., 2003; National Collaborating Centre for Mental Health, 2005). Of note, simple provision of an educational handout appears ineffective (Ehlers et al., 2003; Scholes, Turpin, & Mason, 2007; Turpin, Downs, & Mason, 2005). There are no similar CBT studies in military personnel, and there would be numerous logistical barriers to delivering CBT while deployed. Nevertheless, the promise of being able to shorten the duration of symptoms (and, presumably, of dysfunction) is appealing, even if the effects on long-term PTSD prove to be limited.

THE POSTDEPLOYMENT PERIOD

Although coming home from a difficult deployment is generally a huge relief, many service members find parts of this process difficult, particularly in the first weeks to months after return (Adler et al., 2009; Adler, Zamorski, & Britt, 2011). Redeploying service members experiencing transition difficulties or reintegration problems represent a heterogeneous group. Some are fundamentally healthy people having more or less normal reactions to major changes in their physical and social environment. In addition, there are some individuals with minor psychosocial difficulties or with self-limiting distress. Finally, there is an important minority with a broad range of diagnosable deployment-related mental health problems.

These three groups map roughly to Bonanno's (2004) concept of resistance, resilience, and recovery after traumatic events. Each group has different needs. The first (resistant) group does not need professional help. The second (resilient) group might benefit from watchful waiting or perhaps some education or supportive therapy. The third (ill) group needs formal mental health care. Educational programming has to tell those in the first two groups to worry less and those in the last group to worry more about their mental health. An additional challenge is that the needs of individuals within a given group will also vary substantially, due to differences in personality, deployment and other life experiences, the timing relative to return from deployment, and the social environment. The central challenge of the postdeployment period is to find ways to match programs to the diverse and changing needs of this heterogeneous population.

Decompression and Reintegration Programs

There is a strong consensus that the early phases of reintegration after a difficult deployment are associated with at least some discomfort in many returning service members (Adler et al., 2009, 2011). Some authors (Fontana & Rosenheck, 1994) have suggested that in addition to being temporarily unpleasant, negative reintegration experiences may be potentially toxic, in the sense that they cause mental health problems. This argument is grounded in homecoming experience of U.S. veterans of the Vietnam War (Shay, 2002), and it is supported by the observation that negative homecoming experiences were strongly associated with current psychopathology (Fontana & Rosenheck, 1994).

However, this research is bias prone, relying largely on cross-sectional surveys done years after the end of the war. Even when one ignores the very real risk of recall bias, reliably interpreting the direction of causation here is impossible. Although it is plausible that negative homecoming experiences resulted in later mental health problems, it is virtually certain that those who had mental health problems had more difficult homecoming experiences because they were mentally ill at the time or because a common substrate (e.g., negative affectivity) confers susceptibility to negative homecoming experiences as well as mental health problems. Notwithstanding Fontana and Rosenheck's (1994) audacious assertion that theirs is a "causal" model, no amount of theoretical rigor or statistical wizardry can exclude these important sources of bias in cross-sectional research done years after the events of interest.

The best longitudinal research on this topic in U.S. soldiers returning from Iraq showed that transition problems and mental health problems are indeed separate (though correlated) constructs; transition problems alone shortly after return did not independently predict later mental health problems (Adler et al., 2011). Whether transition experiences are simply unpleasant or truly toxic, military organizations have taken an interest in making transition easier for service members and their families, through third-location decompression (TLD) programs, educational programming, and a graded return to home life once home.

Third-Location Decompression Programs

In the past, the gradual winding down of hostilities and the long return home by sea meant that the transition home occurred more gradually, in theory permitting redeploying service members to deal with some of the challenging aspects of the reintegration process sequentially rather than simultaneously. TLD programs attempt to achieve the same result by providing returning service members a brief pause in a restful location on the way home. This usually involves some educational programming (Garber & Zamorski, 2012; Hacker Hughes et al., 2008), making it difficult to disentangle the benefits of such programming from the nonspecific rest and recreation benefits of the decompression per se.

The stated purpose of Canada's TLD program is to make the reintegration process easier for redeploying personnel and their families; the program is not framed as a preventive measure against PTSD. Since the program's inception in 2006, more than 20,000 service members returning from a combat and peace support mission in Kandahar Province, Afghanistan, have spent 5 days in a hotel in Cyprus, receiving 3 to 4 hours of educational programming (including a version of the U.S. Battlemind program; Adler et al., 2009). The main focus of the program, however, is rest and recreation.

Support for the TLD concept among Canadian participants is high, with 95% agreeing that "some form of TLD is a good idea" (Garber & Zamorski, 2012, p. 397). Overall satisfaction with the program as a whole is also high, with 81% finding it valuable and 83% recommending it for future rotations to Afghanistan. Educational programming is well received, with 74% being satisfied at the end of the program. Approximately 1,800 participants from two TLD rotations were resurveyed 6 months after return; satisfaction was, if anything, higher with the passage of time (Garber & Zamorski, 2012). The most consistently identified benefits of the program were that it had made the reintegration process easier (74%) and that it had helped participants realize that there was nothing wrong with getting help for mental health problems (75%); this is also a central message of the Battlemind program (Adler et al., 2009).

Other nations have reported favorable responses to their TLD programs, even though the content of these programs differs substantially (Garber & Zamorski, 2012; Hacker Hughes et al., 2008). For example, satisfaction is high with the U.K. program, which takes place within a restricted number of military-only areas in Cyprus and lasts a mere 36 hours (N. Jones, Burdett, Wessely, & Greenberg, 2011).

Although a definitive randomized trial has not been conducted, there are strong data to suggest that TLD programs are well received by redeploying service members and are perceived to have made the reintegration process easier for them. Whether this level of evidence is sufficient to sustain a TLD program depends on how it is framed. If it is conceptualized as a medical intervention to prevent mental health problems, stronger evidence of efficacy (e.g., a randomized trial) might be required. If it is instead cast as a human resources benefit (e.g., midtour leave), the consistently favorable evaluation of TLD may suffice.

Postdeployment Educational Programs

These educational programs aim to help returning service members better understand the reintegration process, to normalize it, to make sense of the confusing ambivalence that characterizes it, and to help service members prevent conflicts and problems by enhancing adaptive coping (Adler et al., 2009). There is generally also some discussion of warning signs of mental health problems and how to access care if needed. The evaluation of nearly all such programs consists (at most) of brief user acceptability ratings immediately afterward rather than careful assessment of the target outcomes of easier reintegration or prevention of mental health problems. An exception to this is an observational study from the United Kingdom that showed that nonreceipt of a homecoming brief was indeed associated with poorer mental health (Iversen et al., 2008). This study also showed that only those who viewed the briefing as being helpful showed evidence of benefit, suggesting that the quality of the briefing matters.

A randomized controlled trial of a novel psychoeducational approach (Battlemind; Adler et al., 2009) showed favorable acceptability ratings and evidence of modest efficacy several months later across several psychosocial outcomes, though only in those who had heavy combat exposure. The program (particularly the video version) is strongly rooted in American culture (accents, idioms, settings) and the American experience in Operation Enduring Freedom in Afghanistan. But, as noted previously, Canadians (including Francophone Canadians) also found the program valuable, and a high-quality U.K. trial of Battlemind versus standard psychoeducation briefings, delivered during decompression, found that those in the Battlemind group were less likely to misuse alcohol than those in the control arm 4 to 8 months after receiving the brief (Mulligan et al., 2012).

The U.S. Marine Corps uses a different educational paradigm, called the Warrior Transition Program (U.S. Marine Corps, 2008). The program is said to have high user acceptability ratings (Hawes, 2003), though the single qualitative evaluation of the program showed decidedly uneven satisfaction (Buchanan, 2005). There are no published evaluations of its mental health impact.

Graded Return to Work

The last commonly used approach to easing the reintegration process consists of human resources policies that make the return to home life a little more gradual once the service member is home. The central feature of these policies is several days to several weeks of work before commencing postdeployment leave; this is used for various tasks related to wrapping up the deployment (e.g., cleaning and returning equipment, medical exams, paperwork).

There has been only limited evaluation of these approaches; researchers in the United Kingdom (Academic Centre for Defence Mental Health, 2009) showed no association between completion of a heterogeneous set of decompression/reintegration interventions and postdeployment mental health status. Australia reported a small study on the outcomes of service members who, for various reasons, happened to complete a TLD program, a reintegration program (along the lines of the above), both, or neither (Field, 2005). Reasonable satisfaction was found with the interventions, though those who had both TLD and reintegration valued the decompression portion more highly. There was no difference in distress scores 6 months after their return. One consistent comment on reintegration policies in general is that reservists and individual reinforcements from other bases object to having to spend additional time away from their families when the reintegration approach occurs at a base far from their home (Academic Centre for Defence Mental Health, 2009; Field, 2005).

Postdeployment Screening

Postdeployment mental health screening is widely performed but highly controversial. This section reviews the theoretical rationale for screening, the findings of mental health screening programs in both military and non-military settings, and the remaining uncertainties and controversies in this important area.

The argument for postdeployment mental health screening is as follows: Mental health problems are highly prevalent and are leading causes of disability, impaired productivity, and impaired well-being (Demyttenaere et al., 2004). Mental health problems are thus of interest to any large employer, but they are of particular interest to the military for three reasons. First, they can be a consequence of military activities, so the military has a due-diligence or duty of care requirement to minimize these problems to the extent possible. Second, they can cause deficits in areas such as memory, concentration, judgment, reasoning, and goal-directed behavior, which can influence operational safety and effectiveness. Finally, they are strong risk factors for separation from military service (Creamer et al., 2006; Hoge et al., 2002, 2005) and this at a time when most military forces are experiencing unusual pressures for retention of experienced staff.

As alluded to above, some deployments are associated with an increased risk of a broad range of mental health problems, particularly PTSD, depression, and their comorbidities (Institute of Medicine, 2000). Effective treatments for many common mental health problems exist, but only a minority of those who could benefit from care actually receive care (Fikretoglu, Guay, Pedlar, & Brunet, 2008; Hoge et al., 2004; Sareen et al., 2007). Many barriers have been identified to explain this gap (Fikretoglu et al., 2008; Hoge et al., 2004; Sareen et al., 2007), but one of the most important appears to be that many mentally ill individuals do not appear to realize they have a problem for which they need help. This problem may account for approximately 90% of unmet need (Fikretoglu et al., 2008).

Widely available, brief screening tests with acceptable performance characteristics exist (Brown, Leonard, Saunders, & Papasouliotis, 2001; Löwe, Kroenke, & Gräfe, 2005; Ouimette, Wade, Prins, & Schohn, 2008), and some have been cross-validated in military populations and even in the postdeployment context (Bliese, Wright, Adler, Thomas, & Hoge, 2004). Initially, there was concern that few personnel would disclose their problems. The experience, though, has been otherwise. In the United States, 27% of soldiers returning from Iraq disclosed symptoms suggestive of one or more psychosocial problems on their 3- to 6-month postdeployment screening (Milliken, Auchterlonie, & Hoge, 2007); in Canada, 12% of service members who returned from deployment in support of the mission in Afghanistan have reported symptoms suggestive of one or more common mental health problems (Zamorski, 2011). The issue of deception during postdeployment screening was directly explored by a randomized trial that showed that anonymous screening resulted in only slightly higher rates of reported symptoms, and it was the least affected individuals who were most likely to underreport (Thomas, Bliese, Adler, & Wright, 2004). However, a more recent study showed larger differences (McLay et al., 2008).

Some have argued that even if problems are identified by screening, stigma, lack of confidence in the military, or other barriers will prevent those identified during screening from actually accessing care (Rona et al., 2005). This is not the case in the United States; 35% of U.S. Iraq and Afghanistan returnees sought formal care for a mental health problem in the first year after their return (Hoge, Auchterlonie, & Milliken, 2006). The largest fraction of individuals who did seek care consisted of those for whom no follow-up had been recommended during the screening; they disproportionately sought care in the first month after screening, suggesting that it may have influenced later care seeking in those who did not initially disclose problems or who refused care. U.S. surveys have also shown substantial levels of support for mental health screening among the rank and file (Warner, Appenzeller, Mullen, Warner, & Grieger, 2008). In Canada, 30% of a large, diverse cohort of previously deployed personnel sought specialty mental health care over an average of 4.5 years after their return (Boulos & Zamorski, 2011). The unique contribution of screening to this high rate of care seeking is unclear and is difficult to assess without a randomized trial.

For screening to work, the system must have the capacity to deliver a sufficient volume of high-quality care, should individuals present for it. This is a major problem in the United States (U.S. Department of Defense Task Force on Mental Health, 2007): Iraq returnees seeking mental health care in the first year after return received only 3 visits each, on average, including primary care visits (Hoge et al., 2006). This seems unlikely to be sufficient to meet the likely substantial clinical needs of this population, approximately 17% of which reported symptoms suggestive of PTSD (Milliken et al., 2007). In Canada, however, service members with mental health problems were significantly more likely than their general population counterparts to have received mental health care in the previous 12 months (Zamorski et al., 2006). This suggests that although service members may have special barriers to care, special access to care can overcome them.

Proponents of screening also point to high-quality studies that show that screening for depression and high-risk drinking can be effective in primary care settings, although only if certain conditions are met (U.S. Preventive Services Task Force, 2004). This has led several national groups to recommend such screening (U.S. Preventive Services Task Force, 2004). Screening for PTSD has also been shown to be superior to usual care in adults with serious physical trauma (Zatzick et al., 2004). There is preliminary evidence of benefit for screening in the primary care setting for unexplained physical symptoms (Dickinson et al., 2003), which are common after some deployments (Hyams, Wignall, & Roswell, 1996).

The weakest link in the chain of evidence supporting postdeployment screening is the uncertainty about whether earlier treatment results in a more favorable long-term outcome. Certainly, early treatment should be able to truncate the period of suffering, which can be prolonged. In 2002, Canadian Forces members with service-related PTSD had a median delay between symptom onset and initiation of treatment of 5.5 years (Fikretoglu, Brunet, Guay, & Pedlar, 2007). Whether early treatment is truly easier or more likely to result in remission is unclear.

In general terms, screening programs may also have harmful effects, which should be considered in their evaluation (U.S. Preventive Services Task Force, 2004). In the context of cancer screening, false positives can understandably cause worry, and there is evidence that such worry may persist even after the definitive test is reassuring (Brewer, Salz, & Lillie, 2007). Although harm is, in theory, a possible effect with mental health screening, none of the high-quality trials have shown any evidence of such effects (U.S.

Preventive Services Task Force, 2004). However, some have argued that labeling false positives as being "unwell" may bring with it the possibility of stigmatization (Rona et al., 2005), with all of its negative effects.

The criticism of postdeployment screening that is hardest to dismiss is that it is wasteful. The same resources devoted to screening might be better applied elsewhere. Cost–benefit analysis requires information on costs and benefits, neither of which are known here. Some have proposed that screening has ancillary benefits, such as providing reassurance, encouragement, and advice. Postdeployment screening also provides useful health surveillance data. These ancillary benefits should be explicitly evaluated if they are to be used to justify screening.

If a screening program is implemented, when should it be timed relative to redeployment? In returning service members after a difficult deployment, the apparent prevalence of mental health problems appears to have a steady, almost linear increase, at least over the first year after return (Hoge, 2006; Hoge et al., 2006; Zamorski, 2011). Screening immediately after deployment identifies many individuals who have what appear to be self-limiting problems but misses many who will develop problems later (Milliken et al., 2007). On the other hand, screening later misses an opportunity to intervene early for those with early onset disorders.

Some nations hedge their bets and screen both immediately after deployment and again 3 to 6 months later, but the incremental value of this approach is uncertain. In Canada, screening occurs only once, 3 to 6 months after return, but mechanisms other than screening are getting at least some of those with early onset problems into care. For example, more than half of those with symptoms of depression or of PTSD were already in care at the time of their screening (Zamorski, 2011).

The United Kingdom experimented with screening for mental disorders in the general military population (i.e., not specifically after return from a deployment) using a brief postal questionnaire (Rona, Jones, French, Hooper, & Wessely, 2004). The survey was completed by 67% of those invited, and the 27% who had one or more positive screening tests received a letter inviting them to follow up with their military general practitioner; a random sample of those who screened negative were also encouraged to follow up. Overall, less than 30% of those invited actually did so. Those who screened positive were significantly less likely to follow up than those who screened negative. Qualitative research (French, Rona, Jones, & Wessely, 2004) on potential barriers to follow-up identified the key theme as being "lack of confidence" in the military and in its health care system.

Although the design of the U.K. study was very thoughtful and rigorous, the design of the screening program itself was less so. Those studies that have shown value in mental health screening have used a much more intensive approach, including a face-to-face encounter with a primary care clinician at the time of screening, more clinically oriented screening tests, informing the provider of the results of the tests, and systematic efforts to ensure follow-up (U.S. Preventive Services Task Force, 2004). It is also possible that different results would be seen in a system in which service members had greater confidence in the military and its health care system. It is particularly noteworthy that other postdeployment screening studies have shown that those who screen positive are more likely to follow up (Hoge et al., 2006; Milliken et al., 2007) rather than less likely, as seen in the U.K. study (Rona et al., 2004). This suggests that the propensity to seek care after screening depends on the screening process itself and the context in which it is applied.

In summary, as with predeployment screening and TLD programs, randomized trials should be done to assess the value of postdeployment screening. Nevertheless, there is growing evidence to refute the common criticisms that useful screening tests do not exist, that service members will not disclose their problems, or that they will fail to seek help if they do (Rona et al., 2005). There are randomized trial data for screening for depression, problem drinking, and PTSD in other settings that cannot be summarily dismissed just because they are from a different context. Whether the existing evidence is strong enough to sustain a postdeployment screening program is a matter about which reasonable minds might differ. Moreover, what works in one country and context may not work in others. In particular, the prevalence rate of postdeployment mental health problems must be high enough in the screened population to justify the effort and to minimize the burden of false positives.

Admittedly, the foregoing section on screening may not appear to be directly related to building resilience per se. But it does reflect the reality that until such time as resilience can be reliably ensured, mechanisms must be in place to help those in whom resilience mechanisms fail. An imperfect but growing evidence base supports postdeployment screening. This discussion of the postdeployment period began with pointing out that one of the main challenges of building resilience during this period is the diversity of human needs in a mixed population of resistant, resilient, and ill individuals. The strongest philosophical appeal of postdeployment screening is that it is based on an individual assessment of needs and individual targeting of interventions.

Other Potentially Promising Interventions

The positive psychology literature that shows that some remarkably simple interventions that focus attention on the positive aspects of life and on personal strengths can result in sustained improvements in well-being; these benefits accrue to both mentally ill and mentally well individuals (Seligman, Steen, Park, & Peterson, 2005). Such interventions might provide a useful tool to offer to everyone returning from a deployment. Expressive writing about emotional experiences also shows significant and consistent efficacy with remarkably little effort or professional involvement. Benefits are again seen in those with and without mental health problems (Pennebaker, 1997, 1999; van Emmerik, Kamphuis, & Emmelkamp, 2008); some investigators are exploring the potential value of this tool in soldiers returning from combat deployments (Baddeley & Pennebaker, 2011). Computer-based interventions (particularly those delivered via the Internet) also show promise in a broad range of mood and anxiety disorders (Andersson et al., 2005; Carlbring et al., 2005, 2007), including PTSD (Knaevelsrud & Maercker, 2007; Litz, Engel, Bryant, & Papa, 2007).

CONCLUSION

The topic for this chapter unfortunately did not lend itself to theoretical coherence. Instead of forcing these observations about a diverse group of interventions into some unfamiliar framework, we use this Conclusion to highlight some themes about military resilience that might not otherwise emerge in this book.

Do Whatever It Takes to Keep Service Members Well

Military operations obviously require physically and mentally fit service members. This book deals largely with trying to understand the psychological processes that underlie resilience. This focus on psychological processes is valid in that it is clear that these are important predictors of resilience, if not the true mechanisms by which resilience occurs.

But military organizations are not interested in psychological processes per se; they are interested instead in accomplishing their military mission, and they will do whatever it takes to keep service members healthy and functional in order to ensure readiness, operational effectiveness, and force sustainability. "Whatever it takes" could be a psychoeducational intervention, a pill, a screening program, a human resources policy. Military leaders are presumably interested in whatever is most effective and efficient, not whatever is most interesting or theoretically coherent.

Short-Term Performance Versus Long-Term Mental Health

In the section on predeployment screening, the two facets of resilience were described. Both short-term performance and long-term mental health are important, but the two may require different approaches and will require different evaluation strategies. Interventions that enhance performance may be valuable, but one cannot assume that they will improve long-term mental health.

Resilience-Building Interventions Must Be Evidence Based

Theory should guide the development of interventions, but theory alone is not enough to establish their effectiveness. Many theoretically attractive approaches have proven to be useless or even harmful (e.g., some applications of CISD). Randomized controlled trials will often be required to establish efficacy, particularly if the intervention is resource intensive, if there are risks involved, or if the outcomes are health related. Of course, observational data may still provide practical guidance. For example, if predeployment psychoeducation is to be provided, it makes sense to use the Battlemind program as a template, given the encouraging results seen in nonrandomized trials. Finally, the content of evidence-based interventions (e.g., short-term CBT) may inform the development of new interventions (e.g., group psychoeducation), but the efficacy of these new interventions cannot be assumed.

The Importance of Context

Although fundamental psychological processes do not differ substantially from country to country or from deployment to deployment, the military and societal contexts clearly do. The differential effect of interventions such as postdeployment Battlemind and debriefing according to combat exposure suggests that this is an essential part of this context. Thus, interventions that work in one context may not work in another. The effectiveness of postdeployment screening, for example, hinges on service members disclosing their problems, seeking care, and receiving effective care once it is sought; differences in these areas may explain differences in the deployment-related screening experiences of different countries. Thus, even where programs of proven efficacy exist, implementation into new contexts will require adaptation and validation.

The Importance of Content

It should be clear from the mixed results reported in this chapter that some interventions appear to work better than others. Although context matters, the content of the intervention itself and the precise way it is delivered are also paramount. Thus, it is misleading to say that "postdeployment mental health briefings don't work" or "debriefing is ineffective." The evident U.S. success with these two interventions is likely related to the care with which the interventions were developed and implemented.

Different People Need Different Things at Different Times

People differ. Service members are likely to be almost as diverse as the host population from which they are drawn. Needs are also likely to vary across the deployment cycle. Accordingly, it is likely that different strategies will be needed to address the different needs of different individuals and that these will have to be appropriately timed. Group psychoeducation will thus always be a blunt tool that will never meet the needs of everyone all the time.

One-on-one interventions such as screening or short-term CBT may overcome this limitation, but these are often resource intensive. The challenge is to find the most efficient ways possible to leverage the benefits of such precious one-on-one time with service members. Positive psychology interventions, expressive writing, and computer-based interventions are appealing because little or no professional time may be required in their application. In addition, such interventions can be applied at the individual level, when and where they are needed.

Service Members Are People, Too

Much is made of the important differences between work and culture in the military and in the general population. Such differences certainly exist, but it seems likely that when it comes to fundamental psychological processes, human needs, learning, and effective care, service members think and act first and foremost as human beings. For this reason, high-quality research evidence from the civilian setting, such as that on screening for depression, cannot be dismissed out of hand.

Finding the Right Mix of Professional and Nonprofessional "Care"

The responsibility for resilience is shared among leaders, health professionals, and service members themselves. Each has something essential to offer, and the right mix will depend on the task at hand and the context in which it occurs. Using less costly and more widely available trained unit personnel in lieu of clinicians for triage and support (à la TRiM) is appealing, but military organizations must take steps to ensure that this is effective and safe.

The Need to Have Reasonable Expectations

Finally, it is important that commanders and researchers do not lose track of what they are up against, in that building resilience is like trying to ensure performance of difficult and morally troubling tasks in an extreme environment at great personal risk. And they are trying to ensure that the mental health of those who are asked to do these things remains sound. This is no small task. The ability of military forces to intervene is limited by some important knowledge gaps. For example, what psychological processes truly result in the phenomenon of resilience, as opposed to being merely associated with it? Which of these are amenable to change? And what is the best way of achieving this?

Until these knowledge gaps are closed, those who are working in the field of resilience have to have reasonable expectations as to the efficacy of the possible interventions. All who work in this field have to accept that service-related mental health problems will inevitably occur in a certain fraction of those exposed to significant adversity—science simply lacks the technology to reliably prevent these problems. For this reason, there is a need to be careful not to oversell the various resilience-building programs, while at the same time celebrating and promoting those small successes that are found.

REFERENCES

Academic Centre for Defence Mental Health. (2009). *UK Decompression Survey final report*. London, England: Kings College.

Adler, A. B., Bliese, P. D., McGurk, D., Hoge, C. W., & Castro, C. A. (2009). Battlemind debriefing and Battlemind training as early interventions with soldiers returning from Iraq: Randomization by platoon. *Journal of Consulting and Clinical Psychology, 77*, 928–940. doi:10.1037/a0016877

Adler, A. B., Litz, B. T., Castro, C. A., Suvak, M., Thomas, J. L., Burrell, L., . . . Bliese, P. D. (2008). A group randomized trial of critical incident stress debriefing provided to U.S. peacekeepers. *Journal of Traumatic Stress, 21*, 253–263. doi:10.1002/jts.20342

Adler, A. B., Zamorski, M. A., & Britt, T. W. (2011). The psychology of transition: Adapting to home after deployment. In A. B. Adler, P. D. Bliese, & C. A. Castro (Eds.), *Deployment psychology: Evidence-based strategies to promote mental health in the military* (pp. 153–174). Washington, DC: American Psychological Association. doi:10.1037/12300-006

Andersson, G., Bergström, J., Holländare, F., Carlbring, P., Kaldo, V., & Ekselius, L. (2005). Internet-based self-help for depression: Randomised controlled trial. *The British Journal of Psychiatry, 187*, 456–461. doi:10.1192/bjp.187.5.456

Baddeley, J. L., & Pennebaker, J. W. (2011). A postdeployment expressive writing intervention for military couples: A randomized controlled trial. *Journal of Traumatic Stress, 24*, 581–585. doi:10.1002/jts.20679

Bisson, J. I., Brayne, M., Ochberg, F. M., & Everly, G. S., Jr. (2007). Early psychosocial intervention following traumatic events. *The American Journal of Psychiatry, 164*, 1016–1019. doi:10.1176/appi.ajp.164.7.1016

Bliese, P. D., Wright, K., Adler, A. B., Thomas, J. L., & Hoge, C. W. (2004). *Screening for traumatic stress among re-deploying soldiers* (Report No. 2004-001). Heidelberg, Germany: U.S. Army Medical Research Unit–Europe.

Bonanno, G. A. (2004). Loss, trauma, and human resilience: Have we underestimated the human capacity to thrive after extremely aversive events? *American Psychologist, 59,* 20–28. doi:10.1037/0003-066X.59.1.20

Boulos, D. B., & Zamorski, M. A. (2011). *Cumulative incidence of PTSD and other mental disorders in Canadian Forces personnel deployed in support of the mission in Afghanistan, 2001–2008.* Ottawa, Ontario, Canada: Department of National Defence.

Brewer, N. T., Salz, T., & Lillie, S. E. (2007). Systematic review: The long-term effects of false-positive mammograms. *Annals of Internal Medicine, 146,* 502–510.

Brewin, C. R. (2005). Risk factor effect sizes in PTSD: What this means for intervention. *Journal of Trauma & Dissociation, 6,* 123–130. doi:10.1300/J229v06n02_11

Brewin, C. R., Andrews, B., & Valentine, J. D. (2000). Meta-analysis of risk factors for posttraumatic stress disorder in trauma-exposed adults. *Journal of Consulting and Clinical Psychology, 68,* 748–766. doi:10.1037/0022-006X.68.5.748

Britt, T. W., Davison, J., Bliese, P. D., & Castro, C. A. (2004). How leaders can influence the impact that stressors have on soldiers. *Military Medicine, 169,* 541–545.

Brown, R. L., Leonard, T., Saunders, L. A., & Papasouliotis, O. (2001). A two-item conjoint screen for alcohol and other drug problems. *Journal of the American Board of Family Practice, 14,* 95–106.

Buchanan, D. (2005). *Warrior Transition Program: Needs assessment Marines in Operation Iraqi Freedom 2004–2005* (Master's thesis, Miami University). Retrieved from http://drc.ohiolink.edu/handle/2374.OX/19184

Burwell, D. G. (1999). *Special Forces assessment and selection program development for Force XXI.* Unpublished master's thesis, U.S. Army Command and General Staff College.

Carlbring, P., Gunnarsdottir, M., Hedensjo, L., Andersson, G., Ekselius, L., & Furmark, T. (2007). Treatment of social phobia: Randomised trial of Internet-delivered cognitive-behavioural therapy with telephone support. *The British Journal of Psychiatry, 190,* 123–128. doi:10.1192/bjp.bp.105.020107

Carlbring, P., Nilsson-Ihrfelt, E., Waara, J., Kollenstam, C., Buhrman, M., Kaldo, V., . . . Andersson, G. (2005). Treatment of panic disorder: Live therapy vs. self-help via the Internet. *Behaviour Research and Therapy, 43,* 1321–1333. doi:10.1016/j.brat.2004.10.002

Creamer, M., Carboon, I., Forbes, A. B., McKenzie, D. P., McFarlane, A. C., Kelsall, H. L., & Sim, M. R. (2006). Psychiatric disorder and separation from military service: A 10-year retrospective study. *The American Journal of Psychiatry, 163,* 733–734. doi:10.1176/appi.ajp.163.4.733

Demyttenaere, K., Bruffaerts, R., Posada-Villa, J., Gasquet, I., Kovess, V., Lepine, J. P., . . . Chatterji, S. (2004). Prevalence, severity, and unmet need for treatment of mental disorders in the World Health Organization World Mental Health Surveys. *JAMA, 291,* 2581–2590. doi:10.1001/jama.291.21.2581

Department of National Defence. (1994). *Canadian Forces Administrative Order (CFAO) 34-55: Management of critical incident stress in the Canadian Forces.* Ottawa, Ontario, Canada: Author.

Dickinson, W. P., Dickinson, L. M., deGruy, F. V., Main, D. S., Candib, L. M., & Rost, K. (2003). A randomized clinical trial of a care recommendation letter intervention for somatization in primary care. *Annals of Family Medicine, 1,* 228–235. doi:10.1370/afm.5

Ehlers, A., & Clark, D. (2003). Early psychological interventions for adult survivors of trauma: A review. *Biological Psychiatry, 53,* 817–826. doi:10.1016/S0006-3223(02)01812-7

Ehlers, A., Clark, D. M., Hackmann, A., McManus, F., Fennell, M., Herbert, C., & Mayou, R. (2003). A randomized controlled trial of cognitive therapy, a self-help booklet, and repeated assessments as early interventions for posttraumatic stress disorder. *Archives of General Psychiatry, 60,* 1024–1032. doi:10.1001/archpsyc.60.10.1024

Fertout, M., Jones, N., Greenberg, N., Mulligan, K., Knight, T., & Wessely, S. (2011). A review of United Kingdom Armed Forces' approaches to prevent postdeployment mental health problems. *International Review of Psychiatry, 23,* 135–143. doi:10.3109/09540261.2010.557770

Field, C. (2005). *Ration packs to the Sunday roast: An analysis of the Australian Defence Forces experience with postdeployment reintegration.* Unpublished thesis for postgraduate Diploma of Psychology, Monash University, Melbourne, Victoria, Australia.

Fikretoglu, D., Brunet, A., Guay, S., & Pedlar, D. (2007). Mental health treatment seeking by military members with posttraumatic stress disorder: Findings on rates, characteristics, and predictors from a nationally representative Canadian military sample. *Canadian Journal of Psychiatry/Revue canadienne de psychiatrie, 52,* 103–110.

Fikretoglu, D., Guay, S., Pedlar, D., & Brunet, A. (2008). Twelve month use of mental health services in a nationally representative, active military sample. *Medical Care, 46,* 217–223. doi:10.1097/MLR.0b013e31815b979a

Fontana, A., & Rosenheck, R. (1994). Posttraumatic stress disorder among Vietnam theater veterans: A causal model of etiology in a community sample. *Journal of Nervous and Mental Disease, 182,* 677–684. doi:10.1097/00005053-199412000-00001

French, C., Rona, R. J., Jones, M., & Wessely, S. (2004). Screening for physical and psychological illness in the British Armed Forces: II: Barriers to screening—learning from the opinions of Service personnel. *Journal of Medical Screening, 11,* 153–161. doi:10.1258/0969141041732247

Garber, B. G., & Zamorski, M. A. (2012). Evaluation of a third-location decompression program for Canadian Forces members returning from deployment in Afghanistan. *Military Medicine, 177,* 397–403.

Girard, M. L., & Scholtz, D. C. (2005, October). *Trial of the psychological screening program for sniper selection in the Canadian Forces*. Paper presented at the meeting of the International Military Testing Association, Singapore.

Gould, M., Greenberg, N., & Hetherton, J. (2007). Stigma and the military: Evaluation of a PTSD psychoeducational program. *Journal of Traumatic Stress, 20*, 505–515. doi:10.1002/jts.20233

Greenberg, N., Cawkill, P., & Sharpley, J. (2005). How to TRiM away at post traumatic stress reactions: Traumatic risk management—now and the future. *Journal of the Royal Naval Medical Service, 91*, 26–31.

Greenberg, N., Jones, E., Jones, N., Fear, N. T., & Wessely, S. (2011). The injured mind in the UK Armed Forces. *Philosophical Transactions of the Royal Society Series B: Biological Sciences, 366*, 261–267. doi:10.1098/rstb.2010.0210

Greenberg, N., & Langston, V. (2007). *A cluster randomised controlled trial to determine the efficacy of TRiM (Traumatic Risk Management) in achieving a positive culture change, reducing organisational distress and improving unit response to traumatic events*. London, England: King's Centre for Military Health Research, Kings College London.

Greenberg, N., Thomas, S. L., Iversen, A., Unwin, C., Hull, L., & Wessely, S. (2003). Do military peacekeepers want to talk about their experiences? Perceived psychological support of UK military peacekeepers on return from deployment. *Journal of Mental Health, 12*, 565–573. doi:10.1080/096382303 10001627928

Grossman, D., & Christensen, L. W. (2004). *On combat: The psychology and physiology of deadly conflict in war and in peace*. Millstadt, IL: PPCT Research.

Hacker Hughes, J., Cameron, F., Eldridge, R., Devon, M., Wessely, S., & Greenberg, N. (2005). Going to war does not have to hurt: Preliminary findings from the British deployment to Iraq. *British Journal of Psychiatry, 186*, 536–537. doi:10.1192/bjp.186.6.536

Hacker Hughes, J. G., Earnshaw, N. M., Greenberg, N., Eldridge, R., Fear, N. T., French, C., . . . Wessely, S. (2008). Use of psychological decompression in military operational environments. *Military Medicine, 173*, 534–538.

Hawes, M. W. (2003). *Policy for return and reunion of Marines (ALMAR 032/03)*. Washington, DC: United States Marine Corps.

Hoge, C. W. (2006). *Post-traumatic stress disorder and traumatic brain injury: Hearing before the Subcommittee on Health of the Committee on Veterans' Affairs, House of Representatives*, 109th Congress, 2nd session (2006) (statement of Colonel Charles W. Hoge, United States Army). Retrieved from http://democrats.veterans.house.gov/hearings/schedule109/sep06/9-28-06/CharlesHoge.html

Hoge, C. W., Auchterlonie, J. L., & Milliken, C. S. (2006). Mental health problems, use of mental health services, and attrition from military service after returning from deployment to Iraq or Afghanistan. *JAMA, 295*, 1023–1032. doi:10.1001/jama.295.9.1023

Hoge, C. W., Castro, C. A., Messer, S. C., McGurk, D., Cotting, D. I., & Koffman, R. L. (2004). Combat duty in Iraq and Afghanistan, mental health problems, and barriers to care. *The New England Journal of Medicine, 351*, 13–22. doi:10.1056/NEJMoa040603

Hoge, C. W., Lesikar, S. E., Guevara, R., Lange, J., Brundage, J. F., Engel, C. C., Jr., . . . Orman, D. T. (2002). Mental disorders among U.S. military personnel in the 1990s: Association with high levels of health care utilization and early military attrition. *The American Journal of Psychiatry, 159*, 1576–1583. doi:10.1176/appi.ajp.159.9.1576

Hoge, C. W., Toboni, H. E., Messer, S. C., Bell, N., Amoroso, P., & Orman, D. T. (2005). The occupational burden of mental disorders in the U.S. military: Psychiatric hospitalizations, involuntary separations, and disability. *The American Journal of Psychiatry, 162*, 585–591. doi:10.1176/appi.ajp.162.3.585

Hyams, K. C., Wignall, F. S., & Roswell, R. (1996). War syndromes and their evaluation: From the U.S. Civil War to the Persian Gulf War. *Annals of Internal Medicine, 125*, 398–405.

Institute of Medicine. (2000). *Protecting those who serve: Strategies to protect the health of deployed U.S. forces.* Washington, DC: National Academy Press.

Iversen, A. C., Fear, N. T., Ehlers, A., Hacker Hughes, J., Hull, L., Earnshaw, M., . . . Hotopf, M. (2008). Risk factors for post-traumatic stress disorder among UK Armed Forces personnel. *Psychological Medicine, 38*, 511–522. doi:10.1017/S0033291708002778

Jones, E., Hyams, K. C., & Wessely, S. (2003). Screening for vulnerability to psychological disorders in the military: An historical survey. *Journal of Medical Screening, 10*, 40–46. doi:10.1258/096914103321610798

Jones, N., Burdett, H., Wessely, S., & Greenberg, N. (2011). The subjective utility of early psychosocial interventions following combat deployment. *Occupational Medicine, 61*, 102–107. doi:10.1093/occmed/kqq182

Knaevelsrud, C. & Maercker, A. (2007). Internet-based treatment for PTSD reduces distress and facilitates the development of a strong therapeutic alliance: A randomized controlled clinical trial. *BMC Psychiatry, 7*, Article 13. doi:10.1186/1471-244X-7-13

Leardmann, C. A., Smith, T. C., Smith, B., Wells, T. S., & Ryan, M. A. (2009). Baseline self reported functional health and vulnerability to post-traumatic stress disorder after combat deployment: Prospective US military cohort study. *British Medical Journal, 338*, b1273. doi: 10.1136/bmj.b1273

Litz, B. T., Engel, C. C., Bryant, R. A., & Papa, A. (2007). A randomized, controlled proof-of-concept trial of an Internet-based, therapist-assisted self-management treatment for posttraumatic stress disorder. *The American Journal of Psychiatry, 164*, 1676–1684. doi:10.1176/appi.ajp.2007.06122057

Löwe, B., Kroenke, K., & Gräfe, K. (2005). Detecting and monitoring depression with a two-item questionnaire (PHQ-2). *Journal of Psychosomatic Research, 58*, 163–171. doi:10.1016/j.jpsychores.2004.09.006

McAllister, P. D., Blair, S. P., & Philpott, S. (2004). Op Telic—a field mental health team in the general support medical setting. *Journal of the Royal Army Medical Corps, 150,* 107–112.

McLay, R. N., Deal, W. E., Murphy, J. A., Center, K. B., Kolkow, T. T., & Grieger, T. A. (2008). On-the-record screenings versus anonymous surveys in reporting PTSD. *The American Journal of Psychiatry, 165,* 775–776. doi:10.1176/appi.ajp.2008.07121960

McNally, R. J., Bryant, R. A., & Ehlers, A. (2003). Does early psychological intervention promote recovery from posttraumatic stress? *Psychological Science in the Public Interest, 4,* 45–79.

Milliken, C. S., Auchterlonie, J. L., & Hoge, C. W. (2007). Longitudinal assessment of mental health problems among active and reserve component soldiers returning from the Iraq war. *JAMA, 298,* 2141–2148. doi:10.1001/jama.298.18.2141

Mitchell, J. T., & Everly, G. S., Jr. (2001). *Critical incident stress debriefing: An operations manual for CISD, debriefing, and other group crisis intervention services* (3rd ed.). Ellicott City, MD: Chevron.

Mulligan, K., Fear, N. T., Jones, N., Alvarez, H., Hull, L., Naumann, U., . . . Greenberg, N. (2012). Postdeployment Battlemind training for the U.K. Armed Forces: A cluster randomized controlled trial. *Journal of Consulting and Clinical Psychology, 80,* 331–341. doi:10.1037/a0027664

Mulligan, K., Jones, N., Woodhead, C., Davies, M., Wessely, S., & Greenberg, N. (2010). Mental health of UK military personnel while on deployment in Iraq. *British Journal of Psychiatry, 197,* 405–410. doi:10.1192/bjp.bp.110.077263

National Collaborating Centre for Mental Health. (2005). *Post-traumatic stress disorder: The management of PTSD in adults and children in primary and secondary care* (National Clinical Practice Guideline No. 26). Trowbridge, England: Cromwell Press.

Nevin, R. L. (2009). Low validity of self-report in identifying recent mental health diagnosis among U.S. service members completing Predeployment Health Assessment (PreDHA) and deployed to Afghanistan, 2007: A retrospective cohort study. *BMC Public Health, 9,* 376. doi:10.1186/1471-2458-9-376

Ouimette, P., Wade, M., Prins, A., & Schohn, M. (2008). Identifying PTSD in primary care: Comparison of the Primary Care-PTSD screen (PC-PTSD) and the General Health Questionnaire-12 (GHQ). *Journal of Anxiety Disorders, 22,* 337–343. doi:10.1016/j.janxdis.2007.02.010

Pennebaker, J. W. (1997). Writing about emotional experiences as a therapeutic process. *Psychological Science, 8,* 162–166. doi:10.1111/j.1467-9280.1997.tb00403.x

Pennebaker, J. W. (1999). The effects of traumatic disclosure on physical and mental health: The values of writing and talking about upsetting events. *International Journal of Emergency Mental Health, 1,* 9–18.

Reivich, K. J., Seligman, M. E., & McBride, S. (2011). Master resilience training in the U.S. Army. *American Psychologist, 66,* 25–34. doi:10.1037/a0021897

Ritchie, E. C. (2007). Update on combat psychiatry: From the battle front to the home front and back again. *Military Medicine, 172,* 11–14.

Rona, R. J., Hooper, R., Jones, M., Hull, L., Browne, T., Horn, O., . . . Wessely, S. (2006). Mental health screening in armed forces before the Iraq war and prevention of subsequent psychological morbidity: Follow-up study. *British Medical Journal, 333,* 991. doi:10.1136/bmj.38985.610949.55

Rona, R. J., Hyams, K. C., & Wessely, S. (2005). Screening for psychological illness in military personnel. *JAMA, 293,* 1257–1260. doi:10.1001/jama.293.10.1257

Rona, R. J., Jones, M., French, C., Hooper, R., & Wessely, S. (2004). Screening for physical and psychological illness in the British Armed Forces: I: The acceptability of the programme. *Journal of Medical Screening, 11,* 148–152. doi:10.1258/0969141041732193

Rose, S., Bisson, J., & Wessely, S. (2003). A systematic review of single-session psychological interventions ("debriefing") following trauma. *Psychotherapy and Psychosomatics, 72,* 176–184. doi:10.1159/000070781

Rundell, J. R. (2006). Demographics of and diagnoses in Operation Enduring Freedom and Operation Iraqi Freedom personnel who were psychiatrically evacuated from the theater of operations. *General Hospital Psychiatry, 28,* 352–356. doi:10.1016/j.genhosppsych.2006.04.006

Sandweiss, D. A., Slymen, D. J., Leardmann, C. A., Smith, B., White, M. R., Boyko, E. J., . . . Smith, T. C. (2011). Preinjury psychiatric status, injury severity, and postdeployment posttraumatic stress disorder. *Archives of General Psychiatry, 68,* 496–504. doi:10.1001/archgenpsychiatry.2011.44

Sareen, J., Cox, B. J., Afifi, T. O., Stein, M. B., Belik, S. L., Meadows, G., & Asmundson, G. J. G. (2007). Combat and peacekeeping operations in relation to prevalence of mental disorders and perceived need for mental health care: Findings from a large representative sample of military personnel. *Archives of General Psychiatry, 64,* 843–852. doi:10.1001/archpsyc.64.7.843

Scholes, C., Turpin, G., & Mason, S. (2007). A randomised controlled trial to assess the effectiveness of providing self-help information to people with symptoms of acute stress disorder following a traumatic injury. *Behaviour Research and Therapy, 45,* 2527–2536. doi:10.1016/j.brat.2007.06.009

Seligman, M. E., & Fowler, R. D. (2011). Comprehensive Soldier Fitness and the future of psychology. *American Psychologist, 66,* 82–86. doi:10.1037/a0021898

Seligman, M. E., Steen, T. A., Park, N., & Peterson, C. (2005). Positive psychology progress: Empirical validation of interventions. *American Psychologist, 60,* 410–421. doi:10.1037/0003-066X.60.5.410

Sharpley, J. G., Fear, N. T., Greenberg, N., Jones, M., & Wessely, S. (2008). Predeployment stress briefing: Does it have an effect? *Occupational Medicine, 58,* 30–34. doi:10.1093/occmed/kqm118

Shay, J. (2002). *Odysseus in America.* New York, NY: Scribner.

Smith, T. C., Ryan, M. A., Wingard, D. L., Slymen, D. J., Sallis, J. F., & Kritz-Silverstein, D. (2008). New onset and persistent symptoms of post-traumatic stress disorder self reported after deployment and combat exposures: Prospective population based US military cohort study. *British Medical Journal, 336,* 366–371. doi:10.1136/bmj.39430.638241.AE

Thomas, J. L., Bliese, P. D., Adler, A. B., & Wright, K. M. (2004). *Reporting psychological symptoms: Anonymity matters (a little)* (Report No. 2004-003). Heidelberg, Germany: U.S. Army Medical Research Unit–Europe.

Turpin, G., Downs, M., & Mason, S. (2005). Effectiveness of providing self-help information following acute traumatic injury: Randomised controlled trial. *The British Journal of Psychiatry, 187,* 76–82.

U.S. Department of Defense Task Force on Mental Health. (2007). *An achievable vision: Report of the Department of Defense Task Force on Mental Health.* Falls Church, VA: Defense Health Board.

U.S. Marine Corps. (2008). Warrior transition brief: Redeployment operational stress brief for Marines. Retrieved from http://www.public.navy.mil/ia/Documents/WTP_FLYER_30MAR11.pdf

U.S. Office of the Surgeon General. (2003). *Operation Iraqi Freedom (OIF) Mental Health Advisory Team (MHAT) report.* Washington, DC: U.S. Army Medical Command.

U.S. Office of the Surgeon General. (2006). *Final report: Mental Health Advisory Team (MHAT) IV: Operation Iraqi Freedom 05–07.* Washington, DC: U.S. Army Medical Command.

U.S. Office of the Surgeon General. (2008). *Mental Health Advisory Team (MHAT) V: Operation Iraqi Freedom 06–08 (Iraq); Operation Enduring Freedom 8 (Afghanistan).* Washington, DC: U.S. Army Medical Command.

U.S. Preventive Services Task Force. (2004). *Guide to clinical preventive services, 3rd edition: Periodic updates.* Retrieved from http://webapp1.dlib.indiana.edu/cgi-bin/virtcdlib/index.cgi/6468753/FID1/start.pdf

van Emmerik, A. A., Kamphuis, J. H., & Emmelkamp, P. M. (2008). Treating acute stress disorder and posttraumatic stress disorder with cognitive behavioral therapy or structured writing therapy: A randomized controlled trial. *Psychotherapy and Psychosomatics, 77,* 93–100. doi:10.1159/000112886

van Emmerik, A. A., Kamphuis, J. H., Hulsbosch, A. M., & Emmelkamp, P. M. (2002). Single session debriefing after psychological trauma: A meta-analysis. *Lancet, 360,* 766–771. doi:10.1016/S0140-6736(02)09897-5

Vogt, D. S., Proctor, S. P., King, D. W., King, L. A., & Vasterling, J. J. (2008). Validation of scales from the Deployment Risk and Resilience Inventory in a sample of Operation Iraqi Freedom veterans. *Assessment, 15,* 391–403. doi:10.1177/1073191108316030

Warner, C. H., Appenzeller, G. N., Mullen, K., Warner, C. M., & Grieger, T. (2008). Soldier attitudes toward mental health screening and seeking care upon return from combat. *Military Medicine, 173,* 563–569.

Warner, C. H., Appenzeller, G. N., Parker, J. R., Warner, C. M., & Hoge, C. W. (2011). *American Journal of Psychiatry, 168*, 378–385. doi:10.1176/appi.ajp. 2010.10091303

Wright, K. M., Thomas, J. L., Adler, A. B., Ness, J. W., Hoge, C. W., & Castro, C. A. (2005). Psychological screening procedures for deploying U.S. forces. *Military Medicine, 170*, 555–562.

Zamorski, M. A. (2011). *Report on the findings of the enhanced postdeployment screening of those returning from Op ARCHER/Task Force Afghanistan as of 11 February 2011*. Ottawa, Ontario, Canada: Department of National Defence.

Zamorski, M. A., Galvin, M. A., & Humeniuk, T. W. (2007, October). *Findings of an intensive predeployment screening program for Canadian Forces members deployed to Afghanistan in 2003–2005*. Redeployment Paper presented at Wounds of War: Lowering Suicide Risk in Returning Troops, NATO Advanced Research Workshop, Klopeiner See, Austria.

Zamorski, M. A., Uppal, S., Boddam, R., & Gendron, F. (2006, November). *The prevalence of mental health problems in the Canadian armed forces: Comparison with the Canadian general population*. Poster session presented at the meeting of the Canadian Psychiatric Association, Toronto, Ontario, Canada.

Zatzick, D., Roy-Byrne, P., Russo, J., Rivara, F., Droesch, R., Wagner, A., . . . Katon, W. (2004). A randomized effectiveness trial of stepped collaborative care for acutely injured trauma survivors. *Archives of General Psychiatry, 61*, 498–506. doi:10.1001/archpsyc.61.5.498

8

RESILIENCE IN MILITARY FAMILIES: A REVIEW OF PROGRAMS AND EMPIRICAL EVIDENCE

KATHLEEN M. WRIGHT, LYNDON A. RIVIERE, JULIE C. MERRILL, AND OSCAR A. CABRERA

The engagement of the U.S. military in conflicts in Afghanistan and Iraq since 2001 has involved the deployment of hundreds of thousands of military personnel and highlights the demands placed on service members. However, those who deploy are not the only ones affected by the military lifestyle; their families are also affected, particularly by the stress related to combat deployment. Given this context, the psychological resilience of military families becomes a critical asset. In delineating a framework for family resilience, Walsh (2006) identified three key processes: *belief systems* (i.e., meaning making, positivity, and spirituality), *organizational patterns* (i.e., flexibility, connectedness, and social resources), and *communication* (i.e., clarity, collaborative problem solving, and emotional expression). These processes may be viewed within a systems theory framework (Bronfenbrenner, 1977), as the challenges of military life affect the resilience of the individual family

This chapter was coauthored by an employee of the Department of Defense, U.S. Walter Reed Army Institute of Research as part of official duty and is considered to be in the public domain. Any views expressed herein do not necessarily represent the views of the United States government, and the author's participation is not meant to serve as an official endorsement.
http://dx.doi.org/10.1037/14190-008
Building Psychological Resilience in Military Personnel: Theory and Practice, R. R. Sinclair and T. W. Britt (Editors)

member as well as the family as a unit. This chapter explores the demands that military families face and how families respond to them and then reviews existing programs designed to promote psychological resilience.

THE CHALLENGES OF MILITARY LIFE:
KEY ISSUES AND STRESSORS

Military families are part of a unique organization. This section explores findings regarding four common challenges that are part of their lifestyle: residential mobility, spouse employment, deployment separation, and reintegration of the service member. After exploring the lifestyle demands, we summarize factors that can lead to adaptation and successful functioning and recommend future research directions on resilience in military families.

Residential Mobility

Residential relocations are a feature of life, not only in the military but in the U.S. society at large. Census data indicate that around 2% of U.S. residents moved to a different state between 2008 and 2009 (U.S. Census Bureau, 2010). Military families also tend to relocate at least once every 2 to 3 years (Defense Manpower Data Center, 2009; Orthner & Rose, 2005), and they are 3 times more likely than nonmilitary families to move out of the country over the course of a year (Hosek, Asch, Fair, Martin, & Mattock, 2002).

Research examining civilian relocation has found that frequent moves are associated with a number of negative consequences for well-being, particularly in children. These include lack of a regular site for pediatric medical care (Fowler, Simpson, & Schoendorf, 1993); increased likelihood of school suspension, expulsion, or failing a grade (Simpson & Fowler, 1994); earlier initiation into illicit drug use (DeWit, 1998); susceptibility to depression (Gilman, Kawachi, Fitzmaurice, & Buka, 2003); and poorer self-rated health later in life (Bures, 2003). Other studies have found that the relationship between residential mobility and negative outcomes (e.g., attempted suicide, cigarette and alcohol use, teen pregnancy) in children is largely explained by family disadvantages (e.g., poverty) that preexisted relocation (Pribesh & Downey, 1999) or by exposure to adverse childhood experiences (Dong et al., 2005). These findings suggest that the role residential mobility plays in negative outcomes for children is unclear and may depend on the quality and functioning of the family as a system.

In addition, findings in the civilian literature concerning family disadvantages, family dysfunction, and residential mobility may be relevant for only some military families. Perhaps supportive military environments and the screening out of dysfunctional service members result in more stable family units (Jensen, Lewis, & Xenakis, 1986). In fact, one study that examined parental perceptions of the effects of number of relocations on military adolescent behavior found a positive relationship between the two (Weber & Weber, 2005). This is not to say that frequent residential mobility is not a concern. An earlier study found that adults who grew up in the military identified moving as the most stressful aspect of military life (Ender, 2002). However, there may be differences in the ability to cope with the stress of relocations that depend on the patterns of organization and communication within the family unit.

In support of this view of differences in family functioning, the few studies that have examined the consequences of residential mobility for adult well-being have mainly focused on women in the civilian population, and evidence from these studies is mixed. Some researchers found residential mobility did not necessarily lead to poor psychological well-being (Magdol, 2002) or problems with psychological adjustment (Pihl & Caron, 1980). In addition, Makowsky, Cook, Berger, and Powell (1988) found that women reported better well-being if the move was voluntary. This distinction is germane for military populations. Although there are relocations that may be welcomed by military spouses, many undoubtedly are not welcomed. Spouses may experience some negative consequences because of involuntary moves. However, there is little research that examines family attributes or resilience processes that facilitate the ability to cope with relocation.

Spouse Employment

Residential mobility also has consequences for military spouse employment. In fact, Census data indicate that unemployment rates are higher for both male and female military spouses than for their civilian counterparts (Lim, Golinelli, & Cho, 2007). Fifty-three percent of active-duty officer spouses and 56% of the spouses of enlisted military personnel are employed (Office of the Deputy Under Secretary of Defense, 2008) compared with 70% of civilian spouses (Bureau of Labor Statistics, 2010). In addition, military spouses earn less than civilian spouses even when accounting for education and geographical differences (Lim et al., 2007). Interestingly, military spouses tend to be better educated than civilian spouses (Harrell, Lim, Castaneda, & Golinelli, 2004); their lower earnings may reflect their inability to remain in a job long enough to advance, because service members move frequently.

Harrell et al. (2004) also found that a third of the military spouses who were not employed or looking for work indicated that they faced barriers to employment, such as limited job availability, employer bias against military spouses, day care problems, and military lifestyle demands. In addition, separation from extended family members who could provide child care and the taxing nature of service members' jobs may make it difficult for their spouses to have a job and fulfill their parenting responsibilities (Harrell et al., 2004). Even when they are employed, it may be in their family's best interest that they find work with flexible hours so that they can adjust to the uncertain demands of the service member's job (Hosek et al., 2002). This may result in reduced career investment and have consequences for future employment and compensation. Harrell et al. (2004) questioned whether spouses who are unemployed decide not to work or whether the demands of their spouses' military service make it difficult to hold a desirable job. The finding of Angrist and Johnson (2000) that spouses worked less during the service member's deployment provides some support for the involuntary nature of military spouses' disengagement from the labor force. Spouse unemployment may result in unintended consequences for the family unit if it affects the psychological adjustment and well-being of the primary caretaker.

Deployment Separation

Separation from the service member is one of the greatest demands of the military lifestyle on military families. Separations can occur because of field-training exercises, military school attendance, and peacekeeping or combat deployments (Burell, Adams, Durand, & Castro, 2006). Deployment separations also carry the implicit risk of injury or death of service members, which is likely a source of anxiety for the family members who remain at home. In addition, Figley (1993) noted that separations cause disruptions in family routines and the assumption of additional responsibilities required by assuming the role of a single parent. Loneliness and longing were found to characterize the separations reported in Van Breda's (1997) sample of South African Navy spouses. These issues may explain why spouses of nondeployed soldiers are generally more likely to have a favorable view of the army than are spouses of currently deployed or redeployed soldiers (Booth, Segal, & Bell, 2007; Orthner & Rose, 2005).

Although some studies have found that military spouses are relatively unaffected by separation from their service member (e.g., Nice, 1983), others have found elevated depression levels (Burrell et al., 2006; Medway, Davis, Cafferty, Chappell, & O'Hearn, 1995) and increased diagnoses of depression disorders related to deployment separation (Mansfield et al., 2010). Deployment separation has also been implicated in the development of postpartum depression (Robrecht, Millegan, Leventis, Crescitelli, & McLay, 2008) and in increased diagnoses of sleep problems, anxiety, acute stress reactions, and adjustment disorders for army spouses (Mansfield et al., 2010). Younger spouses appear to be particularly vulnerable to deployment separations (Rosen, Westhuis, & Teitelbaum, 1994), which may reflect fewer years of marriage, less time to adapt to the military environment, and lower rank of the service member. One recent study found that spouses who grew up in military families, had previous deployment experience, and were wives of officers coped better with deployment separations than did wives without these experiences (Padden, Connors, & Agazio, 2011). Although the studies did not address resilience processes within the family, it is possible that belief systems and patterns of organization and communication may be influencing the ability to cope with separation. For example, some spouses may be able to cope more effectively because they have learned a shared reality that normalizes and provides context to the deployment separation. In addition, given past experience they also may be more flexible and open to change and more connected to social support than spouses without such assets.

Both the separation itself and the anticipation of the separation appear to affect the psychological well-being of military family members. A longitudinal study of navy spouses found significantly elevated depression levels before the actual separation that remained elevated throughout the deployment (Nice, 1983). Comparable data from the National Military Family Association (NMFA) indicated that, of families, 15% identified the notification about the impending deployment as the most stressful time; 25% reported the beginning of the deployment and 29% reported the middle of the deployment was the most stressful time (NMFA, 2005). However, family differences in perceptions about the deployment and the stress levels related to those concerns, as well as trajectories for families over the course of the deployment cycle, have not been explored to determine contributing factors and corresponding psychological outcomes. In addition, many studies examine the effects of deployment separation on the spouse remaining at home without considering the impact of the family on the returning service member and the change in family interaction patterns during the postdeployment period.

In addition to the body of research examining psychological adjustment in spouses of deployed service members, some studies have addressed the effects of separation on their children by investigating rates of child maltreatment. Rates of child maltreatment tend to be lower in the military than in the general population (McCarroll, Ursano, Fan, & Newby, 2004; Rentz et al., 2007). However, there is evidence of a rise in military child maltreatment rates in the period of increased deployments since September 11, 2001 (McCarroll, Fan, Newby, & Ursano, 2008; Rentz et al., 2007), whereas the rate in nonmilitary families was unchanged (Rentz et al., 2007).

These findings were substantiated in another study that showed rates of child maltreatment were significantly higher in the families of deployed than of nondeployed soldiers (Gibbs, Martin, Kupper, & Johnson, 2007). Children may also have other difficulties coping with separation. For example, behavioral changes (Chartrand, Frank, White, & Shope, 2008; Kelley et al., 2001; Orthner & Rose, 2005), increased anxiety (Lester et al., 2010), deterioration in academic performance (Orthner & Rose, 2005), and sadness (Rosen, Teitelbaum, & Westhuis, 1993) have been reported in both U.S. and Canadian samples. Survey of Army Families data (SAF V; Orthner & Rose, 2005) found sadness was exceeded only by fear of harm to the deployed parent and approximately 25% of school-age children were depressed because of parental separation. Children also were reported to do less well as the deployment length increased (Chandra et al., 2010). However, it is difficult to determine whether child maltreatment rates and child psychological adjustment during the parent's deployment are a direct effect of the deployment or a broader manifestation of existing problems within the family that may have intensified during the separation.

Other studies show that parental deployment is associated with symptoms of posttraumatic stress disorder (PTSD) among children (Barnes, Davis, & Treiber, 2007), as well as increased admission rates to a psychiatric hospital (Levai, Kaplan, Daly, & McIntosh, 1993). It should be noted when looking at child outcomes as a result of separation that some data indicate younger children and boys fare less well (Orthner & Rose, 2005), but other research has found the opposite (Chandra et al., 2010). An important study that begins to identify processes affecting negative outcomes in children of deployed service members found the critical factor for children's adjustment seems to be the psychological well-being of the parent who is present (Flake, Davis, Johnson, & Middleton, 2009). This finding indicates that the child's symptoms may partly reflect the strain of separation experienced by the parent who remains at home. It reinforces the family systems perspective of family functioning, which considers the family as a unit and assesses the interplay among family members.

Reintegration

Despite the joy that family members experience when the service member returns home, reintegration can be a stressful transition. The Survey of Army Families (SAF V; Orthner & Rose, 2005) assessed reintegration issues and found that over half of spouses rated their reunion adjustment as having gone well; however, approximately 20% indicated that the adjustment had been difficult. Adapting to personality and mood changes in the returning service member, reestablishing co-parenting and household responsibilities, sharing the disciplining of children, and adjusting to household routines were found to be key reasons for difficult transitions.

The marital relationship can also be affected by the mental health of the returning service member (see Figley, 1993). SAF V data (Orthner & Rose, 2005) showed that about 25% of spouses reported low marital satisfaction, which corresponds to the percentage indicating moderate to severe marital problems. Symptoms such as sleep disorders and sexual problems were predictive of poorer marital satisfaction in service members and spouses (Goff, Crow, Reisbig, & Hamilton, 2007). In addition, research in both U.S. and non-U.S. samples has found that spouses or cohabiting partners of service members may be secondarily traumatized by the service members' PTSD (Dirkzwager, Bramsen, Adèr, & van der Ploeg, 2005; Manguno-Mire et al., 2007), which may in turn have mental health consequences for their children.

Future Research Directions

Although there is evidence suggesting the military lifestyle can be burdensome for military families, more research is needed to determine the contributing factors. In particular, longitudinal research is recommended because the psychological impact of such challenges as residential mobility or postdeployment reintegration may attenuate or exacerbate over time. Thus, studies that assess the well-being trajectory of military families as they experience the demands of the military lifestyle may provide insight into factors affecting their resilience and identify family attributes that either contribute to worsening problems and symptoms or serve to protect and strengthen the family.

In terms of children's outcomes, many studies used mothers' reports of their children's behavior. Although some of these findings were enhanced by teacher corroboration, direct reports from children may contribute to a better understanding of their experiences. Additionally, we found no studies that investigated secondary traumatization in children. A further research limitation is that surveys of spouses and children from military families typically use small convenience samples of army and navy families and no marine and air force families, which hampers the generalizability of findings. Finally, although there are some research findings from military families in other countries, much of the military family research has been conducted with U.S. samples. An important direction for future research is multinational collaborative studies of military families and their deployment cycle experiences. Such studies could provide important data on national differences and similarities in deployment experiences and the support provided to families.

RESPONSE OF MILITARY FAMILIES TO CHALLENGES: WHY MANY FAMILIES BOUNCE BACK

Having explored some of the challenges faced by military families, we now address how military families respond to these demands. Factors that can lead to adaptation and competent functioning, thus building psychological resilience and the ability to bounce back after experiencing stressful events, are particularly relevant for military families, given the current context of combat deployments.

Military Family Resilience Processes

We examine family resilience using the framework of belief systems, organizational patterns, and communication identified by Walsh (2006) as key processes that will provide an organizing focus for the discussion of studies of military families. Family belief systems are defined as shared realities that facilitate meaning making (normalizing and contextualizing adversity and distress), positivity (hope, courage, perseverance, and active initiative), and spirituality (larger values or purpose, faith, and healing rituals). These belief systems enable families to be resilient in the face of challenges, and some findings from research with military spouses support this assertion. For example, 66% of spouses of active-duty service members reported that their understanding of the necessity and importance of the deployment was an important or very important influence on their ability to cope with a spouse's deployment (Defense Manpower Data Center, 2009), demonstrating the positive effect of meaning making. In addition, Everson (2005) found that spouses' internal belief-based resources, such as seeking spiritual support and making meaning of adversity, predicted higher quality of life for spouses of soldiers deployed more than 6 months than for spouses of nondeployed soldiers or spouses without similar internal resources. Thus, these positive outcomes of meaning making, quality of life, and seeking spiritual support reinforce military family resilience.

Viewing the family as an organizational unit and considering the organizational patterns within the family, Walsh (2006) suggested that flexibility (openness to change, adaptive, and partner equality), connectedness (mutual support and respect), and social resources (social network support, work/family balance) promote and maintain resilience in the face of stressful events. According to Patterson and McCubbin (1984), psychological distress during deployment separation was lower for navy spouses with gender role flexibility, as it allowed them to keep the family functioning as a unit and to more easily accept the demands of the military lifestyle. Military spouses also report the importance of flexibility when asked to describe what contributes to being a successful military family member (cf. Bauernfeind, 2008). In addition, family cohesion (i.e., bonding, unity) was identified by McCubbin and McCubbin (1988) in their research with military families as one of three important coping resources.

Studies have found the value and necessity of social resources in the management of military demands. For example, spouses reported that military and civilian formal supports, as well as high levels of informal support, contributed to their ability to cope with deployment (Defense Manpower Data Center, 2009). In addition, Van Breda (2001) concluded that maintaining resilience across the deployment cycle requires emotional stability, which is reinforced by strong formal and informal social network support. Similarly, Sherwood (2008) found that Canadian military couples, when asked what makes their marriages strong, reported respect, intimacy, and commitment as key components. These positive outcomes of lower psychological distress, successful coping with military family life, emotional stability, and self-defined strong marriages align with family resilience and reinforce viewing the family as a unit.

The third building block of family resilience is communication processes that entail open emotional expression and collaborative problem solving (Walsh, 2006). Many support websites, programs, and guides discuss the importance of effective communication for military families. For example, military spouses who were more informed about the army reported better coping (Westhuis, Fafara, & Ouellette, 2006). When asked, "What do you feel is needed for military families in order for them to continue to be successful before, during, and after the deployment cycle?" both spouses and parents of service members reported that effective and clear communication from the service member, from military spouse resources (including the service member's unit), and among the family members themselves was key to a positive deployment experience (NMFA, 2005). Furthermore, communication between deployed personnel and their spouses and children at home has been linked to family functioning. For example, Chandra et al. (2011) found that the quality of family communication during deployments was predictive of child and caregiver well-being, as well as fewer household and parenting problems. However, although positive family outcomes have been identified as important building blocks of resilience, the processes by which these outcomes occur require further research and elaboration in the context of demands of the military lifestyle.

Military Family Resilience Outcomes

The majority of military family research does not study resilience per se; instead, constructs such as adaptation, satisfaction, and other "competent functioning" indicators serve as proxies for family resilience. For example, Allen, Rhoades, Stanley, and Markman (2010) found that marital satisfaction, confidence in marital strength, or positive bonding did not significantly differ between army couples who had or had not experienced a deployment in the past year. Additionally, Karney and Crown (2007) found that despite increased deployment tempo, divorce rates have remained stable. However, the relationships between marital satisfaction, divorce rates, and more direct indicators of family resilience are unclear.

Studies that identify predictors of positive outcomes following stressful events also inform military family resilience. For example, in a study of Vietnam veterans, Hendrix, Jurich, and Schumm (1995) found aspects of the family environment (e.g., cohesion, expressiveness) predicted parental and marital satisfaction. Correspondingly, Wood, Scarville, and Gravino (1995) reported that army spouses were better adjusted during a deployment if they had a positive outlook (i.e., optimism) and multiple sources of support (i.e., job, friends, church, and children). More recently, Pittman, Kerpelman, and McFadyen (2004) found that Operations Desert Shield and Desert Storm–era army spouses reported greater postdeployment marital quality and satisfaction if they also reported a high level of personal and family functioning during the deployment (i.e., successfully manage the household tasks, obtain necessary transportation, shop for necessities, manage their health, handle loneliness, and maintain the safety and security of their home). These studies indicate that resilience factors can serve as protective family traits.

Relationships between military stressors and positive family outcomes have also been found in non-U.S. samples across the deployment cycle. For example, in spouses of Israeli veterans with mental health concerns, Mikulincer, Florian, and Solomon (1995) found the spouses who reported fewer negative emotions and better health also reported greater postwar marital intimacy. Likewise, Desivilya and Gal (1996) found positive outcomes in garrison Israeli military personnel, noting that couples who perceived the military job as beneficial, were aware of the possibility and severity of work–family conflict, used both organizational and family support, and reported high relationship quality were more likely to have higher family life satisfaction and coping effectiveness.

Future Research Directions

Research on resilience in military families is just beginning with regard to issues faced by families in more recent conflicts. For example, for military personnel who were deployed to conflicts in Iraq and Afghanistan, the role of enhanced means of electronic communication between deployed service members and their families at home and the way in which this communication has affected family resilience are unclear and complex (Greene, Buckman, Dandeker, & Greenberg, 2010), as is defining the components of family communication quality (Durham, 2010). Changes in deployment policies and the rapid turnaround time for units participating in current conflicts are other areas that should be explored from the perspective of resilience processes and outcomes for service members and their families.

In addition, although there is some civilian literature that addresses resilience in children, there is little comparable research on resilience in children from military families. Once again, a systems theory framework could be applied to research in this area. Studies ideally would use prospective, longitudinal designs, allowing researchers to identify characteristics of families and couples that help them adapt in the face of military demands such as combat deployment. Such a perspective could help identify factors that in turn affect the adaptation and coping of their children. Cultural variations in military family resilience and the social processes that encourage the development of resilience are additional gaps in the literature. They should be an avenue for future research, given the multinational nature of military collaborations that are a part of ongoing peacekeeping and combat deployments.

SINGLE PARENTS: CHALLENGES AND RESILIENCE

We turn now to single-parent families in the military, a group that may benefit from programs that promote psychological resilience. Department of Defense data indicate that approximately 5.4% ($n = 74,086$) of active-duty military service members are classified as single parents; this compares to an overall civilian rate of approximately 11.4% (U.S. Department of Defense, 2005). Given the predominance of men in military service, it is not surprising to find a higher percentage of single-parent households in the military headed by men (69%), in contrast to trends in the civilian community, where only 16% fit this pattern (Bowen & Orthner, 1986; Coles, 2002). Thus, a nontrivial minority of military families must adapt successfully to the demands of the institution but with fewer internal resources. One might expect that single-parent families would be more vulnerable to adverse outcomes, due to the demands of the military lifestyle. Given this potential vulnerability, it is surprising that research on single-parent military families is scarce; therefore, general conclusions regarding this population can only be approximated.

Prior civilian research has shown that organizational demands can result in negative outcomes (e.g., depression, irritability, fatigue) for families (Greenhaus & Beutell, 1985; Rogers & May, 2003). Family resilience involves blunting the negative impact of these organizational demands by mustering the family's capabilities and resources (Patterson, 2002b). Thus, for single-parent families in the military, resilience can be understood as the interplay among (a) unique demands of the organization (Edwards & Rothbard, 2000; Kelley, 2006); (b) social, emotional, and logistical deficits created by the absence of a second parent (Bowen, Orthner, & Zimmerman, 1993; Heath & Orthner, 1999); and (c) availability of community and organizational resources to supplement the family's internal capabilities (Adams, Jex, & Cunningham, 2006; Bowen, 1989; Bowen & Orthner, 1986).

Challenges to Family Resilience

As discussed, one of the most stressful demands placed on military families is that of extended separation from deployment that includes possible exposure to physical and psychological trauma (Adams et al., 2005; Bowen, 1989; Burrell et al., 2006). Some studies suggest that the experience of deployment is different for intact versus single-parent families. For example, Kelly, Herzog-Simmer, and Harris (1994) found that prior to a deployment, single-parent military mothers reported higher levels of separation anxiety and lower family cohesiveness than did military mothers from intact families.

In addition, the impact of military organizational demands does not appear to fall equally on single fathers and single mothers. Bowen et al. (1993) reported that single fathers experienced lower overall family adaptation to the demands of the military workplace; adaptation in these families was compromised by lower perceived work predictability and differing perceptions of the availability of social and organizational supports. Similar findings were noted by Schumm, Bell, Rice, and Perez (1996): Single fathers reported greater distress arising from lower work predictability, demands of the military workplace, work stress, and work–family conflict. Schumm et al. concluded that single fathers seem to have more difficulty reconciling the demands of work and family than do single mothers, who appear to show better adaptability to organizational demands. It is noteworthy that this is contrary to what has been reported in studies of civilian single-parent families (Hilton, Desrochers, & Devall, 2001).

Resilience and Adaptation

Some studies have found that support services pioneered by the military can help bolster existing capabilities within the single-parent military family (Bowen et al., 1993). Overall, the use of such services appears to increase resilience in these families, with many adjusting relatively well to organizational demands and challenges (Bowen & Orthner, 1986; Heath & Orthner, 1999). However, the impact of resource availability differs depending on the gender of the head of household. For single fathers, family resources (e.g., strength, optimism) and community resources (e.g., social support) appear to be predictive of family adaptation to work demands, whereas organizational support factors (e.g., emergency financial assistance, housing) do not seem to play as strong a role (Bowen et al., 1993; Heath & Orthner, 1999). For single mothers, family, community, and organizational resources all play key differential roles in predicting family adaptability (Bowen et al., 1993).

Future Research Directions

Given the organizational demands of the military, the structure of single-parent families may lead one to expect instability and compromised functioning. However, the existing literature indicates that these families show considerable resilience in meeting the challenges of military life (Bowen & Orthner, 1986; Heath & Orthner, 1999). Although the military can do little to reduce demands on the single parent, it has targeted interventions to bolster family resilience by augmenting capabilities and resources. These interventions include extensive support services (e.g., child care), as well as substantial fringe benefits (e.g., health care; Bowen et al., 1993; Kelley, 2006). A more detailed assessment of resilience factors in single-parent families may identify coping strategies and other key resilience processes that contribute to improvements in functioning. In addition, program evaluations assessing the effectiveness and usefulness of interventions targeted to single-parent families are recommended to determine the components that foster resilience.

Certainly, much work is needed to improve this area of research. Relatively few studies have assessed single-parent military families, and fewer still have examined resilience and adaptation in these families. Because men constitute the majority of single parents in the military, additional study is recommended to gain better insight into the intersection of work and family. This is particularly important, given that organizational demands have a greater impact on family functioning and levels of distress for single fathers (Kelley, 2006). Finally, further research is needed to assess the impact of the increased operational tempo that has accompanied the wars in Iraq and Afghanistan, with particular attention to the effects of more frequent and multiple deployments.

INTERVENTIONS: DEVELOPING RESILIENCE

We have reviewed the demands of military life and examined the literature on resilience to identify components that may protect families from stress. Characteristics and skills of resilient families that include clear organizational patterns, open communication, encouragement of empathy and problem solving, and the ability to develop a shared sense of meaning after adverse events have been examined (Palmer, 2008; Walsh, 2006). These processes have been demonstrated to improve family functioning, psychological health, and coping in family-based prevention research (Lester, 2012). Here, we review several programs that focus on building and maintaining resilience skills in families as they cope with the challenges of the military lifestyle.

Spouse Battlemind Training

Spouse Battlemind Training is a resilience-building program that synthesizes adaptive measures to confront deployment-related stress for military families (Walter Reed Army Institute of Research [WRAIR], 2007). Battlemind Training (BMT) initially focused on soldier and leader training and combat transitions. However, consistent feedback from soldiers receiving BMT included requests for equivalent training for spouses. The WRAIR developed and fielded predeployment and postdeployment BMT for spouses in 2007, and the training is now integrated into the U.S. Army's Deployment Cycle Support Program and offered to military families. Survey findings from two different program evaluations conducted with spouses and soldiers who attended the training indicated high ratings on satisfaction, relevance, and usefulness (Riviere, Clark, Cox, Kendall-Robbins, & Castro, 2007; Spouses' Battlemind Training Evaluations, 2008).

Spouse BMT emphasizes the ability of the family to face the service member's deployment with resilience and strength. To this end, independence (e.g., the ability to accomplish essential household functions, alone if necessary) and resiliency (e.g., the ability to overcome setbacks and obstacles and to maintain positive thoughts during times of adversity) became the focal points of the training. There are currently two training modules that can be attended by spouses, either alone or with the service member. The predeployment module is given 1 to 2 months prior to deployment, and the postdeployment module is conducted soon after the service member returns home. The modules occur in small-group sessions allowing for interaction and discussion among the group participants, and they are conducted by a trained facilitator.

The main objective of predeployment Spouse BMT is to prepare the military family for the demands and challenges of the service member's deployment. Major training areas include developing skills to keep the family strong, identifying challenges that are common before and during deployment, and focusing on actions that spouse and soldier can take to reduce deployment concerns. On the other hand, the objective of postdeployment Spouse BMT is to prepare the family for reunion and the reintegration of the service member. Key areas for the postdeployment module include identifying ways the soldier and family may have changed as a result of the deployment, emphasizing compromise, and focusing on spouse and soldier actions to reduce or eliminate reintegration concerns. Each letter of Battlemind represents a skill with an associated topic area. For example, Independence (represented by the letter *I*) becomes a teaching point about the necessity for the spouse to make independent decisions while the soldier is deployed. Potential conflict areas are then discussed, such as the soldier feeling excluded from the decision-making role and the spouse feeling resentful at giving it up. Actions each member of the couple can take are illustrated; in this case, willingness to compromise on the part of the spouse and respect and appreciation for managing the household on the part of the soldier.

Spouse BMT promotes resilience by building on existing strengths and skills that spouses already may have and can share with others and by discussing specific actions to guide behavior. The training uses examples that military families can relate to, highlights the potential for misunderstood reactions, encourages giving and receiving assistance, and identifies cues for when to seek help, as well as available resources. Although Spouse BMT has been fielded with spouses of active-duty soldiers, it can be tailored for National Guard and Reserve component spouses, as well as spouses from other services.

SOFAR: A Program for the Military Reserves

Strategic Outreach to Families of All Reservists (SOFAR) is a psycho-educational and community-based outreach program established to provide free and confidential support services to families of deployed reservists. These services are available beginning with the mobilization of the service member and extending up to 4 months postdeployment. Licensed clinical providers volunteer their time to conduct individual counseling for the program or to conduct support groups with a preventive focus, addressing such topics as stress and anger management and coping skills across the deployment cycle. The clinical provider also makes referrals to appropriate resources, should additional or extended services be required. In addition, SOFAR includes preventive services for children and adolescents and has published a project guide aimed at parents, teachers, pediatricians, and other community resources (Levin & Iskols Daynard, 2005). Child and adolescent preventive services primarily address difficulties associated with deployment separation, as well as coping with deployment-related injury or the death of the service member.

Although both Spouse BMT and SOFAR focus on developing resilience in military families during the stressful transitions surrounding deployment,

Spouse BMT tends to be prevention oriented. SOFAR is more treatment oriented and focuses on identifying families that may require additional help, such as clinical referral or other treatment services. In addition, the needs of children and adolescents are addressed through a community-based orientation that provides information to be used in particular contexts. For example, the program has developed guides for schools to support children and their families in dealing with the deployment of a parent and for pediatricians who treat children whose parents are deployed. These guides review the deployment cycle, discuss age-specific reactions that children may experience, recommend specific strategies that can support families, and include extensive information about available resources. Although Spouse BMT and SOFAR are targeted to different populations, they can be adapted to the needs of both reservist and active-duty military families. The community-based approach of SOFAR is an advantage because it expands the circle of awareness and involvement within the community that may facilitate access to services for those families who need them.

Talk, Listen, Connect: Helping Families During Military Deployment

A national program, originating from a Sesame Street Workshop, has been designed specifically for children ages 3 to 5 and their parents (Sesame Street Workshop, 2007). The Talk, Listen, Connect program was developed in consultation with an advisory board of mental health, child development, and military program experts, as well as focus groups conducted with military families. The program is built on the premise that service members who have deployed to Iraq and Afghanistan are typically young and that many have children less than 5 years of age (U.S. Department of Defense, 2003). It is believed to fill a critical need for young families who may not have readily available resources. The program's objectives include empowering caregivers by providing them with practical strategies to help their children cope and by raising their awareness about possible reactions children may have in response to the deployment.

The Talk, Listen, Connect program is designed to develop resilience and provide stability during a time of separation and change by giving parents tools and strategies they may need to help their children cope with deployment. A multimedia outreach kit has been developed for parents and preschoolers; it is oriented toward helping young children cope with experiences across the deployment cycle. The kit is available for military families through extensively advertised distribution routes on military installations. Research conducted with a national sample of 367 spouses of service members indicated that more than 80% of families found the kit to be effective in helping them support their children in coping with deployment. In addition, spouses reported that their own feelings of depression and hopelessness had decreased and that their children exhibited fewer negative behaviors and more constructive family interactions during deployment (Sesame Street Workshop, 2007).

Future Research Directions

In summary, each of the three programs focuses on building resilience in military families to help them cope with the demanding conditions surrounding deployment. In addition, there is some evidence that participants appreciate and will use resources that can help them support their families across the deployment cycle. However, there has been little systematic, longitudinal research that assesses whether the programs actually contribute to the development of resilience and how they affect processes in the family system that lead to improved functioning. For each program, there is potential for studies that can identify factors affecting resilience outcomes for the family as a unit. Peer-reviewed empirical support for intervention and prevention programs for military families would provide some assurance of their efficacy as well as identify new directions for further development.

Although evidence-based interventions for family-centered community care are limited, a recent approach has adapted an existing evidence-based preventive intervention designed to promote positive psychological functioning in families during times of adversity. This approach is currently being examined in a demonstration project with military families (Lester, 2012). Results may provide valuable information concerning the development of resilience, as well as guidance on implementation of such programs in a military context and the generalizability of family-centered civilian programs to the military community.

SUMMARY AND CONCLUSIONS

Three themes emerged as we explored the demands faced by military families, examined components of psychological resilience, considered the needs of single-parent families, and described several resilience-building programs. First, each section emphasized the need for additional research on military families. For example, as the unique demands faced by military families were reviewed, empirical findings for each of the four significant challenges were summarized. However, there was no integrated body of literature that addressed how military families develop and maintain resilience in the face of military lifestyle demands; rather, scattered efforts provided tantalizing hints about the ability of military families to maintain their equilibrium.

The second theme that emerged was that little is known about what constitutes family resilience. What enables military families to bounce back to a healthy psychological state from a stressful situation, and what protects families from adverse outcomes? There are proposals as to what constitutes the building blocks or processes of resilience (Walsh, 2006), and Patterson's model of adaptation (2002a) describes the components of resilience as applied to family systems. Yet, there is no solid theoretical framework to guide research in more clearly identifying the relevant attributes of family resilience and how these attributes contribute to positive outcomes. There is also little research about how to build and maintain family resilience for those families who have more difficulty than most in coping with the military lifestyle. Although several programs that are designed to promote family resilience were described, there are no longitudinal studies that assess whether the programs actually contribute to the development of resilience and how they affect the functioning of family members.

There is a growing literature on family-to-work conflict suggesting that family resilience may be associated with certain work outcomes (Hammer, Cullen, Neal, Sinclair, & Shapiro, 2005). In the last few years, family researchers have considered the positive spillover between work and family roles such that skills learned and used in each of these roles may be beneficial across both contexts. Similarly, work–family conflict and the resulting stress of one family member can affect the functioning of the family system. This research has examined the crossover effects of work and family experiences and functioning from a systems theory perspective (Bronfenbrenner, 1977), which considers the individual in relation to family, work, and work–family systems. These systems are believed to be interrelated, so there is interplay and potential impact across systems. Conceptualizing research with military families using this perspective may help identify factors of resilience and the effects on the work–family relationship.

Finally, the third theme is that existing literature on military families demonstrates the requirement for these families to be strong and resourceful and to have the ability to survive and bounce back from chronic military lifestyle demands as well as from extremely adverse situations. Research with military families using a systems theory perspective as a framework could contribute knowledge about the development and maintenance of resilience to help families cope with the challenges of military life.

REFERENCES

Adams, G. A., Durand, D. B., Burrell, L., Teitelbaum, J. M., Pehrson, K. L., & Hawkins, J. P. (2005). Direct and indirect effects of operations tempo on outcomes for soldiers and spouses. *Military Psychology, 17,* 229–246. doi:10.1207/s15327876mp1703_6

Adams, G. A., Jex, S. M., & Cunningham, C. J. L. (2006). Work–family conflict among military personnel. In C. A. Castro, A. B. Adler, & T. W. Britt (Eds.), *Military life: The psychology of serving in peace and war. Vol. 3: Military family* (pp. 169–192). Westport, CT: Praeger Security International.

Allen, E. S., Rhoades, G. K., Stanley, S. M., & Markman, H. J. (2010). Hitting home: Relationships between recent deployment, posttraumatic stress symptoms, and marital functioning for Army couples. *Journal of Family Psychology, 24*, 280–288. doi:10.1037/a0019405

Angrist, J. D., & Johnson, J. H., IV (2000). Effects of work-related absences on families: Evidence from the Gulf War. *Industrial and Labor Relations Review, 54*, 41–58. doi:10.2307/2696031

Barnes, V. A., Davis, H., & Treiber, F. A. (2007). Perceived stress, heart rate, and blood pressure among adolescents with family members deployed in Operation Iraqi Freedom. *Military Medicine, 172*, 40–43.

Bauernfeind, T. (2008, March 11). *The American military wife: History in the making.* Retrieved from http://www.af.mil/news/story.asp?id=123089683

Booth, B., Segal, M. W., & Bell, D. B. (with Martin, J. A., Ender, M. G., Rohall, D. E., & Nelson, J.). (2007). *What we know about Army families: 2007 update.* Retrieved from http://www.army.mil/fmwrc/documents/research/WhatWeKnow2007.pdf

Bowen, G. L. (1989). Satisfaction with life in the military. *Armed Forces & Society, 15*, 571–592. doi:10.1177/0095327X8901500406

Bowen, G. L., & Orthner, D. K. (1986). Single parents in the U.S. Air Force. *Family Relations, 35*, 45–52. doi:10.2307/584281

Bowen, G. L., Orthner, D. K., & Zimmerman, L. I. (1993). *Family adjustment of single parents in the U.S. Army: An empirical analysis of work stressors and adaptive resources* (DTIC Report ADA273208). Research Triangle Park, NC: Research Triangle Institute.

Bronfenbrenner, U. (1977). Toward an experimental ecology of human development. *American Psychologist, 32*, 513–531. doi:10.1037/0003-066X.32.7.513

Bureau of Labor Statistics. (2010). *Employment characteristics of families–2009.* Retrieved from http://www.bls.gov/news.release/famee.htm

Bures, R. M. (2003). Childhood residential stability and health at midlife. *American Journal of Public Health, 93*, 1144–1148. doi:10.2105/AJPH.93.7.1144

Burrell, L. M., Adams, G. A., Durand, D. B., & Castro, C. A. (2006). The impact of military lifestyle demands on well-being, Army, and family outcomes. *Armed Forces & Society, 33*, 43–58. doi:10.1177/0002764206288804

Chandra, A., Lara-Cinisomo, S., Jaycox, L. H., Tanielian, T., Burns, R. M., Ruder, T., & Han, B. (2010). Children on the homefront: The experience of children from military families. *Pediatrics, 125*, 16–25. doi:10.1542/peds.2009-1180

Chandra, A., Lara-Cinisomo, S., Jaycox, L. H., Tanielian, T., Han, T. B., Burns, R. M., & Ruder, T. (2011). *Views from the homefront: The experiences of youth and spouses from military families.* Santa Monica, CA: RAND Corporation.

Chartrand, M. M., Frank, D. A., White, L. F., & Shope, T. R. (2008). Effect of parents' wartime deployment on the behavior of young children in military families. *Archives of Pediatric Adolescent Medicine, 162,* 1009–1014. doi:10.1001/archpedi.162.11.1009

Coles, R. L. (2002). Black single fathers: Choosing to parent full-time. *Journal of Contemporary Ethnography, 31,* 411–439. doi:10.1177/0891241602031004002

Defense Manpower Data Center. (2009). *2008 survey of active duty spouses: Tabulations of Responses* (DMDC Report No. 2008-041). Arlington, VA: Author.

Desivilya, H. S., & Gal, R. (1996). Coping with stress in families of servicemen: Searching for "win-win" solutions to a conflict between the family and the military organization. *Family Process, 35,* 211–225. doi:10.1111/j.1545-5300.1996.00211.x

DeWit, D. J. (1998). Frequent childhood geographic relocation: Its impact on drug use initiation and the development of alcohol and other drug-related problems among adolescents and young adults. *Addictive Behaviors, 23,* 623–634. doi:10.1016/S0306-4603(98)00023-9

Dirkzwager, A. J. E., Bramsen, I., Adèr, H., & van der Ploeg, H. M. (2005). Secondary traumatization in partners and parents of Dutch peacekeeping soldiers. *Journal of Family Psychology, 19,* 217–226. doi:10.1037/0893-3200-19.2.217

Dong, M., Anda, R. F., Felitti, V. J., Williamson, D. F., Dube, S. R., Brown, D. W., & Giles, W. H. (2005). Childhood residential mobility and multiple health risks during adolescence and adulthood. *Archives of Pediatric & Adolescent Medicine, 159,* 1104–1110. doi:10.1001/archpedi.159.12.1104

Durham, S. W. (2010). In their own words: Staying connected in a combat environment. *Military Medicine, 175,* 554–559.

Edwards, J. R., & Rothbard, N. P. (2000). Mechanisms linking work and family: Clarifying the relationship between work and family constructs. *Academy of Management Review, 25,* 178–199.

Ender, M. G. (Ed.). (2002). *Military brats and other global nomads: Growing up in organization families.* Westport, CT: Praeger.

Evans, M. A., & Rosen, L. N. (2000). Demographic and psychosocial risk factors for preterm delivery in an active duty pregnant population. *Military Medicine, 165,* 49–53.

Everson, R. B. (2005). *Quality of life among Army spouses: Parenting and family stress during deployment to Operation Iraqi Freedom* (Doctoral dissertation, Florida State University). Retrieved from http://etd.lib.fsu.edu/theses_1/available/etd-04072005-181319/unrestricted/rbe_dissertation.pdf

Figley, C. R. (1993). Coping with stressors on the home front. *Journal of Social Issues, 49,* 51–71. doi:10.1111/j.1540-4560.1993.tb01181.x

Flake, E. M., Davis, B. E., Johnson, P. L., & Middleton, L. S. (2009). The psychosocial effects of deployment on military children. *Journal of Developmental & Behavioral Pediatrics, 30,* 271–278. doi:10.1097/DBP.0b013e318aac6e4

Fowler, M. G., Simpson, G. A., & Schoendorf, K. C. (1993). Families on the move and children's health care. *Pediatrics, 91*, 934–940.

Gibbs, D. A., Martin, S. L., Kupper, L. L., & Johnson, R. E. (2007). Child maltreatment in enlisted soldiers' families during combat-related deployments. *JAMA, 298*, 528–535. doi:10.1001/jama.298.5.528

Gilman, S. E., Kawachi, I., Fitzmaurice, G. M., & Buka, S. L. (2003). Socioeconomic status, family disruption and residential stability in childhood: Relation to onset, recurrence and remission of major depression. *Psychological Medicine, 33*, 1341–1355. doi:10.1017/S0033291703008377

Goff, B. S. N., Crow, J. R., Reisbig, A. M. J., & Hamilton, S. (2007). The impact of individual trauma symptoms of deployed soldiers on relationship satisfaction. *Journal of Family Psychology, 21*, 344–353. doi:10.1037/0893-3200.21.3.344

Greene, T., Buckman, J., Dandeker, C., & Greenberg, N. (2010). How communication with families can both help and hinder service members' mental health and occupational effectiveness on deployment. *Military Medicine, 175*, 745–749.

Greenhaus, J. H., & Beutell, N. J. (1985). Sources of conflict between work and family roles. *Academy of Management Review, 10*, 76–88.

Hammer, L. B., Cullen, J. C., Neal, M. B., Sinclair, R. R., & Shafiro, V. (2005). The longitudinal effects of work–family conflict and positive spillover on depressive symptoms among dual-earner couples. *Journal of Occupational Health Psychology, 10*, 138–154. doi:10.1037/1076-8998.10.2.138

Harrell, M. C., Lim, N., Castaneda, L. W., & Golinelli, D. (2004). *Working around the military*. Santa Monica, CA: RAND Corporation.

Heath, D. T., & Orthner, D. K. (1999). Stress and adaptation among male and female single parents. *Journal of Family Issues, 20*, 557–587. doi:10.1177/019251399020004007

Hendrix, C. C., Jurich, A. P., & Schumm, W. R. (1995). Long-term impact of Vietnam War service on family environment and satisfaction. *Families in Society, 76*, 498–506.

Hilton, J. M., Desrochers, S., & Devall, E. L. (2001). Comparison of role demands, relationships, and child functioning in single-mother, single-father, and intact families. *Journal of Divorce & Remarriage, 35*, 29–56. doi:10.1300/J087v35n01_02

Hosek, J., Asch, B. J., Fair, C. C., Martin, C., & Mattock, M. (2002). *Married to the military: The employment and earnings of military wives compared with those of civilian wives*. Santa Monica, CA: RAND Corporation.

Jensen, P. S., Lewis, R. L., & Xenakis, S. N. (1986). The military family in review: Context, risk, and prevention. *Journal of the American Academy of Child Psychiatry, 25*, 225–234. doi:10.1016/S0002-7138(09)60230-2

Karney, B. R., & Crown, J. S. (2007). *Families under stress: An assessment of data, theory, and research on marriage and divorce in the military*. Retrieved from http://www.rand.org/content/dam/rand/pubs/monographs/2007/RAND_MG599.pdf

Kelley, M. L. (2006). Single military parents in the new millennium. In C. A. Castro, A. B. Adler, & T. W. Britt (Eds.), *Military life: The psychology of serving in peace and war. Vol. 3: Military family* (pp. 93–114). Westport, CT: Praeger Security International.

Kelley, M. L., Herzog-Simmer, P., & Harris, M. A. (1994). Effects of military-induced separation on the parenting stress and family functioning of deployed mothers. *Military Psychology, 6*, 125–138. doi:10.1207/s15327876mp0602_4

Kelley, M. L., Hock, E., Smith, K. M., Jarvis, M. S., Bonney, J. F., & Gaffney, M. A. (2001). Internalizing and externalizing behavior of children with enlisted Navy mothers experiencing military-induced separation. *Journal of the American Academy of Child & Adolescent Psychiatry, 40*, 464–471. doi:10.1097/00004583-2000104000-00016

Lester, P. (2012). War and military children and families: Translating prevention science into practice. *Journal of the American Academy of Child & Adolescent Psychiatry, 5*, 3–5. doi:10.1016/j.jaac.2011.10.008

Lester, P., Peterson, K., Reeves, J., Knauss, L., Glover, D., Mogil, C., . . . Beardslee, W. (2010). The long war and parental combat deployment: Effects on military children and at-home spouses. *Journal of the American Academy of Child & Adolescent Psychiatry, 49*, 310–320. doi:10.1016/j.jaac.2010.01.003

Levai, M., Kaplan, S., Daly, K., & McIntosh, G. (1994). The effect of the Persian Gulf crisis on the psychiatric hospitalization of Navy children and adolescents. *Child Psychiatry & Human Development, 24*, 245–254. doi:10.1007/BF02353200

Levin, D. E., & Iskols Daynard, C. (2005). *The "so far" guide for helping children and youth cope with the deployment of a parent in the military reserves.* Needham, MA: Psychoanalytic Couple and Family Institute of New England.

Lim, N., Golinelli, D., & Cho, M. (2007). *"Working around the military" revisited: Spouse employment in the 2000 Census data* (RAND Corporation Report). Retrieved from http://rand.org/pubs/monographs/2007/RAND_MG566.pdf

Magdol, L. (2002). Is moving gendered? The effects of residential mobility on the psychological well-being of men and women. *Sex Roles, 47*, 553–560. doi:10.1023/A:1022025905755

Makowsky, P. P., Cook, A. S., Berger, P. S., & Powell, J. (1988). Women's perceived stress and well-being following voluntary and involuntary relocation. *Journal of Family and Economic Issues, 9*, 111–122. doi:10.1007/BF00986934

Manguno-Mire, G., Sautter, F., Lyons, J., Myers, L., Perry, D., Sherman, M., . . . Sullivan, G. (2007). Psychological distress and burden among female partners of combat veterans with PTSD. *Journal of Nervous and Mental Disease, 195*, 144–151. doi:10.1097/01.nmd.0000254755.53549.69

Mansfield, A. J., Kaufman, J. S., Marshall, S. W., Gaynes, B. N., Morrissey, J. P., & Engel, C. C. (2010). Deployment and the use of mental health services among U.S. Army wives. *The New England Journal of Medicine, 362*, 101–109. doi:10.1056/NEJMoa0900177

McCarroll, J. E., Fan, Z., Newby, J. H., & Ursano, R. J. (2008). Trends in U.S. Army child maltreatment reports: 1990–2004. *Child Abuse Review, 17,* 108–118. doi:10.1002/car.986

McCarroll, J. E., Ursano, R. J., Fan, Z., & Newby, J. H. (2004). Comparison of U.S. Army and civilian substantiated reports of child maltreatment. *Child Maltreatment, 9,* 103–110. doi:10.1177/1077559503261262

McCubbin, H. I., & McCubbin, M. A. (1988). Typologies of resilient families: Emerging roles of social class and ethnicity. *Family Relations, 37,* 247–254. doi:10.2307/584557

Medway, F. J., Davis, K. E., Cafferty, T. P., Chappell, K. D., & O'Hearn, R. E. (1995). Family disruption and adult attachment correlates of spouse and child reaction to separation and reunion due to Operation Desert Storm. *Journal of Social and Clinical Psychology, 14,* 97–118. doi:10.1521/jscp.1995.14.2.97

Mikulincer, M., Florian, V., & Solomon, Z. (1995). Marital intimacy, family support, and secondary traumatization: A study of wives of veterans with combat stress reaction. *Anxiety, Stress, & Coping, 8,* 203–213. doi:10.1080/10615809508249373

National Military Family Association. (2005). *Report on the cycles of deployment: An analysis of survey responses from April through September, 2005.* Alexandria, VA: Author.

Nice, D. S. (1983). The course of depressive affect in Navy wives during family separation. *Military Medicine, 148,* 341–343.

Office of the Deputy Under Secretary of Defense. (2008). *2008 demographic report.* Retrieved from http://prhome.defense.gov/rfm/mcfp/Reports.aspx

Orthner, D. K., & Rose, R. (2005). *Survey of Army Families V survey report.* Alexandria, VA: Army Research Institute.

Padden, D. L., Connors, R. A., & Agazio, J. G. (2011). Stress, coping, and well-being in military spouses during deployment separation. *Western Journal of Nursing Research, 33,* 247–267. doi:10.1177/0193945910371319

Palmer, C. (2008). A theory of risk and resilience factors in military families. *Military Psychology, 20,* 205–217. doi:10.1080/08995600802118858

Patterson, J. M. (2002a). Integrating family resilience and family stress theory. *Journal of Marriage and Family, 64,* 349–360. doi:10.1111/j.1741-3737.2002.00349.x

Patterson, J. M. (2002b). Understanding family resilience. *Journal of Clinical Psychology, 58,* 233–246. doi:10.1002/jclp.10019

Patterson, J. M., & McCubbin, H. I. (1984). Gender roles and coping. *Journal of Marriage and Family, 46,* 95–104. doi:10.2307/351868

Pihl, R. O., & Caron, M. (1980). The relationship between geographic mobility, adjustment, and personality. *Journal of Clinical Psychology, 36,* 190–194. doi:10.1002/1097-4679(198001)36:1<190::AID-JCLP2270360123>3.0.CO;2-S

Pittman, J. F., Kerpelman, J. L., & McFadyen, J. M. (2004). Internal and external adaptation in Army families: Lessons from Operations Desert Shield and Desert Storm. *Family Relations, 53,* 249–260. doi:10.1111/j.0197-6664.2004.0001.x

Pribesh, S., & Downey, D. B. (1999). Why are residential and school moves associated with poor school performance? *Demography, 36,* 521–534. doi:10.2307/2648088

Rentz, E. D., Marshall, S. W., Loomis, D., Casteel, C., Martin, S. L., & Gibbs, D. A. (2007). Effects of deployment on the occurrence of child maltreatment in military and nonmilitary families. *American Journal of Epidemiology, 165,* 1199–1206. doi:10.1093/aje/kwm008

Riviere, L. A., Clark, J. C., Cox, A. L., Kendall-Robbins, A., & Castro, C. A. (2007, August). Spouse Battlemind Training: Elements and strengths. In C. A. Castro & J. L. Thomas (Co-chairs), *Battlemind training system: Supporting soldiers through the deployment cycle.* Symposium conducted at the meeting of the American Psychological Association, San Francisco, CA.

Robrecht, D. T., Millegan, J., Leventis, L. L., Crescitelli, J. A., & McLay, R. N. (2008). Spouse military deployment as a risk factor for postpartum depression. *Journal of Reproductive Medicine, 53,* 860–864.

Rogers, S. J., & May, D. C. (2003). Spillover between marital quality and job satisfaction: Long-term patterns and gender differences. *Journal of Marriage and Family, 65,* 482–495. doi:10.1111/j.1741-3737.2003.00482.x

Rosen, L. N., Teitelbaum, J. M., & Westhuis, D. J. (1993). Children's reactions to the Desert Storm deployment: Initial findings from a survey of Army families. *Military Medicine, 158,* 465–469.

Rosen, L. N., Westhuis, D. J., & Teitelbaum, J. M. (1994). Patterns of adaptation among Army wives during Operations Desert Shield and Desert Storm. *Military Medicine, 159,* 43–47.

Schumm, W. R., Bell, D. B., Rice, R. E., & Perez, M. M. V. (1996). Trends in single parenting in the U.S. Army. *Psychological Reports, 78,* 1311–1328. doi:10.2466/pr0.1996.78.3c.1311

Sesame Street Workshop. (2007). Helping children cope with deployment: New research reveals Sesame Street Workshop's Talk, Listen, Connect Initiative is helping military families [Press release]. Retrieved from http://www.sesameworkshop.org/aboutus/inside_press.php?contentId=18062688

Sherwood, E. M. (2008). *Marital strength in Canadian military couples: A grounded theory approach* (Doctoral dissertation). Retrieved from http://dspace1.acs.ucalgary.ca/bitstream/1880/4640/3/Sherwood_PhD.pdf

Simpson, G. A., & Fowler, M. G. (1994). Geographic mobility and children's emotional/behavioral adjustment and school functioning. *Pediatrics, 93,* 303–309.

Spouses' Battlemind Training evaluations: 2008 [Data file]. Washington, DC: Walter Reed Army Institute of Research.

U.S. Census Bureau. (2010). *Annual geographical mobility rates, by type of movement: 1947–2009.* Retrieved from http://www.census.gov/population/socdemo/migration/tab-a-1.pdf

U.S. Department of Defense. (2003). *2003 demographics report*. Arlington, VA: Military Family Resource Center.

U.S. Department of Defense. (2005). *2005 demographics report*. Arlington, VA: Military Family Resource Center.

Van Breda, A. D. (1997). Experience of routine husband absences in the South African Navy. *Social Work/Maatskaplike Werk, 33*, 154–164.

Van Breda, A. D. (2001). *Resilience theory: A literature review*. Retrieved from http://www.vanbreda.org/adrian/resilience/resilience_theory_review.pdf

Walsh, F. (2006). *Strengthening family resilience* (2nd ed.). New York, NY: Guilford Press.

Walter Reed Army Institute of Research. (2007). *Walter Reed Army Institute of Research Battlemind Training*. Retrieved from http://www.battlemind.org/

Weber, E. G., & Weber, K. W. (2005). Geographic relocation frequency, resilience, and military adolescent behavior. *Military Medicine, 170*, 638–642.

Westhuis, D. J., Fafara, R. J., & Ouellette, P. (2006). Does ethnicity affect the coping of military spouses? *Armed Forces & Society, 32*, 584–603. doi:10.1177/0095327X06287050

Wood, S., Scarville, J., & Gravino, K. (1995). Waiting wives: Separation and reunion among Army wives. *Armed Forces & Society, 21*, 217–236. doi:10.1177/0095327X9502100204

9

COMPREHENSIVE SOLDIER FITNESS: UNDERSCORING THE FACTS, DISMANTLING THE FICTION

PAUL B. LESTER, SHARON McBRIDE, AND RHONDA L. CORNUM

Though the U.S. Army may place stock in its physical fitness programs and actively dedicates significant resources toward ensuring that soldiers maintain their physical fitness, it has until recently done little programmatically to address the need for and importance of psychological fitness. The rise of behavioral health problems associated with a decade of war in Iraq and Afghanistan underscores this need (Milliken, Auchterlonie, & Hoge, 2007; U.S. Department of the Army, 2010). Army programs designed to address behavioral health problems in a preventive fashion have little or no documented efficacy, and success is often defined by the number of soldiers who participated in the training rather than a change in the targeted behavior (Cornum & Lester, 2012).

The U.S. Army's Comprehensive Soldier Fitness program (CSF) is a step toward addressing some of these problems. At the strategic level, CSF is a cultural change agent that answers a key question facing the army: How does

This chapter was coauthored by employees of the U.S. Department of Defense as part of official duty and is considered to be in the public domain. Any views expressed herein do not necessarily represent the views of the United States government, and the authors' participation is not meant to serve as an official endorsement.
http://dx.doi.org/10.1037/14190-009
Building Psychological Resilience in Military Personnel: Theory and Practice, R. R. Sinclair and T. W. Britt (Editors)

an organization of over 1.1 million people go about making psychological fitness as important as physical fitness? Operationally, CSF is a vehicle that provides commanders with a trained cadre to lead group-level resilience training locally; this cadre—known as Master Resilience Trainers, or MRTs—is armed with high-quality training packages that can be delivered from a variety of platforms and in both garrison and combat environments.

Tactically, CSF helps individual soldiers "get left of the boom" (i.e., teaches them how to psychologically prepare for and address challenges and adversity); adversity need not necessarily be related to combat, given that the military occupations offer a host of unique challenges. The program does so first by helping the individual soldier become aware of his or her psychological fitness via completing a 105-question survey. This survey is known as the Global Assessment Tool, or GAT, and every soldier is provided with tailored feedback based on how he or she answers the questions. Upon completion of the GAT, soldiers are provided a menu of online training modules; each module targets a specific skill to improve psychological health. There are currently 27 modules, and the CSF program plans to expand its library for the next few years. Additionally, soldiers improve their psychological fitness by attending training hosted by their local unit and typically proctored by MRTs. Last, the army has institutionalized resilience training across its education system. Recognizing that the reinforcement is necessary for making organizational changes stick, the army's senior leadership directed that resilience and psychological fitness be discussed at every professional development training course offered to leaders. These four components of the program—the GAT, online training modules, MRTs, and the institutional training—are the cornerstones of the CSF program and represent the army's programmatic approach toward a promotion model of psychological health.

Therefore, our purpose in this chapter is to more closely examine the CSF program. We begin by offering the philosophical roots of CSF. We then provide a brief overview of the empirical literature of the Penn Resilience Program, the program on which CSF was largely based. Next, we provide details about each of the cornerstones outlined previously. Later, we address several of the criticisms leveled against CSF. We end this chapter with an overview of CSF's program evaluation initiative and an outline of several considerations for the future.

THE PHILOSOPHICAL UNDERPINNINGS OF COMPREHENSIVE SOLDIER FITNESS

CSF is a holistic training program designed to bolster existing and develop nascent cognitive resources and communication and reasoning skills in order to help soldiers thrive in the face of challenges inherent in army life. The program focuses its training effort along the five prime dimensions of human health and fitness endorsed by the World Health Organization (1948): physical, social, emotional, spiritual, and family. Taking its cue from the positive psychology literature, CSF is a strengths-based program in that it promotes the development of characteristics that better enable soldiers to deal with stressors. Although CSF assumes that every soldier should be reasonably fit in all five dimensions, it encourages soldiers to identify and leverage their own individual strengths. *Resilience* is a key programmatic term and is conceptualized as a global construct related to overall physical and psychological health. Soldiers who are physically and psychologically fit are best prepared to face adversity and bounce back from it because they have (a) the cognitive resources available to process challenges appropriately, (b) the emotional mastery necessary to withstand stress, (c) the social and familial networks available to be called upon in trying times, (d) the ability to find purpose and meaning in serving as a soldier, and (e) the physical stamina to endure hardship. Though a stated objective of the program is to develop resilient soldiers, the program also recognizes that being psychologically and physically fit is a lifelong process that changes over time as the context and the needs of the individual soldier and context also change. To address these changes, much of CSF training focuses on developing metacognitive skills because doing so helps soldiers understand how and why they think a certain way or have a certain belief. Quite simply, if soldiers are readily able to employ their metacognitive skills, then it follows that they will more easily adapt as the context changes. With practice, they will learn to challenge their underlying assumptions about problems they face in order to realize an optimal pathway toward a solution.

Although it is important to understand what CSF is, it is equally important to understand what it is not. CSF is not a medical program designed to treat psychopathology. Stated bluntly, there is a robust and well-resourced organization charged with that mission—the U.S. Army Medical Department—and soldiers diagnosed with a particular psychopathology receive the best medical treatment available. In fact, given the stigma against behavioral health care in the army (U.S. Department of the Army, 2010), the CSF program has purposefully distanced itself from the army medical community out of concern that soldiers would resist CSF training if they believed that it was a medical program. The stigma against behavioral health care is strong (U.S. Department of the Army, 2010). Doctors, clinical psychologists, licensed clinical social workers, and chaplains—those officers most often relied upon to enact medical treatments and social programs in the army—are not typically tapped to deliver CSF training, though they are encouraged to be familiar with the vocabulary and constructs of the program. Rather, CSF training is sponsored, managed, and led by unit leadership in order to maximize emphasis on the importance of being psychologically and physically fit.

Similarly, CSF training is not designed to be delivered in response to a specific negative event, such as following a training accident or combat death. The U.S. Army Medical Command's Combat Stress Control teams have this mission; those teams largely focus on providing psychological health care during and following discrete crises. To insert CSF training after a crisis ends completely misses the point that CSF is a prevention-oriented program. It is much harder to shape how a soldier approaches a crisis and cognitively processes solutions after the crisis has occurred, because the potential damage is already done. There may be value in reviewing behavior in a post hoc fashion in order to prepare the soldier for future challenges; Combat Stress Control teams are well prepared for this mission.

CSF is not a panacea—for anything. The program will not bring about an end to low base rate behavioral problems, such as suicide and violent crime within the army. It will not cure posttraumatic stress disorder (PTSD). It will not solve the army's alarmingly high number of soldiers who are prescribed psychotropic medication for behavioral health problems. It will not cure addiction of any kind, especially those commonly prevalent in soldiers: alcohol abuse (Lande, Marin, Chang, & Lande, 2008), tobacco addiction (Grier, Knapik, Canada, Canham-Chervak, & Jones, 2010), and illicit drug use (Lacy et al., 2008). It will not prevent a divorce from happening or make a soldier a great parent.

But CSF will help some percentage of soldiers avoid these outcomes by helping them approach challenges and adversity in a more positive, more prosocial manner. Stated differently, CSF is a cognitive approach to preventative psychological and physical health in which soldiers are trained to use their cognitive resources toward good actions—good for themselves, good for their families, good for the army. Perhaps most important, CSF goes well beyond what critics of the program (e.g., Eidelson, Pilisuk, & Soldz, 2011) often point to—that merely thinking positive thoughts ultimately gets you nowhere without constructive action. In fact, as we show below, CSF trains soldiers to actually apply their CSF skills toward problem solving within a framework repeatedly shown to be efficacious in a variety of settings.

THE EMPIRICAL UNDERPINNINGS OF COMPREHENSIVE SOLDIER FITNESS

A core organizing principle of CSF is that the program's training is based upon evidence of training effectiveness, and this principle is operationalized through four organizational maxims. First, soldier time is valuable; it should be treated as such, and therefore CSF shall provide effective training in the shortest period of time required to get the desired results. Second, if for some

reason that novel training cannot be assessed for efficacy prior to incorpora-
tion into the CSF program (e.g., due to needs of the force, a directive from
the army senior leadership, or emerging requirements critical to combat success), CSF shall assess the training's effectiveness over time. Third, evidence
of training effectiveness in a civilian population (vs. a military population)
may be initially acceptable, but ultimately the training must be tested on a
U.S. Army population if the training is to become an enduring component of
the CSF program. Fourth, CSF will stop using a particular training regimen if
the evidence suggests that it is not effective or if it causes harm.

With this organizing principle in mind, it is useful to understand the
empirical foundations on which CSF was built. As is discussed later in this
chapter, evidence of CSF's effectiveness is forthcoming. Seligman (2011a,
2011b) pointed out that several courses of action on how to proceed with CSF
were presented to the army's most senior leadership, including pilot testing the
components of the current program prior to implementation. Given the exi-
gent circumstances inherent with war, the army's leadership decided not to wait
for pilot testing and instead accepted the empirical evidence already gathered
by the Penn Resilience Program; this evidence was treated as a proxy until such
time that a proper program evaluation could be conducted. As Eidelson et al.
(2011) pointed out, there are certainly risks associated with launching a training program without evidence of effectiveness—the training might cause more
harm than good—and the army's senior leadership understood this risk quite
well (Seligman, 2011a). Below, we outline some of the empirical evidence that
the army senior leadership weighed as it made its decision.

As has been widely reported, CSF was largely derived from a program
designed to decrease depression and anxiety in schoolchildren and young
adults; this program is known as the Penn Resilience Program (PRP; Reivich,
Seligman, & McBride, 2011). There is a parallel program known as APEX
that focuses on doing the same for young adults and college students (Reivich,
Shatte, & Gillham, 2003). The basic principle of PRP and APEX is that there
are many aspects of resilience and psychological health that are teachable
(Reivich & Shatte, 2002; Seligman, 1990). There is no shortage of empirical
evidence in support of this principle; there are 19 controlled studies to date that
show various levels of efficacy for the program (e.g., Gillham, Hamilton, Freres,
Patton, & Gallop, 2006; Gillham et al., 2007; Gillham, Reivich, Jaycox, &
Seligman, 1995). Further, a meta-analysis published by Brunwasser, Gillham,
and Kim (2009) suggests that PRP does in fact reduce depressive symptoms up
to 12 months postintervention.

Perhaps most important, PRP is an effective train-the-trainer program
(Challen, Noden, West, & Machin, 2009). In most cases, PRP trainers taught
the material to teachers who participated in the research, and these teachers
in turn taught the PRP material to their students over a given length of time.

And, the effects (e.g., decreased depression and anxiety) were measured not at the teacher level but at the proper referent level: the students. This validated train-the-trainer approach is critical for the army and is quite simply the most important reason why the army selected PRP as the foundational program for CSF. Perspective here is important, and the army senior leadership grappled with a critical question: How could the U.S. Army—with more than 1.1 million soldiers—diffuse the critical components of CSF across an entire population without an effective train-the-trainer program? Hiring thousands of trained psychologists was out of the question; the army force structure, budget, and applicant pool could not support such an endeavor. Although it is true that recent advances in distance learning might be helpful here—and, in fact, CSF does incorporate some distance learning into its program via online training modules discussed later in the chapter—there is no substitute for a seasoned noncommissioned officer (NCO) working face-to-face with his or her soldiers to impart CSF skills.

When taken together, PRP served as a good foundation on which to build CSF for two reasons: (a) PRP is one of the most heavily researched and evidenced psychological intervention that targets areas important to the army, and (b) PRP is a validated train-the-trainer program. Although Brunwasser et al. (2009) pointed out that the statistical effects of such programs are small (effect sizes ranging from .11 to .21, 6–12 months postintervention), the practical impact of those effects is tremendous when one considers that, like CSF, PRP was designed to be a population-wide intervention. As discussed earlier, CSF and PRP are not designed to be the panacea to end depression, anxiety, or traumatic stress. Rather, they are designed to "move the needle" just a little by giving people the cognitive skills to think through problems and manage their emotions.

THE CORNERSTONES

The cornerstones of the CSF program consist of the GAT, the MRT course, the Comprehensive Resilience Modules, and the Institutional Resilience Training. We describe each below.

The Global Assessment Tool

The GAT is a 105-question, psychometrically valid questionnaire completed annually by every soldier not deployed to combat. The GAT is a web-based program administered via CSF's information technology platform, known as the Soldier Fitness Tracker, or SFT. The GAT was authored by Chris Peterson and Nansook Park from the University of Michigan and

Colonel Carl Castro, a highly regarded U.S. Army research psychologist. Approximately 90% of the questions included on the GAT were adapted or adopted wholesale from existing scales published in the peer-reviewed psychology literature, and the remaining 10% were written by the authors. The GAT was developed and tested in 2009 and was released for use by all soldiers on October 1, 2009 (for a lengthy review of the origins of the GAT and the SFT, see Fravell, Nasser, & Cornum, 2011; Peterson, Park, & Castro, 2011).

From a policy perspective, the GAT has been quite successful. As of this writing, the GAT has been completed more than 2 million times since its launch in 2009, a rate of one GAT completion approximately every 30 seconds since its release. Not everyone completes the GAT at the same time: CSF typically sees completions range from 2,000 to over 25,000 per day depending on time of year and operational tempo across the army. Soldiers are notified via a variety of methods that they are due for another GAT completion (e.g., electronically, through unit chain of command). Soldiers may elect to take the GAT every 90 days. Though unit chains of command know when soldiers must retake the GAT, they do not have access to a particular soldier's score; this is done to protect soldier privacy, and soldiers cannot be compelled to provide their GAT scores to anyone. As a matter of policy, only the U.S. Army chief of staff may direct CSF to turn over a soldier's GAT score to anyone other than the soldier who completed the GAT, and to date this has never happened. Further, this policy has successfully rebuffed several attempts by investigators to obtain GAT scores in both criminal and suicide investigations.

Privacy of the GAT is a critical component to the CSF program. If soldiers do not believe that their privacy will be maintained, they are simply less likely to provide honest responses to the questions. The GAT was designed to serve as a self-awareness tool, as it provides a snapshot of fitness along the four psychosocial dimensions of CSF (social, emotional, spiritual, and family). Feedback on the physical dimension is not currently provided, though this shortcoming will be rectified in the near future via data provided from sources external to CSF (e.g., physical fitness test scores, blood pressure, body mass index). The GAT was never designed to be a surveillance tool for commanders, and, despite repeated requests from leaders, CSF policy does not allow for command access to individual- or unit-level scores because this is not very useful from a macro perspective. Data analyses show that there is a wide distribution of GAT scores within units and few if any reliable differences between large organizations. These analyses underscore the fact that the GAT is a tool for the individual soldier and is of little use for organizational leaders as a macro measure of unit psychological health.

Soldiers receive feedback in a variety of formats. First, they receive their mean scores in a bar chart format, and if they have taken the GAT previously, they also see how their current scores compare with their last five GAT results. Second, soldiers receive a very broad narrative on how to interpret their scores. Third, soldiers also receive a more narrowly tailored narrative that makes specific recommendations for development and effort based on their GAT scores. Fourth, soldiers may elect to compare their scores to others along demographic lines (e.g., military rank, gender, deployment status, age); this final feedback is provided to soldiers to help them better understand their scores. For example, a young soldier may score low on several of the dimensions and may not feel good about his or her performance, but the soldier may also learn that others in his or her age group scored similarly. Stated another way, this function provides perspective. Finally, we point out that soldiers are offered web links and phone numbers of behavioral health care providers should they wish to speak with a professional immediately upon receiving their scores.

Though feedback is provided along the four psychosocial dimensions of health, the GAT derives those scores based on 16 subscales. The emotional dimension consists of adaptability, good coping, bad coping, catastrophic thinking, character strengths, depression, optimism, positive affect, and negative affect. The family dimension is bifurcated as family satisfaction and family support. The social dimension consists of engagement, friendship, loneliness, and organization trust. The spiritual component of the GAT is treated as a unidimensional construct. A list of subscales, anchors, references, sample items, and reliabilities is provided in Table 9.1.

Master Resilience Trainer Course

MRTs deliver evidence-based resilience training to NCOs through a 10-day course. As discussed earlier, the MRT course is based on content from the PRP and other empirically validated training from the field of positive psychology. The course teaches resilience fundamentals and also teaches students how to teach these concepts to others. PRP skills make up the majority of the curriculum. However, the course also includes the application of these skills to the specific challenges of each phase of the deployment cycle and a review of personal and professional skills that maximize individual and unit performance; we encourage interested readers to review Greenberg's chapter in this volume (Chapter 7) for further discussion of resilience across the deployment cycle. The overarching goal of MRT training is to equip the force members with a set of skills that promote overall well-being and performance by better preparing them to handle challenges and adversity.

Key concepts underlying resilience have been studied since the 1970s, and research supports the notion that aspects of resilience can be taught (Seligman, 1990). The MRT course curriculum was developed in 2009 by the

TABLE 9.1
Scales and Constructs Measured by the Global Assessment Tool (GAT)

Dimension/ subscale	No. items	Scale range	Example question	Author(s)	Reliability estimates
Emotional fitness	77				$\alpha T_1 = .97$ $\alpha T_2 = .97$
Adaptability	3	1 = *Not like me at all* 5 = *Very much like me*	I can usually fit myself into any situation.	Developed by Professors C. Peterson and N. Park	$\alpha T_1 = .68$ $\alpha T_2 = .69$
Bad Coping	4	1 = *Not like me at all* 5 = *Very much like me*	I usually keep my emotions to myself.	Adapted by Professors C. Peterson and N. Park from previous research (e.g., Carver et al., 1989)	$\alpha T_1 = .70$ $\alpha T_2 = .71$
Good Coping	4	1 = *Not like me at all* 5 = *Very much like me*	When something stresses me out, I try to solve the problem.	Adapted by Professors C. Peterson and N. Park from previous research (e.g., Carver et al., 1989)	$\alpha T_1 = .85$ $\alpha T_2 = .88$
Catastrophizing	7	1 = *Not like me at all* 5 = *Very much like me*	When bad things happen to me, I expect more bad things to happen.	Adapted by Professors C. Peterson and N. Park from previous research (e.g., Peterson et al., 2001)	$\alpha T_1 = .78$ $\alpha T_2 = .81$
Character	24	0 = *Never* 5 = *Always*	Bravery or courage	Peterson (2007); Peterson & Seligman (2004)	$\alpha T_1 = .98$ $\alpha T_2 = .98$
Depression	10	1 = *Not at all* 5 = *Every day*	Feeling down, depressed, or hopeless	Kroenke et al. (2001); Spitzer et al. (1999)	$\alpha T_1 = .91$ $\alpha T_2 = .92$
Negative Affect	11	1 = *Never* 5 = *Most of the time*	Anxious/Nervous	Watson et al. (1988)	$\alpha T_1 = .79$ $\alpha T_2 = .81$
Positive Affect	10	1 = *Never* 5 = *Most of the time*	Joyful	Watson et al. (1988)	$\alpha T_1 = .89$ $\alpha T_2 = .91$
Optimism	4	1 = *Strongly disagree* 5 = *Strongly agree*	Overall, I expect more good things to happen to me than bad.	Scheier et al. (1994)	$\alpha T_1 = .74$ $\alpha T_2 = .74$

(continues)

TABLE 9.1

Scales and Constructs Measured by the Global Assessment Tool (GAT)   *(Continued)*

Dimension/subscale	No. items	Scale range	Example question	Author(s)	Reliability estimates
Family fitness	5				$\alpha T_1 = .76$ $\alpha T_2 = .78$
Family Satisfaction	2	1 = *Not at all satisfied* 5 = *Extremely satisfied*	How satisfied are you with your marriage/relationship?	Developed by the Directorate of Basic Combat Training's Experimentation and Analysis Element, Fort Jackson, SC	$\alpha T_1 = .79$ $\alpha T_2 = .81$
Family Support	3	1 = *Strongly disagree* 5 = *Strongly agree*	My family supports my decision to serve in the Army.	Developed by the Directorate of Basic Combat Training's Experimentation and Analysis Element, Fort Jackson, SC	$\alpha T_1 = .81$ $\alpha T_2 = .83$
Social fitness	18				$\alpha T_1 = .88$ $\alpha T_2 = .89$
Engagement	4	1 = *Not like me at all* 5 = *Very much like me*	I would choose my current work again if I had the chance.	Peterson et al. (2005); Wrzesniewski et al.(1997)	$\alpha T_1 = .84$ $\alpha T_2 = .84$
Friendship	6	0 = *No* 1 = *Yes*	I have someone to talk to when I feel down.	Developed by Professors C. Peterson and N. Park.	$\alpha T_1 = .66$ $\alpha T_2 = .69$
Loneliness	3	1 = *Never* 5 = *Most of the time*	How often do you feel close to people?	Russell (1996); Russell et al. (1978)	$\alpha T_1 = .76$ $\alpha T_2 = .78$
Organizational Trust	5	1 = *Strongly disagree* 5 = *Strongly agree*	Overall, I trust my immediate supervisor.	Mayer et al. (1995); Sweeney et al. (2009)	$\alpha T_1 = .88$ $\alpha T_2 = .89$
Spiritual fitness	5	1 = *Not like me at all* 5 = *Very much like me*	My life has lasting meaning.	Fetzer Institute/National Institute on Aging Working Group (1999)	$\alpha T_1 = .81$ $\alpha T_2 = .83$
Organizational context	35				
Transformational Leadership	14	1 = *Not at all* 5 = *Frequently, if not always*	Spends time teaching and coaching.	Avolio et al. (1995); Bass & Avolio (2000)	$\alpha T_1 = .97$ $\alpha T_2 = .98$
Unit Cohesion	21	1 = *Strongly disagree* 5 = *Strongly agree*	Soldiers in this unit have enough skills that I would trust them with my life in combat.	Adapted by Professors C. Peterson and N. Park from previous research (e.g., Griffith, 2002).	$\alpha T_1 = .97$ $\alpha T_2 = .98$

University of Pennsylvania in collaboration with U.S. Army personnel from the CSF program, the Walter Reed Army Institute of Research, and the U.S. Military Academy at West Point. The PRP curriculum (which serves as the foundation for the MRT course) focuses on a subset of the evidence-based protective factors that Masten and Reed (2002) identified as contributing to resilience: optimism, problem solving, self-efficacy, self-regulation, emotional awareness, and strong relationships. As the course was being adapted from PRP, specific emphasis was given to modifying the content for a military population. Modifications included identifying specific and unique aspects of military life and incorporating them into the program as case studies, examples, and practical exercises.

MRT was designed to serve as a program of instruction for mid-level NCOs and, in particular, drill and platoon sergeants. The rationale for targeting this audience was simple. Once trained, these NCOs would incorporate the CSF skills into their leadership style and also teach them to their soldiers. Data from PRP studies suggest that young adults (the group that junior soldiers overwhelmingly represent) benefit most from the skills included in this program (Brunwasser et al., 2009).

A key element of successful classroom-based training is an instructor who is motivated, demonstrates a good depth of knowledge, and has good communication skills. Unit leaders are directed to recommend that their top NCOs attend MRT training in order to ensure that the unit's MRT can effectively train these skills. These NCOs hold the rank of E6 or above (ideally in a leadership position), are in good standing, and demonstrate a willingness to serve as a resilience trainer. Additionally, they need to display the capability to effectively facilitate and lead small group instruction. Combat experience and college education are preferred, along with current or prior experience in trainer-type positions. Finally, MRTs should have at least 1 year remaining at their current duty station after completing MRT training. This ensures that they can return to their unit and effectively develop and execute an implementation plan for resilience training.

The first 5 days of the course introduce foundational elements of MRT. Instruction is given both in large-group plenary sessions and in smaller breakout sessions. The breakout sessions include group discussions, role-plays, and exercises that allow participants to apply and practice what they have learned in the larger plenary session. This deepens their understanding of the skills and prepares them to present the skills when they return to their units as certified resilience trainers. The next 3 days of the course focus on training the students how to teach these skills. Table 9.2 presents an overview of the foundational MRT course skills and the theoretical basis for each, as published in the psychological literature. For a more detailed description of these skills, see Reivich et al. (2011).

TABLE 9.2
Master Resilience Trainer (MRT) Skills and Theoretical Foundations

MRT skill	Description	Theoretical basis in the psychological literature
Activating event → thoughts → consequences	Identify thoughts about an activating event and the consequences of those thoughts.	Activating event → beliefs → consequences (Ellis, 1962)
Avoid thinking traps	Identify and correct counter-productive patterns in thinking through the use of critical questions.	Errors in logic (Beck, 1976; Burns, 1999; Ellis, 1962); explanatory style (Peterson & Seligman, 1984)
Detecting icebergs	Identify deep beliefs and core values that fuel out-of-proportion emotion and evaluate the accuracy and usefulness of these beliefs. Identify deep beliefs and core values that promote rejuvenation.	Underlying assumptions and core beliefs (Beck, 1976; Young, 1994)
Problem solving	Accurately identify what caused the problem and identify solution strategies.	Challenging beliefs (Beck, 1976; D'Zurilla & Goldfried, 1971); explanatory style (Peterson & Seligman, 1984)
Put it in perspective	Stop catastrophic thinking, reduce anxiety, and improve problem solving by identifying the worst, best, and most likely outcomes of a situation.	Decatastrophizing (Beck & Emery, 1985)
Mental games	Change the focus away from counterproductive thinking to enable greater concentration and focus on the task at hand.	Distraction techniques
Real-time resilience	Shut down counterproductive thinking to enable greater concentration and focus on the task at hand.	Externalization of voices (Burns, 1999; Freeman et al., 2004)
Character strengths	Identify strengths in yourself and others to improve teamwork and overcome challenges.	Character strengths (Peterson & Seligman, 2004)
Active constructive responding and praise	Respond to others with authentic, active, and constructive interest to build strong relationships. Give praise to build mastery and winning streaks.	Active constructive responding (Gable et al., 2004; Kamins & Dweck, 1999)

(continues)

TABLE 9.2
Master Resilience Trainer (MRT) Skills and Theoretical Foundations   *(Continued)*

MRT skill	Description	Theoretical basis in the psychological literature
Hunt the good stuff	Look for positive "good stuff" to counter the "negativity bias," to create positive emotion, and to notice and analyze what is good in your life.	Gratitude (Emmons, 2007)
Assertive communication	Communicate clearly and with respect, especially during conflict or challenge. Communicate in a confi-dent, clear, and controlled manner.	Assertive communication
Imagery; goal setting	Learn and engage a system-atic approach to achieving a personally meaningful outcome goal through the development of priorities and actions as well as the application of commitment and monitoring strategies.	Behavioral element of cogni-tive behavioral therapy (Beck, 1976); goal setting theory (Latham & Locke, 1991; Locke & Latham, 1990)
Energy management	Understand the roles of inter-mittent and chronic stress on performance as well as develop cognitive and behavioral techniques to both mobilize and restore energy effectively.	Sports psychology and stress management (Benson & Proctor, 1984)

Day 9 of the course focuses on applying MRT skills to situations that are in large part unique to a career in the military. This includes the application of these skills to the deployment cycle as well as to military leadership and family scenarios. The course concludes on Day 10 with a block of instruction that focuses on performance enhancement. This material is based on con-cepts derived from sports and performance psychology literature. Graduates of the 10-day MRT course are certified as Master Resilience Trainers and are awarded an Army Skill Identifier that is listed within the personnel files that follows soldiers throughout their careers. Course graduates receive a set of digital training materials and are instructed to work with their unit leadership to outline a resilience training plan. This includes identifying and scheduling time on the training calendar to teach a minimum of 2 hours of resilience training every quarter.

Comprehensive Resilience Modules

Upon completing the GAT, soldiers gain access via the Soldier Fitness Tracker to 24 online training modules, which CSF names Comprehensive Resilience Modules, or CRMs. These modules perform several tasks. First, they introduce the soldier to key concepts about resilience and psychological health. Second, they introduce the soldier to specific language used by MRTs, outlined in the previous section. Third, the modules target several simple skills that are later reinforced during didactic instruction led by the MRTs. As of this writing, the modules have been completed over 900,000 times, and over 160,000 soldiers have completed at least one module. Much of the training material for the modules was provided by a steering committee made up of respected scientists and psychologists, including John Cacioppo, Barbara Fredrickson, John and Julie Gottman, Ken Pargament, Karen Reivich, Martin Seligman, and others (see *American Psychologist*, 66(1) for a full listing).

The long-term strategy for the CRMs is to tailor a specific training package of modules to a soldier based on how he or she performs on the GAT. For example, a soldier who could improve on the social and emotion dimensions would receive a decidedly different group of modules than a soldier who could improve on the family and spiritual dimensions. This is critical insofar as CSF recognizes that the developmental needs of a new enlisted recruit are likely very different than those of a commissioned colonel who has 25 years of army experience. Stated another way, CSF hopes to meet the needs of the individual soldier rather than taking a one-size-fits-all approach to training, which is unfortunately quite common in the army. Admittedly, tailoring these distance training packages will take time; cut-off scores will have to be established, and more modules that cover the range of developmental needs will have to be built. CSF launched 12 additional modules in December 2011, and more are on the way.

Institutional Resilience Training

Institutional Resilience Training is CSF material taught in U.S. Army schools attended by soldiers throughout their military careers. Attending various professional development army courses, such as the Basic Noncommissioned Officer Course, the Officer Career Course, the Command and General Staff College, and the Sergeant Major Academy, ensures that emerging leaders are taught what they need to know in order to lead the different levels of the army organization. As part of CSF, these emerging leaders participate in resilience and psychological fitness training as they attend these schools.

As outlined in the introductory portion of this chapter, one goal of CSF is to serve as a change agent designed to shift the conversation across the army toward making psychological fitness every bit as important as physical fitness. Schein's (2004) work on organizational culture and change is critical to understanding why the Institutional Resilience Training serves as a cornerstone of the CSF program. If CSF serves as the embedding program that places focus on resilience and psychological fitness across the army, then the Institutional Resilience Training serves as a reinforcing mechanism because such training is designed to help these emerging leaders manage CSF training within their units. Here, apart from their unit culture, they not only learn CSF skills but also have group discussions about best practices toward making CSF an effective unit-led, unit-managed psychological fitness program. Upon graduation from school, these leaders fan out across the army and impart these best practices to the junior leaders and soldiers under their charge. Table 9.3 shows the schools where CSF is taught and the time spent doing so.

TABLE 9.3
Institutional Resilience Training

Target	School	Typical rank	Years in U.S. Army	Hours spent on CSF training
Officer	Reserve Officer Training Course (ROTC)/United States Military Academy (West Point)	Cadet	0 (done prior to commissioning)	4
Officer	Basic Officer Leader Course (BOLC)	2nd Lieutenant	<1	12
Officer	Captain's Career Course	Captain	4–6	2
Officer	Command and General Staff College	Major	9–11	2
Officer	Pre-Command Course (Battalion and Brigade)	Lieutenant Colonel and Colonel	16–22	1
Officer	Army War College	Colonel	>20	1
Enlisted	Basic Combat Training	Private	<1	2
Enlisted	Warrior Leaders Course	Specialist or Sergeant	2–5	3
Enlisted	Advanced Leaders Course	Staff Sergeant	5–10	2
Enlisted	Senior Leaders Course	Sergeant First Class	8–15	2
Enlisted	Sergeant Majors Academy	Sergeant Major	15–20	2
Enlisted	Pre-Command Course	Command Sergeant Major	15–20	1

Note. CSF = Comprehensive Soldier Fitness.

PROGRAM EVALUATION

As highlighted previously, though the 19 empirical studies and the meta-analysis suggest that the PRP is a somewhat effective program for children and young adults, those studies are no substitute for a proper program evaluation of CSF. As outlined by Lester, McBride, Bliese, and Adler (2011), CSF does have a robust program evaluation that involved eight brigade combat teams, or BCTs—the largest self-sustaining army formation typically sent to combat. Four of the BCTs received enough MRTs to have an MRT/soldier ratio of approximately 1/100 (96 total MRTs). Due to the throughput constraints of the MRT courses offered at the University of Pennsylvania, the Mobile Training Teams, and the course offered at Fort Jackson, South Carolina, many units were not high enough on the army's priority list to receive MRTs until the second or third year of training MRTs. As such, the CSF scientific staff created a "wait-list" control group of four BCTs.

Selection of BCTs was as random as possible, and the inclusion criteria simply stated that the units in each program evaluation group had to be similar. Therefore, three units in each group served a combat deployment over the length of the evaluation, and one BCT in each did not. One BCT in each group was permanently stationed outside the continental United States. All BCTs were from the combat arms in order to get a relatively similar complement of soldier skills (e.g., infantrymen, artillerymen, logisticians) and training and operational tempo (e.g., roughly the same amount of "field" vs. "garrison" time). At the outset, CSF intended to run an active program evaluation across 24 to 36 months, resulting in four to six data collection waves approximately 6 months apart. However, pressure from the BCT leadership who did not have MRTs convinced the CSF leadership to curtail the program evaluation significantly. As such, the design was shortened: Soldiers in each group were directed to take the GAT three times over a 15-month period. Further, the CSF leadership approved incorporating objective outcomes such as behavioral indicators, health care use, and attrition from the army into the analyses; however, access to these data would not granted until after the 15-month evaluation period ended, due to Department of the Army information technology policies.

Membership in the program evaluation team was tightly controlled to maximize objectivity in relation to conclusions about the assessment of the effectiveness of the CSF. Anyone who had a hand in developing components of the CSF training program (e.g., the University of Pennsylvania) or developing the GAT (e.g., the University of Michigan) would be excluded from the program evaluation team. Taking objectivity an additional step, CSF contracted with a civilian company and university outside of the army to analyze all data.

The critical question before the program evaluation team was simple: Does MRT training in operational army units lead to an increase in the self-report positive psychological states and a decrease in the negative psychological states measured by the GAT across time? The team recognized all of the limitations associated with self-report inventories (Hoyle, Harris, & Judd, 2002) but also recognized that the repeated measurement and longitudinal nature of the program evaluation would help keep some of these concerns in check.

Though the details of the results go beyond the scope of the current chapter, we can state that initial evidence suggests that MRT training is effective, even after controlling for the quality of unit leadership, unit cohesion, and a host of demographic variables—all of which easily could have influenced the results. As outlined by Seligman (2011b), when compared with soldiers who did not receive CSF training, soldiers who were trained by MRTs (a) have greater emotional fitness, (b) are more adaptable, (c) think in less catastrophic terms when faced with adversity, (d) employ their core character strengths more often, (e) have better coping skills, (f) are more optimistic, and (g) perceive the army as being more supportive of their family's needs. Further, there is no evidence that training provided by MRTs makes soldiers worse off than if they did not receive the training at all. As stated earlier, more on this program evaluation will be forthcoming in a technical report and peer-reviewed journal article.

CRITICISMS AND RESPONSE

A program of the nature and scope of CSF brings with it a cavalcade of criticism from the media and within the field of psychology. We welcome such criticism as a matter of course, because it provides CSF with opportunities to make the program better over time. Below, we address a few of the more recent criticisms.

As a Solution, CSF Targets an Ill-Defined Problem, and Therefore It Will Not Work

As outlined in this chapter, the "problem" facing the U.S. Army is a general lack of resilience—as suggested by the steep rise in a host of maladaptive behavioral patterns, such as suicide, violent crime, and illicit drug use. These maladaptive patterns are symptomatic of a larger problem below the surface of the army: that many soldiers lack psychological and physical fitness. Given this, we would characterize the problem facing the army as a well-defined one. Institutionally, the army has a choice: do nothing and wait for this lack of fitness to manifest into difficult-to-treat problems, take action before the problems manifest into treatable or untreatable diseases (e.g., the medical care model), or take action before the problems manifest at all (e.g., the preventive health model). Ultimately, CSF has adopted the latter approach—help ensure that those who are relatively healthy stay healthy and help those who are headed down a path toward pathology change their trajectory. Krueger (2011) suggested that such a win-win scenario simply will not work, because what is ultimately good for the organization (army) is not necessarily what is good for the individual (soldier). We take exception with such logic and suggest that both the army as an institution and the individual soldier may benefit from CSF. However, it is too soon to tell— especially since CSF is just now entering its third year of existence—how balanced the benefit will be between the army and the soldier.

Comprehensive Soldier Fitness Collects a Lot of Data on Soldiers, So It Must Be a Research Project

The purpose of collecting data from soldiers via the GAT is to provide a means for self-awareness and generate self-development of the individual soldier, not to drive a research agenda. Historical data are kept within the SFT database to provide each soldier with a historical perspective of how he or she performed on the GAT, and this view is provided on the results page following completion of the GAT. As has been previously reported (Lester et al., 2011; see also within this chapter), data are also used for program-evaluation purposes to determine the efficacy of the program.

Nevertheless, Eidelson et al. (2011) clearly disagreed and stated that "the CSF program is a massive research project. . . . No evidence was provided indicating that CSF received preliminary review by an independent ethics review board" (p. 643). Fortunately, this argument is indefensible because it is clear that Eidelson et al. failed to understand that an independent ethics review is not appropriate for an army-wide training program (Seligman, 2011b; U.S. Department of the Army, 1990). To put this criticism in perspective, the army does not convene an ethics review panel prior to releasing marksmanship training programs or physical fitness training programs—both of which, by army regulation, require that individual-level historical data be collected and maintained. Army Regulation 70-25 is quite clear: The definition of research cannot be extended to include "individual or group training of military personnel such as combat readiness, effectiveness, proficiency, or fitness exercises" (U.S. Department of the Army, 1990). Perhaps Seligman (2011b) said it best by pointing out that CSF

> has the same status as training programs that require all soldiers to attend classes about how to recognize signs of suicide and sexual harassment, to

do morning physical training, how to resist psychologically when cap-tured, or why to wear safety belts when driving. These programs do not require informed consent. (p. 646)

The Spiritual Dimension of CSF Is a Thinly Veiled Attempt to Press a Religious Agenda

The spiritual dimension of CSF is designed to help soldiers find pur-pose and meaning in life—to strengthen their human spirit—not to press a religious agenda. Phipps (2011), however, did not see it that way and stated,

> It is particularly sad to see [CSF] applied to human spirituality. . . . This manipulation of human spirituality for military purposes is more obscene than virtuous and is simply a New Age reworking of the ancient myth that has sent men to their death in battles for millennia—that God is on our side, not theirs. (p. 641)

This concern has been expressed elsewhere in the media (Leopold, 2011).

As a matter of policy, the army actively protects soldiers' religious free-dom; soldiers are able to practice their religion provided that doing so does not impinge on their job requirements. The army is careful not to endorse religion, and the stated mission of the U.S. Army's Chaplaincy is to provide "religious support to America's Army while assisting commanders in ensur-ing the right of free exercise of religion for all soldiers" (U.S. Department of the Army, 2011). Equally, soldiers are neither encouraged nor required to practice any religion at all, and many do not. Rather, CSF treats religion as but one potential pathway to improving quality of life. Further, CSF states in its training that some soldiers find comfort and derive great meaning from their religion, and others do not. Moreover, as discussed elsewhere in this volume, a great deal of both military and civilian research has shown that the ability to find meaning and purpose in one's life is associated with positive mental health outcomes. For example, research on hardiness has addressed this ability without specific regard to religion. Either way, soldiers are encouraged use a variety of vehicles outside of religion (e.g., meditation, interaction in social groups) to find a greater sense of purpose and meaning in their lives as soldiers.

Further, we must point out that the GAT is not a religious test, as some have inaccurately stated (Leopold, 2011). Although it is true that the GAT adapted items from the Brief Multidimensional Measure of Religiousness/ Spirituality (Fetzer Institute/National Institute of Aging Working Group, 1999), only items from the spiritual dimension were incorporated into the GAT taken by soldiers (see Table 9.1 for a sample item). The specific language of each question on the GAT—to include each spiritual fitness item—was vetted not only by our scientists but also independently by a team of attorneys from the U.S. Army's Office of the Judge Advocate General. Further, the feedback given to soldiers in no way suggests that their lack of spiritual fitness means that they are unfit to serve in the army. On the contrary, the feedback merely suggests that spiritual fitness may be an area where the soldiers could grow and develop if they deem spiritual fitness to be an area of psychological fitness on which they choose to work. Because both the army and the CSF respect the right of soldiers to place no emphasis on spiritual fitness at all, all training associated with the spiritual dimension is completed on a voluntary basis. Commands have been directed to ensure that such training be treated as entirely voluntary.

War Is Bad, CSF Helps Soldiers Fight War, So CSF Must Be Bad, Too

We concur that war is bad, and, frankly, we do not enjoy participating in it. In fact, all three of us have served in multiple theaters of war, and, at the extreme, Cornum survived a helicopter crash, bullet wounds, and being held as a prisoner of war (Cornum & Reed, 1993). Therefore, as both soldiers and scientists who have served in combat, we have a fairly solid understanding of both the theoretical and applied components of war, and as medical officers we have witnessed and experienced what war can do to the human psyche. Ask sane people who have experienced war firsthand and you will likely get the same response: They are in no hurry to experience it again.

Those who endorse the war = bad/CSF = bad logic (e.g., Dyckman, 2011; Eidelson et al., 2011; Phipps, 2011) miss a key point about CSF's training regimen. At no time does CSF training delve into turning soldiers into storm troopers or "making someone feel good about killing someone else," as Dyckman (2011, p. 644) suggested. Combat is but one of many contexts that soldiers may or may not face in their army careers. There is not a single skill taught in the CSF training regimen that is specified for use in combat only. Rather, the training is viewed from a more global perspective—like cognitive behavioral therapy (Beck, 1986)—as applicable in all aspects of soldier life. Take, for example, the Active Constructive Responding (ACR; Gable, Reis, Impett, & Asher, 2004; Kamins & Dweck, 1999) module taught to soldiers by MRTs. Here, the MRT focuses on how to employ ACR to strengthen relationships with spouses, friends, and significant others. The MRT typically explains how ACR works, how to do it, and how to teach others to do the same. Perhaps a question is presented by one of the soldiers participating in the training about ACR's use in combat, and the MRT responds by discussing the challenges of employing ACR in long-distance relationships where the primary means of communication is the telephone or e-mail.

"We" Should Focus on Primary Prevention of PTSD Rather Than Look to CSF as Secondary Prevention

Phipps (2011) especially took issue with the notion that members of the psychological field are helping the army develop the CSF program. In particular, he stated that "a true positive psychology should be primarily addressed to eradicating the disease of war, not supporting those who fight it" (Phipps, 2011, p. 642). Here, the notion of primary prevention of PTSD implies that the traumatic event should be altogether avoided in order to prevent the subsequent pathology. And, by extension, doing so means that war should be avoided, or, at a minimum, perhaps people should not volunteer to participate. Krueger (2011) correctly pointed out that "war, by definition, can only be waged if the individual makes a sacrifice for the group. The soldier accepts the risk of being wounded, killed, or captured for the prospect of his or her group overcoming another" (p. 642). His point about acceptance of risk is especially true in the U.S. Army, given that the draft ended decades ago and the army has long since been an all volunteer force.

Nevertheless, laypeople often fail to understand that soldiers neither write nor endorse national policy. Rather, soldiers implement it (Huntington, 1981). And if the national policy is to go to war, then soldiers will go. All of us—laypeople and soldiers—may debate the value, ethics, and justness of war writ large. Furthermore, we may debate the judgment of young people, socioeconomic status and education of people who join the military in general, their patriotism relative to others', and other factors that may or may not influence enlistment decisions. However, to portray soldiers as unaware pawns, as some have recently done, is simply disingenuous. Soldiers are quite intelligent, and they understand that by joining the army they may be required to serve in combat, be exposed to trauma, or be killed.

When taken together, we posit, CSF is philosophically grounded in a reality informed by law, history, and empirical evidence. First, our laws suggest to us that, at least at the organizational/army level, primary prevention will not work simply because those of us who are leaders within the army are not the same leaders who decide to send the army to war. Army senior leaders do shape, weigh, and present both military and diplomatic options toward solving crises, but ultimately the president of the United States is the leader who decides to send the army to combat. Second, our history tells us that we as mankind have failed in "eradicating the disease of war" (Phipps, 2011, p. 642); the United States has engaged in armed conflict in every decade since the 1940s. As such, it would be foolish not to prepare for future conflicts. Third, the empirical evidence suggests that programs such as CSF might be an effective way to better prepare people for soldier life, which includes the stresses and strains of serving in combat. Given these facts, it follows that secondary prevention strategies such as CSF are more viable and proactive than primary prevention, the out-of-reach alternative. Stated another way, though those of us serving in the army should hope for and work toward peace, we also have a duty to prepare for war and further have a duty to prepare those soldiers in our charge for whatever may come their way.

THE WAY AHEAD

CSF has accomplished the initial goals assigned to it. First, the team developed a rapid assessment of each individual's psychological assets, the GAT, in four important domains (emotional, social, family, and spiritual). The scores on the assessment are significantly correlated with objective outcomes, both positive and negative, that are of great interest to the army. This provides strong evidence that psychological fitness is indeed both measurable and important. Second, the team developed a training program for NCOs and junior officers, the MRT program, that allows first-line supervisors and leaders to teach the thinking, communication, and decision-making skills that will improve psychological fitness and performance. Third, in conjunction with the Training and Doctrine Command, we developed some programs of instruction dealing with "resilience" in every leader development school, officer and enlisted. Last, by integrating multiple databases across the army, the team showed that having MRTs doing training in operational units does indeed measurably improve the psychological health of the force. CSF works.

But, much remains to be done that could significantly improve the overall fitness and functioning of the force. In the next few months, soldiers doing their annual GAT will also receive a physical score, based on the information they provided on the periodic health assessment, the results of their annual Army Physical Fitness Test, and lab results and measurements extracted from the medical record. They will get feedback on these results and suggestions for improvements, just as they currently do following the scoring of the psychological domains. The addition of simultaneously assessing psychological and physical health will help to define the relationship between them in a healthy, as opposed to a clinical, military population. Analysis may show, for example, that psychological fitness training has a greater effect on body fat or run time than does more physical therapy or meetings with a dietician.

The current process of teaching these important thinking, communication, and decision-making skills by MRTs is not the optimal way to ensure that these vital skills reside in every soldier. As the value of psychological skills training becomes more apparent to everyone, a strategy to fully embed them into both pre-accession and initial military training, both officer and enlisted, would be most beneficial. The Army National Guard has been the most aggressive in using the "GAT for Trainees" and teaching resilient thinking as part of the required pre-accession training. CSF is working with the recruiting command to increase the MRT population of recruiters; the typical ratio of MRT to soldiers is insufficient in this high-stress, geographically distributed force.

Teaching the MRT skills as a stand-alone process, resulting in an additional skill identifier, is not the best approach when in fact these are skills and knowledge that every member of the force needs. We believe that eventually, as the number of MRTs in initial military training goes up and the skills are embedded more and more into everyday training, every soldier will have had skills training by the time he or she is sergeant or first lieutenant. Then, MRT training could be much shorter, and it could focus on training these junior leaders how to use the skills and teach and reinforce them with their subordinates.

A large gap is getting family members, adult and children, to embrace learning resilience skills in a proactive, preventive manner. Soldiers are directed to do the assessment and training, but family members must volunteer. To date, the participation of family members taking the GAT and taking training, either online or with MRTs provided by the Army Community Service, has been less than 1%. In general, family members come when there is some crisis in their lives, which is the worst time to try to learn and practice new skills. Ways must be found to incentivize family members to build their psychological tool kit before they need it, and the CSF staff is working to identify better ways to reach army families.

We have often been asked, "Will CSF go Joint?" In some ways it already has. On September, 1, 2011, the Chairman of the Joint Chiefs of Staff (CJCS) signed a letter of instruction (CJCSI 3405.01) to the entire force, requiring each service to develop and institute a Total Force Fitness (TFF) framework and program, and CSF lexicon and references are prominent within the document. The five dimensions of strength recognized by CSF fit neatly within the eight domains of fitness described by the TFF instruction. Further, the chairman's instruction emphasizes the need not just of having a program but of having metrics to determine whether the program is accomplishing the intent. Moreover, the U.S. Air Force's Air Combat Command began sending airmen to MRT training in 2010, and in May 2011, the chief of staff of the U.S. Air Force directed the establishment of a Comprehensive Airmen Fitness program across the air force. Comprehensive Airmen Fitness is being instituted in a uniquely air force way, but there are more similarities than differences. A small number of navy and U.S. Marine Corps NCOs and officers have attended the MRT course; these services are in the process of deciding how to accomplish the chairman's intent of TFF. The SFT, which is the software environment that delivers the GAT and the online modules and that tracks completions, already has opening pages for each of the other services, complete with their logo and separate URL, should they want to see the fitness of their own service members without investing millions of dollars and years of development.

REFERENCES

Avolio, B. J., Bass, B. M., & Jung, D. I. (1995). *Multifactor Leadership Questionnaire: Technical report*. Redwood City, CA: Mind Garden.

Bass, B. M., & Avolio, B. J. (2000). *MLQ Multifactor Leadership Questionnaire: Technical report*. Redwood City, CA: Mind Garden.

Beck, A. T. (1976). *Cognitive therapy and the emotional disorders*. New York, NY: International Universities Press.

Beck, A. T. (1986). *Cognitive therapy and the emotional disorders*. New York, NY: International Universities Press.

Beck, A. T., & Emery, G. D. (1985). *Anxiety disorders and phobias: A cognitive perspective*. New York, NY: Basic Books.

Benson, H., & Proctor, H. (1984). *Beyond the relaxation response*. New York, NY: Berkley.

Brunwasser, S. M., Gillham, J., & Kim, E. (2009). A meta-analytic review of the Penn Resiliency Program's effect on depressive symptoms. *Journal of Consulting and Clinical Psychology, 77*, 1042–1054. doi:10.1037/a0017671

Burns, D. D. (1999). *Feeling good*. New York, NY: HarperCollins.

Carver, C. S., Scheier, M. F., & Weintraub, J. K. (1989). Assessing coping strategies: A theoretically based approach. *Journal of Personality and Social Psychology, 56*, 267–283. doi:10.1037/0022-3514.56.2.267

Challen, A., Noden, P., West, A., & Machin, S. (2009). *U.K. Resilience Programme evaluation: Interim report* (Research Report No. DCSF-RR094). London, England: Department for Children, Schools and Families.

Cornum, R., & Copeland, P. (1993). *She went to war*. Novato, CA: Presidio Press.

Cornum, R., & Lester, P. (2012). Comprehensive Soldier Fitness: Why and why now? In J. H. Laurence & M. D. Matthews (Eds.), *The Oxford handbook of military psychology* (pp. 4–14). New York, NY: Oxford University Press.

Dyckman, J. (2011). Exposing the glosses in Seligman and Fowler's (2011) straw-man arguments. *American Psychologist, 66*, 644–645. doi:10.1037/a0024932

D'Zurilla, T. J., & Goldfried, M. R. (1971). Problem solving and behavior modification. *Journal of Abnormal Psychology, 78*, 107–126. doi:10.1037/h0031360

Eidelson, R., Pilisuk, M., & Soldz, S. (2011). The dark side of Comprehensive Soldier Fitness. *American Psychologist, 66*, 643–644. doi:10.1037/a0025272

Ellis, A. (1962). *Reason and emotion in psychotherapy*. Secaucus, NJ: Citadel Press.

Emmons, R. A. (2007). *Thanks! How the new science of gratitude can make you happier.* New York, NY: Springer.

Fetzer Institute/National Institute on Aging Working Group. (1999). *Multidimensional measurement of religiousness/spirituality for use in health research: A report of the Fetzer Institute/National Institute on Aging Working Group.* Kalamazoo, MI: Fetzer Institute.

Fravell, M., Nasser, K., & Cornum, R. (2011). The Soldier Fitness Tracker. *American Psychologist, 66,* 73–76. doi:10.1037/a0021632

Freeman, A., Pretzer, J., Fleming, B., & Simon, K. M. (2004). *Clinical applications of cognitive therapy* (2nd ed.). New York, NY: Kluwer Academic.

Gable, S. L., Reis, H. T., Impett, E. T., & Asher, E. R. (2004). What do you do when things go right? The intrapersonal and interpersonal benefits of sharing positive events. *Journal of Personality and Social Psychology, 87,* 228–245. doi:10.1037/0022-3514.87.2.228

Gillham, J. E., Hamilton, J., Freres, D. R., Patton, K., & Gallop, R. (2006). Preventing depression among early adolescents in the primary care setting: A randomized controlled study of the Penn Resiliency Program. *Journal of Abnormal Child Psychology, 34,* 203–219. doi:10.1007/s10802-005-9014-7

Gillham, J. E., Reivich, K. J., Freres, D. R., Chaplin, T. M., Shatte, A. J., Samuels, B., . . . Seligman, M. E. P. (2007). School-based prevention of depressive symptoms: A randomized controlled study of the effectiveness and specificity of the Penn Resiliency Program. *Journal of Consulting and Clinical Psychology, 75,* 9–19. doi:10.1037/0022-006X.75.1.9

Gillham, J. E., Reivich, K. R., Jaycox, L. H., & Seligman, M. E. P. (1995). Prevention of depressive symptoms in schoolchildren: Two-year follow-up. *Psychological Science, 6,* 343–351. doi:10.1111/j.1467-9280.1995.tb00524.x

Grier, T., Knapik, J. J., Canada, S., Canham-Chervak, M., & Jones, B. H. (2010). Tobacco use prevalence and factors associated with tobacco use in new U.S. Army personnel. *Journal of Addictive Diseases, 29,* 284–293. doi:10.1080/1055 0887.2010.489445

Griffith, J. (2002). Multilevel analysis of cohesion's relation to stress, well-being, identification, disintegration, and perceived combat readiness. *Military Psychology, 14,* 217–239.

Hoyle, R., Harris, M., & Judd, C. (2002). *Research methods in social relations.* New York, NY: Wadsworth.

Huntington, S. (1981). *The soldier and the state: The theory and politics of civil–military relations.* Boston, MA: Belknap Press.

Kamins, M. L., & Dweck, C. S. (1999). Person versus process praise and criticism: Implications for contingent self-worth and coping. *Developmental Psychology, 35,* 835–847. doi:10.1037/0012-1649.35.3.835

Kroenke, K., Spitzer, R. L., & Williams, J. B. W. (2001). The PHQ 9: Validity of a brief depression severity measure. *Journal of General Internal Medicine, 16,* 606–613. doi:10.1046/j.1525-1497.2001.016009606.x

Krueger, J. I. (2011). Shock without awe. *American Psychologist, 66*, 642–643. doi:10.1037/a0025080

Lacy, B. W., Ditzler, T. F., Wilson, R. S., Martin, T. M., Ochikubo, J. T., Roussel, R. R., . . . Vazquez, R. (2008). Regional methamphetamine use among U.S. Army personnel stationed in the continental United States and Hawaii: A six-year retrospective study (2000–2005). *Military Medicine, 173*, 353–358.

Lande, R. G., Marin, D. A., Chang, A. S., & Lande, G. R. (2008). Survey of alcohol use in the U.S. Army. *Journal of Addictive Diseases, 27*, 115–121. doi:10.1080/10550880802122711

Latham, G. P., & Locke, E. A. (1991). Self-regulation through goal setting. *Organizational Behavior and Human Decision Processes, 50*, 212–247. doi:10.1016/0749-5978(91)90021-K

Leopold, J. (2011). *Army's "spiritual fitness" test comes under fire*. Retrieved from http://www.truth-out.org/armys-fitness-test-designed-psychologist-who-inspired-cias-torture-program-under-fire66577

Lester, P. B., McBride, S., Bliese, P. D., & Adler, A. B. (2011). Bringing science to bear: An empirical assessment of the Comprehensive Soldier Fitness program. *American Psychologist, 66*, 77–81. doi:10.1037/a0022083

Locke, E. A., & Latham, G. P. (1990). *A theory of goal setting and task performance.* Englewood Cliffs, NJ: Prentice Hall.

Masten, A. S., & Reed, M. G. (2002). Resilience in development. In C. R. Snyder & S. J. Lopez (Eds.), *The handbook of positive psychology* (pp. 74–88). New York, NY: Oxford University Press.

Mayer, R. C., Davis, J. H., & Schoorman, F. D. (1995). An integrative model of organizational trust. *Academy of Management Review, 20*, 709–734.

Milliken, C. S., Auchterlonie, J. L., & Hoge, C. W. (2007). Longitudinal assessment of mental health problems among active and reserve component soldiers returning from the Iraq war. *JAMA, 298*, 2141–2148. doi:10.1001/jama.298.18.2141

Peterson, C. (2007). *Brief Strengths Test*. Cincinnati, OH: VIA Institute.

Peterson, C., Bishop, M. P., Fletcher, C. W., Kaplan, M. R., Yesko, E. S., Moon, C. H., . . . Michaels, A. J. (2001). Explanatory style as a risk factor for traumatic mishaps. *Cognitive Therapy and Research, 25*, 633–649. doi:10.1023/A:1012945120821

Peterson, C., Park, N., & Castro, C. (2011). Assessment for the U.S. Army Comprehensive Soldier Fitness program. *American Psychologist, 66*, 10–18. doi:10.1037/a0021658

Peterson, C., Park, N., & Seligman, M. E. P. (2005). Orientations to happiness and life satisfaction: The full life versus the empty life. *Journal of Happiness Studies, 6*, 25–41. doi:10.1007/s10902-004-1278-z

Peterson, C., & Seligman, M. E. P. (1984). Causal explanations as a risk factor for depression: Theory and evidence. *Psychological Review, 91*, 347–374. doi:10.1037/0033-295X.91.3.347

Peterson, C., & Seligman, M. E. P. (2004). *Character strengths and virtues: A handbook and classification*. Washington, DC: American Psychological Association.

Phipps, S. (2011). Positive psychology and war: An oxymoron. *American Psychologist, 66*, 641–642. doi:10.1037/a0024933

Reivich, K., & Shatte, A. (2002). *The resilience factor: Seven essential skills for overcoming life's inevitable obstacles*. New York, NY: Broadway Books.

Reivich, K., Shatte, A., & Gillham, J. (2003). *Penn resilience training for college students: Leader's guide and participant's guide*. Unpublished manuscript, University of Pennsylvania.

Reivich, K. J., Seligman, M. E. P., & McBride, S. (2011). Master Resilience Training in the U.S. Army. *American Psychologist, 66*, 25–34. doi:10.1037/a0021897

Russell, D., Peplau, L. A., & Ferguson, M. L. (1978). Developing a measure of loneliness. *Journal of Personality Assessment, 42*, 290–294.

Russell, D. W. (1996). UCLA Loneliness Scale (Version 3): Reliability, validity, and factor structure. *Journal of Personality Assessment, 66*, 20–40. doi:10.1207/s15327752jpa6601_2

Scheier, M. F., Carver, C. C., & Bridges, M. W. (1994). Distinguishing optimism from neuroticism (and trait anxiety, self-mastery, and self-esteem): A reevaluation of the Life Orientation Test. *Journal of Personality and Social Psychology, 67*, 1063–1078. doi: 10.1037/0022-3514.67.6.1063

Schein, E. (2004). *Organizational culture and leadership* (3rd ed.). San Francisco, CA: Jossey-Bass.

Seligman, M. E. P. (1990). *Learned optimism*. New York, NY: Knopf.

Seligman, M. E. P. (2011a). *Flourish: A visionary new understanding of happiness and well-being*. New York, NY: Free Press.

Seligman, M. E. P. (2011b). Helping American soldiers in time of war: Reply to comments on the Comprehensive Soldier Fitness special issue. *American Psychologist, 66*, 646–647. doi:10.1037/a0025156

Spitzer, R. L., Kroenke, K., Williams, J. B. W., and the Patient Health Questionnaire Primary Care Study Group. (1999). Validation and utility of a self-report version of PRIME-MD: The PHQ primary care study. *JAMA, 282*, 1787–1788. doi:10.1001/jama.282.18.1737

Sweeney, P. J., Thompson, V., & Blanton, H. (2009). Trust and influence in combat: An interdependence model. *Journal of Applied Social Psychology, 39*, 235–264. doi:10.111/j.1559-1816.2008.00437.x

U.S. Department of the Army. (1990). Army Regulation 70-25: Use of volunteers as subjects of research. Retrieved from http://armypubs.army.mil/epubs/pdf/R70_25.PDF

U.S. Department of the Army. (2010). *Army health promotion, risk reduction, suicide prevention report 2010*. Retrieved from http://www.armyg1.army.mil/hr/suicide/docs/commanders%20tool%20Kit/HPRRSP_Report_2010_v00.pdf

U.S. Department of the Army. (2011). *Mission of the U.S. Army Chaplaincy*. Retrieved from http://www.army.mil/info/organization/chaplaincy/

Watson, D., Clark, L. A., & Tellegen, A. (1988). Development and validation of brief measures of positive and negative affect: The PANAS scales. *Journal of Personality and Social Psychology, 54*, 1063–1070. doi:10.1037/0022-3514-54.6.1063

World Health Organization. (1948). Preamble to the Constitution of the World Health Organization as adopted by the International Health Conference, New York, June 19–22, 1946, and entered into force on April 7, 1948. Retrieved from http://whqlibdoc.who.int/hist/official_records/constitution.pdf

Wrzesniewski, A., McCauley, C., Rozin, P., & Schwartz, B. (1997). Jobs, careers, and callings: People's relations to their work. *Journal of Research in Personality, 31*, 21–33.

Young, J. E. (1994). *Cognitive therapy for personality disorders: A schema-focused approach* (2nd ed.). Sarasota, FL: Professional Resource Press.

III

MILITARY RESILIENCE: CONCLUSIONS AND FUTURE DIRECTIONS

10

RESILIENCE IN A MILITARY OCCUPATIONAL HEALTH CONTEXT: DIRECTIONS FOR FUTURE RESEARCH

AMY B. ADLER

The concept of resilience reflects a fundamental optimism, a belief that although we experience demands that are a challenge, we are capable of responding positively or rebounding quickly from these demands. The concept also reflects an emphasis on success, the belief that by encouraging, training, and promoting resilience, a desirable outcome can be facilitated in terms of mental health, functioning, and performance.

Focusing on resilience also reflects what most people are predisposed to avoid. Most people don't want to falter significantly under stress; they don't want to suffer, and they don't want to fail in functioning at work or at home.

This chapter was authored by an employee of the Department of Defense, U.S. Walter Reed Army Institute of Research as part of official duty and is considered to be in the public domain. Any views expressed herein do not necessarily represent the views of the United States government, and the author's participation is not meant to serve as an official endorsement.
http://dx.doi.org/10.1037/14190-010
Building Psychological Resilience in Military Personnel: Theory and Practice, R. R. Sinclair and T. W. Britt (Editors)

Perhaps underlying this emphasis on resilience is the expectation, realistic or otherwise, that many demands cannot be minimized. Demands are presumed to be here to stay, and it is presumed worthwhile to build up resilience in order to enhance positive adaptation.

This perspective is echoed in the chapters in this volume on resilience in military personnel. Each chapter emphasizes the importance of resilience and the various factors that can be used to sustain and enhance resilience in service members. The chapters cover a range of related topics, from measuring and defining resilience to identifying predictors of resilience and from the role of leadership to training service members across the deployment cycle. In general, the chapters target individual resilience and address a wide range of variables that can influence the development and maintenance of resilience for service members and their families.

THE OCCUPATIONAL CONTEXT

One of the key themes in this book is that the occupational context is important to consider in understanding the resilience construct or in implementing resilience-focused interventions. Individuals have to respond to stressors that occur as part of their training and participation in a particular job, and being able to respond effectively to these demands can help benefit productivity as well as worker well-being. For high-risk occupations such as the military, the question of resilience is particularly critical in terms of operational effectiveness and service member psychological adjustment. To understand the unique contributions of the occupational context to the topic of resilience, one must examine several assumptions.

First, high-risk occupations such as the military have an explicit emphasis on resilience. In these occupations, being physically and psychologically resilient is a requirement for employment that is integrated into entry-level training regimens. In the army, for example, basic training requires individuals to demonstrate their ability to withstand rigorous physical and psychological demands.

Second, these occupations use core values and language that reflect resilience as central to organizational identity. For example, "personal courage" is one of the U.S. Army's core values, and the slogan "Army Strong" was introduced in U.S. Army advertising in 2006. The language is also embedded in mission statements and creeds, as exemplified by the Soldier's Creed. It states, "I will never accept defeat. I will never quit. I will never leave a fallen comrade. I am disciplined, physically and mentally tough." Including resilience-related words in the language of slogans and creeds demonstrates how resilience is embedded across the military.

Third, the military reinforces resilience. For example, the military conveys the message that resilience is valued by rewarding resilient behavior, formally recognizing individuals who demonstrate resilient performance under difficult conditions. Military leaders also establish a climate in which individual resilience in arduous circumstances is a norm. Phrases such as "embrace the suck" illustrate how the military describes the expectation that service members will encounter difficulties and succeed.

Fourth, individuals who join high-risk occupations such as the military expect some degree of challenging demands, and some may even welcome these demands as a way to test their skills or use their training in the context of an important mission. This positive approach to testing personal strength is particularly relevant for service members who want to join elite units (e.g., Special Forces). Thus, resilience is not just something valued by the larger organization. It is also valued by many of the individuals joining the organization, who want the opportunity to prove themselves and to test their capacity to perform under high-stress conditions. Recruits are not passive recipients of the resilience ethic but active participants who have chosen the military lifestyle (McGurk, Cotting, Britt, & Adler, 2006).

Fifth, the military organization may specifically train individuals to build their resilience. This training can be both direct and indirect. In terms of direct training, the military provides service members with tough and realistic scenarios that provide individuals with an opportunity to perform under difficult conditions. This training can lead to a sense of mastery, which, in turn, can increase feelings of self-efficacy. In terms of indirect training, the military organization can provide service members with explicit information and practice in using resilience-building techniques. In the case of the U.S. Army's Comprehensive Soldier Fitness program, for example, individuals are trained in fundamental resilience skills (Cornum, Matthews, & Seligman, 2011) and are provided specific resilience-based education related to deployments (e.g., Adler, Bliese, McGurk, Hoge, & Castro, 2009).

Direct and indirect resilience training can also be supplemented through organizational resources such as teams, leaders, and policies. Teams are typically an important dimension to building resilience in a high-risk occupation. Teams establish a norm for resilient behavior, and they ensure potential access to social support. This access is important because it facilitates a fundamental resilience skill, seeking social support in times of need. In turn, these teams give individuals the chance to provide social support to others on their team. Teams, or in some cases peers, can also provide an important role in terms of identifying individuals in need of additional mental health assessment (Greenberg & Jones, 2011).

Leaders are another critical asset for facilitating resilience. Several studies have demonstrated that unit-level leadership is associated with the ability of individuals to withstand the demands of difficult work conditions. For example, in a study of combat exposure, soldiers who were exposed to combat stress were less reactive in terms of mental health problems when their unit reported good leadership (e.g., Bliese, Adler, & Castro, 2011; Mental Health Advisory Team IV, 2006).

Finally, organizational policies have the potential to promote resilience. These policies can include training requirements that prioritize resilience, such as the U.S. Army's Comprehensive Soldier Fitness initiative (e.g., Casey, 2011), and policies that reinforce the need for respite between high-stress missions. For example, the United Kingdom's harmony guidelines establish a minimum amount of time needed between deployments for military personnel (cf. Rona et al., 2007). Policies can also provide support to military families. In the case of the United States, for example, supports for military families include resilience training, couples training around the deployment cycle, marital retreats, and rear detachment support.

It is important to note that just as peer support, leadership, and policies can promote resilience, they can also undermine resilience. For example, assessments of leadership ratings in U.S. Army units demonstrate natural variability in leadership ability (Bliese, 2006). When leadership quality is measured, there is typically a range of scores from high to low. This range indicates that the military organization may inadvertently tolerate poor leadership (i.e., some units rate their leaders as relatively low in leadership quality). Indeed, studies are able to demonstrate the association of good social climate and leadership with positive outcomes only because there is a range of leadership quality to measure (e.g., Bliese, 2006; Wright et al., 2009). Thus, although the organization may actively try to ensure that units have good-quality leadership, there is still some natural variability that can impact unit and individual resilience.

Another way in which a military organization may inadvertently undermine resilience is through a disproportionate focus on short-term performance as a mark of resilience. That is, it may be that although individuals are able to perform under duress in the short term, they still experience longer term negative effects on mental health (e.g., Adler, Wright, Bliese, Eckford, & Hoge, 2008). Unless these longer term outcomes are assessed and the organization addresses the impact of stressors on both short- and long-term outcomes, resilience may not be adequately understood or supported. Besides being measured over a longer term, outcomes associated with resilience should be considered from a broad perspective in terms of domain. From an organizational perspective, these outcomes may at first be focused on performance, but long-term health outcomes are also essential markers of resilience. Other markers such as attrition and organizational citizenship behaviors may also be important to consider.

Thus, the military needs to consider factors that build individual and team resilience and factors that detract from resilience. Before launching an aggressive resilience-building strategy, however, the organization needs to consider how focusing on resilience can potentially have a negative impact on service members.

A SHADOW SIDE TO RESILIENCE

Despite the importance of promoting resilience across the military, an unquestioning allegiance to resilience has the potential to become self-defeating for a military organization. The underlying assumptions about resilience and the organizational context described above can be misapplied such that they undermine the very resilience they are designed to sustain. Although resilience is not often talked about in this way, it is important to examine the ways in which resilience can be perceived as having a shadow side. There is little empirical evidence demonstrating this shadow, or negative, side of resilience; however, these potential concerns still must be confronted to minimize their influence.

Although resilience is valued and reinforced in the military, the military can also inadvertently convey the message that faltering in the face of profound stressors signals a lack of resilience. If a lack of resilience is perceived as a larger characterological flaw that is inconsistent with the organization's values, it can become a source of stigma. Even though the definition of resilience explicitly acknowledges that individuals will likely experience a dip in functioning following a significant stressor and thus need to bounce back from this stressor, the depth and duration of this dip are not specified. In the absence of other criteria, the dip is likely to be interpreted as short-lived. Any prolonged dip could potentially signal a lack of resilience and be stigmatized by the group, just as behavioral health problems are stigmatized (Greene-Shortridge, Britt, & Castro, 2007). This stigma can then negatively impact service members if it impedes their willingness to admit to having problems or if it affects the way in which they are regarded by the group. Stigma can then negatively impact an organization's readiness if the organization underestimates the mental health impact of stressors on service members and does not prepare commensurate services and support.

Similarly, if an individual does seek professional help for psychological problems, negative reactions of the unit, the leaders, or the organization can fuel the inadvertent negative side to resilience. For example, if an individual seeks help for a mental health problem, that individual may not be regarded as being as resilient as someone who does not seek help. Service members may perceive negative consequences to treatment seeking, whether in terms of not being trusted by peers or leadership or of career implications (e.g., Gould et al., 2010; Hoge et al., 2004). Thus, positive messages about seeking behavioral health care could get lost amid the enthusiasm of embracing the concept of resilience. In the absence of a concerted information campaign, there is a potential risk for stigma associated with having mental health problems and seeking mental health care to be strengthened when resilience is the primary focus. Still, not all resilience training leads to an increase in stigma; in fact, if stigma is directly addressed, military mental health training (arguably a type of resilience training) can actually reduce concerns about stigma (e.g., Adler et al., 2009).

Another potential problem with focusing on resilience is that assuming external demands are immovable may detract from efforts to reduce these demands. As stated previously, one of the fundamental expectations in understanding resilience in the military is that real-world requirements, such as deployments and combat experiences, are external demands that cannot necessarily be minimized. In addition, some of these demands, such as coming under enemy fire or having a battle buddy be a casualty, may be determined by other forces and be designed to tax service member resilience in the extreme. However, to what extent are other demands associated with the operational context, such as difficult sleeping conditions or extra assignments/taskings, able to be reduced? If the organization focuses only on the responsibility of the individual to be more resilient, this can unintentionally suggest that stressors are immutable. In turn, leaders may be less likely to first examine whether these demands can be reduced or even eliminated. To some extent, this concern is largely theoretical. For example, the military has already addressed the concerns of multiple deployments by increasing the length of time between deployments. In addition, good leaders routinely assess whether a particular mission is worth the risk. Still, the organizational mind-set of emphasizing individual resilience has the potential to result in less effort in reducing unnecessary demands.

Another shadow side to focusing on resilience is that the discussion typically neglects the concept of a limit to resilience. Although resilience is a positive construct and is associated with positive outcomes, it is important to consider that all individuals have a limit to what they can tolerate. Without expressly acknowledging this limit, to what extent is the military organization setting up individuals to have unrealistic expectations about what they should be able to tolerate? To what extent will this approach make it difficult for individuals to accept or acknowledge their own reactions? Indeed, studies have identified acceptance of emotional experiences as a key variable in predicting long-term outcomes (e.g., Baer, Smith, Hopkins, Krietemeyer, & Toney, 2006), but this acceptance can potentially be obstructed if messages about resilience discourage recognition of the darker sides of trauma.

Similarly, if a limit is not acknowledged, to what extent are individuals who encounter that limit likely to engage in self-blame either for failing to have the requisite "right stuff" or for not being sufficiently motivated? Critical (negative) self-talk has also been associated with negative outcomes in several studies (e.g., Mental Health Advisory Team VI, 2009), and such self-blame is not likely to benefit an individual or the military organization. Although service members with combat experience may know from personal experience that all individuals have their limits, realistic limits of resilience should be explicitly acknowledged—or at least the impact of this acknowledgment should be studied to determine recommendations for best practice.

As with many well-meaning interventions, there is the potential for negative outcomes to inadvertently emerge from resilience training intervention programs, and, under ideal conditions, research should be conducted on these interventions with the relevant population and not just adapted from the civilian literature. Such research can empirically examine whether negative outcomes increase as a result of resilience initiatives. Training itself can also anticipate the shadow side of resilience and incorporate these potential concerns into the training material as a way to clarify messages about resilience that the organization wants to convey.

THE WAY AHEAD: THE RESILIENCE AGENDA

Given these caveats, it is important to go beyond a standard conceptualization of resilience when establishing priorities in the military context for the next generation of resilience building and research. First, although positive psychology has much to tell us, there are limits to what positive psychology can impact (Eidelman, Pilisuk, & Soldz, 2011) and inadequate empirical support to assume its efficacy (e.g., Coyne & Tennen, 2010). Specifically, performing in a military context, in which bad things do happen, may entail profound personal sacrifice and require a broad approach to conceptualizing resilience. The approach not only should emphasize optimism, cognitive behavioral techniques, and interpersonal communication strategies, but it should also include how to accept and handle the possibility of failure, how to be open to negative feedback from others, how to function even if you don't feel like it, how to be compassionate to those who falter in their resilience, and how to examine whether service members, military families, teams, and leaders are being asked to do too much.

Second, although resilience training is often treated as a unified construct—as a one-size-fits-all approach—this may not be the right approach. Although any training for an organization like the military has to be efficiently pushed out on a large scale (Castro & Adler, 2011), some of the training can address possible individual differences associated with resilience. Just as there are different types of learners (visual, auditory, and experiential), there are also likely to be individuals who respond to some types of resilience training more than others (cognitive, emotional, and physiological). For example, cognitive-based modules may be more useful to some service members, but others may find a mindfulness-based approach more useful for monitoring emotions or deep breathing techniques more useful for reducing physiological arousal. It may be helpful to ensure that training incorporates all three approaches (cognitive, emotional, and physiological) to reach the widest audience. Currently, most training programs and most studies are oriented to testing out one style of training. It is to the organization's benefit to examine a range of resilience-training mechanisms.

Third, resilience training must address the role that small-group leaders should have in the implementation of resilience-building techniques. Are these techniques best considered at an individual level, or should they be adapted for small-group leaders to train and integrate in the context of normal military training requirements? There are various examples of how this kind of training can be integrated into the occupational context. For instance, in one study of soldiers in basic combat training, performance psychology techniques were tied to specific basic training events and taught in situ (e.g., on the range, at the confidence course, by the rappelling tower). In comparison with an active control, this training resulted in better performance (Hammermeister et al., 2010). This kind of study demonstrates the feasibility of integrating resilience training into the occupational context. Assuming the training does not require a high level of specialization, the material could be presented or at least reinforced by small-group leaders.

Fourth, there is a need for well-designed research that can demonstrate intervention efficacy over time. There is a surprising dearth of well-designed research assessing the efficacy of resilience training. Several considerations have to be taken into account when preparing to conduct a research study. Just as the intervention should be designed or adapted for the occupational setting (Castro & Adler, 2011), so too should the study methods be adapted for the organizational context.

The most appropriate research design may be a group randomized trial rather than a traditional randomized controlled trial, because the intervention is applied to intact groups (Bliese et al., 2011). That is, instead of randomly assigning individuals to different conditions, as is typical of many intervention and treatment studies, the study would randomize by units (e.g., platoons). Most training in the military is conducted in preexisting work groups like platoons, and these groups typically share work objectives, deployment experiences, unit climate, and leadership. Members of these work groups also often are friends and socialize with one another outside of work hours.

By randomizing by work group, the training is more ecologically valid and potentially even more effective. Randomizing platoons mirrors how actual training implementation typically occurs and also has the potential to take advantage of the intact group's cohesion and leadership. This cohesion and leadership may potentiate the impact of the training by having unit members reinforce concepts with one another outside of the training context.

Group randomized trials require appropriate statistical techniques to address group-level variance and may benefit from mixed-effects modeling. Mixed-effects modeling confers the added advantage of specifying and controlling for Level 2 variance (e.g., shared perceptions of unit climate), and thus it may increase the power of the study design to detect differences across intervention conditions (Raudenbush & Liu, 2000).

Furthermore, appropriate expectations about effect sizes should be maintained. If the training is not a targeted training for high-risk groups, the effect is likely to be small in comparison with that for traditional treatment trials (Bliese et al., 2011) but may be larger than that for clinical interventions with high dropout rates (e.g., Hoge, 2011; Zatzick, Koepsell, & Rivara, 2009).

The question of what constitutes an appropriate control group also should be considered carefully. Most studies benefit in terms of internal validity from a comparison group that offers some alternative form of intervention, but it is essential that the appropriate point of comparison does not waste service member time, has credibility, and is relevant. Nevertheless, as some researchers have found, using an active control condition (i.e., an alternative intervention) can mask the presence of an effect from the training of interest (e.g., Brunwasser, Gillham, & Kim, 2009). Thus, ideally, studies should include both an active control and an assessment-only condition. Once a training program's efficacy is demonstrated, dismantling studies should be conducted. Such studies are used to determine which component of a larger training program (or treatment) is responsible for improvements in order to guide the development of a more effective and efficient intervention.

Resilience training studies also should be designed to measure different kinds of outcomes. For example, ratings of training satisfaction are easy to gather and are an important aspect of intervention evaluation. Such ratings should cover both perceptions of the training process (e.g., interesting, interactive) and the degree to which the training content is seen as useful. These measures are important indicators of whether the training is being well received, whether it fills some perceived gap for participants, and whether it is likely to be implemented with enthusiasm should it become mandatory in the organization.

Intervention studies also benefit from assessments of pre- and posttraining changes in attitudes and skills. These results can demonstrate whether short-term changes occur as a result of the training. However, differences between intervention conditions should also be assessed several weeks or months following training. Although such changes may be difficult to observe, they are critical in terms of establishing the long-term efficacy of an intervention. To the extent the training is universally applied (i.e., provided to everyone, not just a treatment-seeking group), there may be a benefit to assessing the degree to which individuals practice the training skill being taught. Practice or skill usage may be an important moderator of training efficacy that has to be included in the analytic plan (e.g., Jha, Stanley, Kiyonaga, Wong, & Gelfand, 2010).

Finally, it is important to ensure that the outcomes selected make sense for the participating organizations. These outcomes may include a measure of psychiatric symptomatology, functioning, well-being, or another outcome of particular interest to that sample. For example, postdeployment resilience training in the U.S. military is often focused on changes in posttraumatic stress disorder (PTSD) symptoms, reflecting the fact that PTSD symptoms are some of the most common symptoms reported postdeployment (e.g., Hoge et al., 2004). In contrast, in the United Kingdom, such studies focus on alcohol-related problems, reflecting the fact that alcohol problem rates are some of the most common symptoms reported postdeployment (e.g., Iversen et al., 2009; King's Centre for Military Health Research, 2010). Similarly, in some cases new measures will have to be developed, as outcomes such as performance on an obstacle course or the subjective experience of transitioning from combat to home (e.g., Adler, Britt, Castro, McGurk, & Bliese, 2011) may not have equivalent measures in the civilian literature.

It should be clear from the preceding discussion that group randomized trials are complex to implement and resource intensive. As a result, there are significant logistical and coordination challenges. The research team needs to ensure that the study does not interfere with the military unit, that it is convenient in terms of scheduling, and that the unit's leadership has been adequately informed. The study staff should also perform treatment integrity checks to make sure that trainers are following the training material.

Given that group randomized trials are resource intensive, not every training program will necessarily be tested by this kind of study design. Instead, researchers may have to rely on a combination of qualitative assessments, quasi-experimental designs, and randomized trials with other populations in order to systematically examine the training's efficacy. Nevertheless, a randomized controlled trial with the population of interest can provide strong evidence about the training's utility.

Finally, in an occupational context such as the military, where team members rely on each other to work effectively in high-demand and high-threat environments, resilience should be considered a group-level phenomenon and not just an individual-level phenomenon. This kind of group-level definition has to take leadership, interpersonal dynamics, and the team into account. Just like a resilient individual, a resilient unit (or organization) could be defined as one that is able to bounce back from adversity. Conceptualizing resilience as a unit-level construct can then shift how training and resilience measurement are conceptualized. For example, in contrast to individual resilience initiatives, training perhaps would focus more on group-oriented problems, group functioning, and skills that could be mastered only as an interdependent group. Perhaps markers of resilience would be measured by group achievement, group variability in morale, and attrition from the organization. By inclusion of a group-level perspective on resilience, the impact of resilience on an organization can be broadened, with training, strategies, and policies implemented across the military organization in order to benefit both the individual service members and their unit.

REFERENCES

Adler, A. B., Bliese, P. B., McGurk, D., Hoge, C. W., & Castro, C. A. (2009). Battlemind debriefing and Battlemind training as early interventions with soldiers returning from Iraq: Randomization by platoon. *Journal of Consulting and Clinical Psychology, 77*, 928–940. doi:10.1037/a0016877

Adler, A. B., Britt, T. W., Castro, C. A., McGurk, D., & Bliese, P. D. (2011). Effect of transition home from combat on risk-taking and health-related behaviors. *Journal of Traumatic Stress, 24*, 381–389. doi:10.1002/jts.20665

Adler, A. B., Wright, K. M., Bliese, P. D., Eckford, R., & Hoge, C. W. (2008). A2 diagnostic criterion for combat-related posttraumatic stress disorder. *Journal of Traumatic Stress, 21*, 301–308. doi:10.1002/jts.20336

Baer, R. A., Smith, G. T., Hopkins, J., Krietemeyer, J., & Toney, L. (2006). Using self-report assessment methods to explore facets of mindfulness. *Assessment, 13*, 27–45. doi:10.1177/1073191105283504

Bliese, P. B. (2006). Social climates: Drivers of soldier well-being and resilience. In A. B. Adler, C. A. Castro, & T. W. Britt (Eds.), *Military life: The psychology of serving in peace and combat. Vol. 2: Operational stress* (pp. 213–234). Westport, CT: Praeger Security International.

Bliese, P. B., Adler, A. B., & Castro, C. A. (2011). Research-based preventive mental health care strategies in the military. In A. B. Adler, P. B. Bliese, & C. A. Castro (Eds.), *Deployment psychology: Evidence-based strategies to promote mental health in the military* (pp. 103–124). Washington, DC: American Psychological Association. doi:10.1037/12300-004

Brunwasser, S. M., Gillham, J. E., & Kim, E. S. (2009). A meta-analytic review of the Penn Resiliency Program's effect on depressive symptoms. *Journal of Consulting and Clinical Psychology, 77*, 1042–1054. doi:10.1037/a0017671

Casey, G. W., Jr. (2011). Comprehensive Soldier Fitness: A vision for psychological resilience in the U.S. Army. *American Psychologist, 66*, 1–3. doi:10.1037/a0021930

Castro, C. A., & Adler, A. B. (2011). Re-conceptualizing combat-related posttraumatic stress disorder as an occupational hazard. In A. B. Adler, P. B. Bliese, & C. A. Castro (Eds.), *Deployment psychology: Evidence-based strategies to promote mental health in the military* (pp. 217–242). Washington, DC: American Psychological Association. doi:10.1037/12300-009

Cornum, R., Matthews, M. D., & Seligman, M. E. P. (2011). Comprehensive Soldier Fitness: Building resilience in a challenging institutional context. *American Psychologist, 66*, 4–9. doi:10.1037/a0021420

Coyne, J. C., & Tennen, H. (2010). Positive psychology in cancer care: Bad science, exaggerated claims, and unproven medicine. *Annals of Behavioral Medicine, 39*, 16–26. doi:10.1007/s12160-009-9154-z

Eidelman, R., Pilisuk, M., & Soldz, S. (2011, March). *The dark side of "Comprehensive Soldier Fitness"*. Retrieved from http://www.opednews.com/articles/The-Dark-Side-of-Comprehe-by-Roy-Eidelson-Marc-110326-492.html

Gould, M., Adler, A., Zamorski, M., Castro, C., Hanily, N., Steele, N., . . . Greenberg, N. (2010). Do stigma and other perceived barriers to mental health care differ across Armed Forces? *Journal of the Royal Society of Medicine, 103*, 148–156. doi:10.1258/jrsm.2010.090426

Greenberg, N., & Jones, N. (2011). Optimizing mental health support in the military: The role of peers and leaders. In A. B. Adler, P. B. Bliese, & C. A. Castro (Eds.), *Deployment psychology: Evidence-based strategies to promote mental health in the military* (pp. 69–101). Washington, DC: American Psychological Association. doi:10.1037/12300-003

Greene-Shortridge, T. M., Britt, T. W., & Castro, C. A. (2007). The stigma of mental health problems in the military. *Military Medicine, 172*, 157–161.

Hammermeister, J., Pickering, M. A., Holliday, B., Williams, J., Harada, C., Ohlson, C., . . . Adler, A. B. (2010, August). Mental skills in basic combat training: A group randomized trial. In A. B. Adler (Chair), *Mental fitness training during basic combat training: Two new studies*. Symposium conducted at the meeting of the American Psychological Association, San Diego, CA.

Hoge, C. W. (2011). Interventions for war-related posttraumatic stress disorder: Meeting veterans where they are. *JAMA, 306*, 549–551. doi:10.1001/jama.2011.1096

Hoge, C. W., Castro, C. A., Messer, S. C., McGurk, D., Cotting, D. I., & Koffman, R. L. (2004). Combat duty in Iraq and Afghanistan, mental health problems, and barriers to care. *The New England Journal of Medicine, 351*, 13–22. doi:10.1056/NEJMoa040603

Iversen, A. C., van Staden, L., Hacker Hughes, J., Browne, T., Hull, L., Hall, J., . . . Fear, N. (2009). The prevalence of common mental disorders and PTSD in the UK military: Using data from a clinical interview-based study. *BMC Psychiatry, 9*, 68–80. doi:10.1186/1471-244X-9-68

Jha, A. P., Stanley, E. A., Kiyonaga, A., Wong, L., & Gelfand, L. (2010). Examining the protective effects of mindfulness training on working memory capacity and affective experience. *Emotion, 10,* 54–64. doi:10.1037/a0018438

King's Centre for Military Health Research. (2010). *King's Centre for Military Health Research: A fifteen year report: What has been achieved by fifteen years of research into the health of the UK Armed Forces?* London, England: Kings College London, University of London.

McGurk, D., Cotting, D. I., Britt, T. W., & Adler, A. B. (2006). Joining the ranks: The role of indoctrination in transforming civilians to service members. In A. B. Adler, C. A. Castro, & T. W. Britt (Eds.), *Military life: The psychology of serving in peace and combat. Vol. 2: Operational stress* (pp. 13–31). Westport, CT: Praeger Security International.

Mental Health Advisory Team IV. (2006). *Mental Health Advisory Team (MHAT) IV Operation Iraqi Freedom 05-07.* Retrieved from http:// www.armymedicine.army.mil/reports/mhat/mhat_iv/MHAT_IV_Report_17NOV06.pdf

Mental Health Advisory Team VI. (2009). *Mental Health Advisory Team (MHAT) IV Operation Iraqi Freedom 05-07.* Retrieved from http://www.armymedicine.army.mil/reports/mhat/mhat_vi/MHAT_VI-OIF_Redacted.pdf

Raudenbush, S. W., & Liu, X. (2000). Statistical power and optimal design for multi-site randomized trials. *Psychological Methods, 5,* 199–213. doi:10.1037/1082-989X.5.2.199

Rona, R. J., Fear, N. T., Hull, L., Greenberg, N., Earnshaw, M., Hotopf, M., & Wessely, S. (2007). Mental health consequences of overstretch in the UK armed forces: First phase of a cohort study. *British Medical Journal, 335,* 603–607. doi:10.1136/bmj.39274.585752.BE

Wright, K. M., Cabrera, O. A., Bliese, P. B., Adler, A. B., Hoge, C. W., & Castro, C. A. (2009). Stigma and barriers to care in soldiers postcombat. *Psychological Services, 6,* 108–116. doi:10.1037/a0012620

Zatzick, D. F., Koepsell, T., & Rivara, F. P. (2009). Using target population specification, effect size, and reach to estimate and compare the population impact of two PTSD preventive interventions. *Psychiatry: Interpersonal and Biological Processes, 72,* 346–359. doi:10.1521/psyc.2009.72.4.346

11

MILITARY RESILIENCE: REMAINING QUESTIONS AND CONCLUDING COMMENTS

ROBERT R. SINCLAIR AND THOMAS W. BRITT

For over a decade, military forces from over two dozen nations have been involved in operations in and around Iraq and Afghanistan. The human and economic costs of these wars have been devastating, and there is good reason to expect that the mental health consequences will last long after the final soldier returns home. The central theme of this book is that resilience plays a central role in the mental health of military personnel and that it is therefore important to understand the nature of resilience, the situational and personal factors associated with higher and lower levels of resilience, and the possible organizational interventions to enhance resilience.

As this volume makes clear, although much is known about resilience, there is a great deal of work yet to be done with respect to developing, protecting, and promoting military resilience. Most of the chapters offer research agendas intended to highlight important unresolved issues related to their particular topics. In this chapter, we highlight several questions and concerns

http://dx.doi.org/10.1037/14190-011
Building Psychological Resilience in Military Personnel: Theory and Practice, R. R. Sinclair and T. W. Britt (Editors)

that either cut across multiple chapters or have not, in our view, received sufficient attention in the military research community. We see these as top priorities for military resilience research and practice.

IMPORTANT ISSUES IN DEFINING AND STUDYING RESILIENCE AMONG MILITARY PERSONNEL

As noted in the Introduction to this volume, researchers have defined the construct of resilience in many ways. In the present volume, *resilience* is defined as the demonstration of positive adaptation following significant adversity, rather than as a trait or capacity residing within the individual. Of course, researchers have examined factors within individuals in order to understand why some people respond adaptively under adversity. These factors include personality traits, attitudes, beliefs, and the ability to execute skills that promote resilience. However, the individual's social environment, both immediate and distal, may also contribute to the demonstration of positive adaptation.

Two issues regarding how resilience has been defined and studied in the present volume are the domains in which positive adaptation should be shown and the research designs necessary to examine determinants of resilience. With regard to the first issue, the chapters herein illustrate that the majority of research on resilience among military personnel and their families has assessed positive adaptation primarily in domains related to mental health symptoms. Therefore, resilience has been studied primarily as military personnel showing reduced mental health symptoms following exposure to different types of stressors (e.g., combat exposure, multiple deployments).

Although mental health symptoms are certainly important indicators of positive adaptation, research on military resilience should assess additional areas, including having a high quality of life, being satisfied with work and relationships, and being able to flourish, in addition to not showing signs of distress. Lester, McBride, and Cornum (see Chapter 9) highlight how the Comprehensive Soldier Fitness (CSF) training provided to U.S. Army soldiers is designed not only to decrease the experience of negative symptoms following highly stressful events but also to enable soldiers to maintain positive psychological health in the wake of these demands. In addition, Adler, Britt, Castro, McGurk, and Bliese (2011) noted that soldiers often have transition-related problems following a deployment above and beyond mental health symptoms, including a sense of anger and alienation, guilt related to events that have happened, a lack of appreciation for the work they did, and the failure to recognize positive ways the deployment may have affected them. Research on resilience should take full advantage of domains resulting from the recent positive psychology movement so as to more thoroughly examine positive adaptation following significant adversity.

The second issue arising from how resilience is defined and studied within military settings is that longitudinal research designs with multiple assessment points are required to best investigate the factors associated with positive adaptation following adversity. Although examples of longitudinal designs are included among the chapters in the present volume, much of the research uses cross-sectional designs in which the experience of stressful events, a hypothesized resilience-promoting factor, and indices of positive adaptation (i.e., mental health symptoms) are assessed at a single point in time. While these designs can provide suggestive evidence that a particular personal, social, or organizational factor is associated with reduced reports of symptoms following exposure to stressors, longitudinal designs are necessary to strengthen causal inferences regarding the role of the hypothesized protective factors.

Some of the most methodologically sophisticated research on resilience includes examining indicators of positive adaptation (typically mental health symptoms) before and at multiple points after exposure to a stressful event (e.g., Bonanno et al., 2012). Different trajectories of adaptation can then be examined with latent growth mixture modeling, and researchers can examine which factors differentiate resilient trajectories (a slight increase in symptoms followed by a return to baseline) from other trajectories that reflect a failure to adapt following stressful events (e.g., trajectories indicating a consistent level of high distress or distress that worsens as time goes by). Conducting this type of research will require following military personnel and their families over extended periods of time, which is a notoriously difficult task (Adler et al., 2011). However, longitudinal designs with multiple assessments will increase our confidence in the resilience-promoting factors that we target for intervention.

Although we think most researchers would agree that longitudinal research is necessary, there remains little consensus on the specific temporal qualities of research designs. For example, is a 1-year time lag between two measurements too short, too long, or just right? How soon after an event (or after completion of a deployment) should outcomes be measured? How long after an event do mental health problems have to be present to indicate resilience problems? The answers to these questions obviously depend on the nature of the stressors, outcomes, and contexts under investigation, but there is little specific guidance for researchers on how to design studies to address these and many other questions related to longitudinal resilience research design. Better guidance on the temporal aspects of longitudinal research design is a critical need for military resilience research, as well as most areas of applied psychology.

CAN MILITARY UNITS BUILD MORE RESILIENT CULTURES?

Another question that emerges from the chapters in the present volume is the role of military culture and unit dynamics in promoting resilience among military personnel. Britt and Oliver (see Chapter 3) highlight the importance of morale and unit cohesion in buffering soldiers from the adverse consequences of stressful events and note the importance of leaders in creating high morale and cohesion. More directly, MacIntyre, Charbonneau, and O'Keefe (Chapter 5) discuss the importance of leader behaviors in promoting resilience among military personnel, and Jex, Kain, and Park (Chapter 4) highlight social support and collective efficacy as factors that should promote positive adaptation under the adversity encountered by military personnel. Furthermore, Wright, Riviere, Merrill, and Cabrera (Chapter 8) highlight the importance of leaders in creating policies that can promote resilience among military families when service members are deployed, and Odle-Dusseau et al. (2013) highlighted how soldiers embedded within "family-friendly" units are less likely to show future symptoms of depression following a combat deployment.

This literature emphasizes that the ability of a service member to demonstrate positive adaptation in the face of adversity is affected by dynamics of the units in which service members are embedded and the behaviors enacted by the leaders in these units. Units that are highly cohesive and in which unit members believe they can perform their mission under high levels of stress are likely to produce more resilient military personnel. As noted in Chapter 9, leader training programs in the military are just beginning to highlight the importance of resilience for mission success (see also Reivich, Seligman, & McBride, 2011), so there is certainly the hope that future leaders will recognize the importance of resilience and understand how their actions can affect the resilience of their unit members. Lester, Harms, Herian, Krasikova, and Beal (2011) recently evaluated the effectiveness of the resilience training for noncommissioned officers (NCOs) in the U.S. Army; they found that soldiers who were a part of a unit with an NCO who had received resilience training scored higher on certain resilience-based skills than soldiers who did not have an NCO who had been through the training. Although these results are preliminary, they do suggest it may be possible to train leaders to engage in behaviors that support the resilience of their soldiers.

In examining the importance of unit factors in resilience, it will be important to emphasize that as a result of exposure to multiple traumatic events during combat operations, many military personnel will develop mental health symptoms that require treatment. If service members are experiencing mental health problems that are interfering with their work or family functioning, leaders will need to emphasize that getting prompt treatment for these problems is a way to promote resilience (Britt & McFadden, 2012) rather than a sign that these service members are not resilient. In addition, unit members need to understand that encouraging fellow service members to get mental health treatment promptly when needed will ultimately contribute to the resilience of their unit. Training leaders and fellow unit members that being resilient does not mean that a service member is immune to symptoms following highly traumatic events will help deal with concerns Adler mentions in Chapter 10 regarding the potential "dark side" of an over-emphasis on resilience.

Although efforts to change military culture to enhance resilience have great potential merit, they are not without challenges. For example, Ruvolo and Bullis (2003) described several "lessons learned the hard way" from an unsuccessful military culture change initiative. They identified several barriers to change, including insufficient organizational knowledge of leaders, lack of communication of the need for change, lack of empowerment among subordinates, poor balance between the needs of different stakeholders, and a need for further senior leader development. Resilience-focused initiatives could encounter several of these challenges, particularly given that senior leaders came from the same general military culture that produced some of the resilience-related challenges in the first place (e.g., stigma about admitting problems). On the other hand, military leaders typically have great concern about factors that affect the health and readiness of their subordinates. This might mean that in some cases it is easier to get buy-in from senior leaders to support culture change. The research community may help address some of these issues through careful study and documentation of the characteristics of successful organizational change initiatives and the positive outcomes they produce.

SORTING OUT THE FACTORS: WHAT REALLY MATTERS FOR BUILDING RESILIENCE?

At the outset of this book, we noted the steadily increasing growth in military resilience research over the past decade. We also noted that there is exponentially more research on resilience in civilian populations than in the military. Taken together, this literature has investigated dozens of personal and situational factors that could influence resilience and resilience-related intervention programs. For example, Fikretoglu and McCreary (2012) reviewed numerous resilience-related definitions, some of which may be more appropriately viewed as antecedents of resilience according to the definition used in this book. Meredith et al. (2011) identified 20 broad categories of empirically supported factors that promote resilience. Similarly, the Global

Assessment Tool measure that is central to the Comprehensive Soldier Fitness program (described by Lester et al. in Chapter 9) assesses over 20 aspects of resilience, and Sinclair, Waitsman, Oliver, and Deese (Chapter 2) identify numerous personality traits potentially related to resilience.

Taken together, all of these reviews suggest that resilience might be an extraordinarily complicated construct to study. However, it is quite likely that many of the resilience factors investigated likely overlap in definition and/or in measurement—problems referred to as the jingle and jangle fallacies in personality research (Sinclair et al., Chapter 2). To build better explanatory models of resilience as well as successful intervention programs, it will be important to overcome these problems, in part by focusing and prioritizing resilience research. Recent methodological developments offer several ways to help resilience researchers accomplish this goal of greater focus.

First, one of the recent trends in organizational psychology has been applications of what is sometimes called dominance analysis or relative weights analysis (e.g., Azen & Budescu, 2003; LeBreton, Hargis, Griepentrog, Oswald, & Ployhart, 2007; LeBreton & Tonidandel, 2008). These techniques involve sets of multivariate analyses that enable researchers to draw stronger conclusions about the relative contributions of several variables to predicting an outcome. Such analyses can be very informative in efforts to sort out which predictors really matter when several are studied simultaneously. Resilience researchers should consider using relative weights analyses to prioritize predictors from the large lists of variables identified in these recent reviews. These analyses would facilitate construction of parsimonious theoretical models and would help focus intervention programs on the most important resilience factors.

Second, many resilience-related resources are likely to be fungible or replaceable. In economics, the idea of fungibility concerns the extent to which one resource may be exchanged for another. Organizational theory scholars (e.g., Katz & Kahn, 1978) have described a related concept called *equifinality*, which highlights the idea that systems can reach the same particular end-state (e.g., high resilience) through a variety of pathways. Applied to resilience, the concepts of equifinality and fungible resources suggest that soldiers likely need some particular resources to be resilient but may not need all of them. Further, there may be multiple combinations of resources associated with high (or low) levels of resilience.

Person-centered methods offer ways to extend resilience research by identifying groups of people with distinct profiles, or combinations of a particular set of variables (e.g., Wang & Hanges, 2011; Wang, Sinclair, Zhou, & Sears, 2012). For example, much of the first half of the book includes discussions of several resilience-related resources, including personality (see Chapter 2), morale and cohesion (Chapter 3), situational factors (Chapter 4), and leadership (Chapter 5). Perhaps soldiers with high morale and transformational leaders do not require the same level of certain resilience-related personality traits to be protected from adverse mental health effects following exposure to potentially traumatic stressors. Or perhaps soldiers with low levels of certain traits do not experience the same level of benefits from leader support. Thus, one might be able to hypothesize a "high morale" profile that is distinct from a "high personal strengths" profile in terms of the variables involved but with similar expected mental health outcomes. Wang and colleagues (2012) described new analytical techniques (e.g., latent class analyses) and design/theory considerations in person-centered research that may be particularly useful for resilience research. We encourage military researchers to consider using these techniques in the future.

THE IMPORTANCE OF STUDYING POSITIVE OUTCOMES THAT RESULT FROM EXPOSURE TO ADVERSITY

The majority of research on resilience, both within and outside the military, focuses on factors that reduce the negative effects of stressful experiences on various outcomes. However, a small body of literature has found that traumatic events can result in perceived benefits by the individual experiencing the event. In nonwork settings, research has examined benefits individuals perceive following highly stressful or traumatic experiences, such as dealing with a life-threatening illness, the effects of a natural disaster, or caring for someone with a debilitating illness (see Helgeson, Reynolds, & Tomich, 2006, for a review). Authors use terms such as *benefit finding, posttraumatic growth*, and *stress-related growth* interchangeably to refer to the perception of positive changes following exposure to stressful events (Helgeson et al., 2006; Park & Fenster, 2004; Weinrib, Rothrock, Johnsen, & Lutgendorf, 2006), and authors have found that benefit finding is related both to features of the stressful event and to personality variables (e.g., optimism; see Affleck & Tennen, 1996).

Benefit finding has been reported by studies of veterans of various military conflicts throughout the 20th century (Aldwin, Levenson, & Spiro, 1994; Elder & Clipp, 1989; Sledge, Boydstun, & Rabe, 1980). Elder and Clipp (1989) examined the positive and negative effects of combat reported by a sample of World War II and Korean War veterans. Sixty to 70% of the men selected "learned to cope with adversity," "exercised self-discipline," and "greater independence," as a result of their involvement in war. Examining prisoners of war in Vietnam, Sledge et al. (1980) found that a majority felt the experience had benefited them by giving them a better perspective on life and increasing their confidence. Britt, Adler, and Bartone (2001) found that engagement in meaningful work during a peacekeeping operation was associated with greater benefit finding months after the deployment. More recently, Wood, Britt, Thomas, Klocko, and Bliese (2011) found that among military personnel deployed to Iraq, perceiving higher levels of benefits was associated with fewer symptoms of PTSD under high combat exposure.

Although reports of benefit finding and growth have been obtained following combat and other military operations, researchers are just beginning to examine whether posttraumatic growth can be facilitated through planful intervention (Tedeschi & McNally, 2011). Researchers caution that military personnel should not feel that they have to experience benefits from traumatic events; instead, researchers emphasize the need to recognize that growing from trauma is a process rather than something that happens at a single point in time (Tedeschi & McNally, 2011). Future research should more thoroughly examine how the benefits of exposure to trauma interact with resilience-promoting factors to influence positive adaptation following adversity.

RESILIENCE CHANGE INITIATIVES: WHAT WORKS? WHY?

Perhaps the single most important need for future military resilience research is program evaluation work. Several authors in this volume address this issue in various ways, noting either that more longitudinal research was needed on resilience factors or that there was only limited research evidence to support certain resilience-focused interventions.

One of the important themes of this book is that there is a continued need for research on both risk and protective factors for resilience and for research to better understand positive and negative resilience-related outcomes. In the literature on occupational health psychology, however, Nielsen, Taris, and Cox (2010) argued for a somewhat different perspective: that we know enough about the general types of factors that contribute to occupational health and what we need is much greater attention to the "design, implementation, and evaluation of interventions" (p. 220). We agree with this perspective. We believe that there are opportunities to do better resilience research to address issues reviewed in this volume but also that more research should focus on interventions. In other words, military resilience research might benefit both from studies that use more sophisticated design, measurement, and analytical strategies and from a stronger emphasis on understanding what kinds of programs work and why they work. Similar issues have been addressed in the literatures on public health (Glasgow & Emmons, 2007) and management (e.g., Shapiro, Kirkman, & Courtney, 2007). These approaches have important differences, but they share a recognition of the need to improve the connections between research to generate scholarly knowledge and organizational practice.

Meredith et al. (2011) reviewed several dozen military and civilian intervention programs focused on resilience. Although it is important to review such programs in terms of the critical risk and protective factors that they emphasize and/or show to be effective (where evaluation work has been conducted), other scholarship could focus on assessing procedural aspects of these interventions shown to be effective. Nielsen, Randall, Holten, and González (2010) provided an example of such scholarship with respect to organizational-level occupational health interventions. They described a conceptual model of what they term the *intervention cycle* that includes five intervention process components: preparation, screening, action planning, implementation, and evaluation. They used this model to evaluate five European occupational health initiatives with respect to the processes used in the intervention. Extending such process evaluation scholarship to existing resilience programs would help identify best practices in process design and could potentially help minimize the number of interventions that "reinvent the wheel" with respect to program design.

There are many pragmatic questions about military resilience interventions that might be informed by further scholarship. For example, military personnel typically have very limited time to devote to new training initiatives (as well as numerous training demands), and because resilience training often focuses on traits and behaviors that are difficult to change, brief, one-time training programs are unlikely to have much lasting effect. What kinds of programs, constructs, and issues are most amenable to brief training programs? Alternately, is there any value in providing soldiers with resilience training that is presented in very brief chunks of time (e.g., 5–10 minutes or even less) but is repeated frequently over the course of a deployment?

Generalizability is another major concern for military resilience research and intervention design. Some resilience training takes place during basic training programs; this includes, for example, several of the studies reviewed in Chapter 2 on personality factors and resilience. As Lester et al. note in Chapter 9, another source of information about resilience training comes from research on populations that resemble military personnel in some ways but differ in others (e.g., research on young adult college students, who might be similar with respect to age and education but who differ dramatically in terms of the kinds of stressors they experience and the cultural context of those stressors). It is unclear whether resilience research conducted in either of these settings is sufficiently generalizable to the context and stressors faced by personnel during combat deployments (and reasonable arguments could be made on either side of this issue). However, the evidence necessary to show that programs are effective for combat-deployed personnel (or post-deployment personnel) is sparse, largely because of the difficulties of obtaining sufficient access to units and then following them over time. These challenges raise additional questions about whether there are particular kinds of training programs or training modalities (e.g., Internet-based training, train-the-trainer systems) more amenable to the deployment environment and/or more likely to produce generalizable findings.

Finally, another important contextual factor may be the trust soldiers have in the process and the data. As Lester et al. acknowledge in Chapter 9, there have been some criticisms of CSF related to privacy concerns and/or whether CSF is assessing the right kinds of content; these criticisms have received attention in the popular press and in professional psychology. Such criticisms, should they become a focus of unit members, may undermine confidence in the CSF program, producing suspicious or cynical soldiers who become immune to the effects of the training. These problems may be further amplified in cohesive units with high levels of stigma about reporting mental health problems. With this in mind, what steps, if any, can be taken to increase the confidence service members have in such programs? Perhaps this will become less of an issue over time, if the CSF program shows more and more successful outcomes.

The pragmatic challenges of implementing organizational interventions are not a new topic. The articles we cite, and many others, deal with this broad set of challenges. However, the fact that they involve difficult problems should not be cause for fatalism. Rather, both academics and military leaders need to improve their approaches by including, for example, a greater emphasis on research that addresses actual military problems and perhaps more military leader training on the need for empirically supported interventions.

HOW CAN CIVILIAN EMPLOYERS CREATE A VETERAN-SUPPORTIVE WORKPLACE?

A final issue for resilience researchers to consider is what happens when veterans return to the civilian workplace. With military deployments in Afghanistan winding down, we expect to see increasing numbers of members of National Guard units returning home and many active duty soldiers transitioning into civilian life. These transitions are, in most cases, cause for celebration, both by the men and women returning from long deployments and by families who have long been separated from their loved ones. Other chapters in this volume discuss some of elements of these transitions with regard to the deployment cycle (e.g., Greenberg, Chapter 7) and the challenges faced by military families (e.g., Wright et al., Chapter 8). In our view, one of the most important but least well understood aspects of the transition process concerns what happens when combat veterans enter the civilian workforce.

The transition from combat-deployed veteran to civilian can be jarring. Combat veterans returning to civilian life face a transition into an environment with completely different stressors as well as completely different daily experiences and behavioral norms. In addition to addressing their own health concerns, returning veterans often have to deal with mental health problems of family members, as deployments are associated with increased family mental health problems (Allen, Rhoades, Stanley, & Markman, 2010; Chandra et al., 2010; White, De Burgh, Fear, & Iversen, 2011).

Obtaining gainful employment may be one of the most pressing needs for veterans, as employment helps people meet financial, support, and esteem needs and provides structure and purpose to life that foster resilience. Many veterans of Operations Enduring Freedom and Iraqi Freedom have, however, returned to communities with limited employment opportunities. They also are more likely to be members of a demographic group with higher unemployment rates, which include young males, African Americans, and those with less than a college education (Bureau of Labor Statistics, U.S. Department of Labor, 2012; U.S. Government Accountability Office, 2005). Problems obtaining employment may be exacerbated for veterans who have knowledge, skills, and abilities that are less readily transferable to the civilian sector (e.g., handling explosive ordnance).

The Obama administration has launched several initiatives to help veterans obtain civilian employment. However, less attention has been paid to organizational policies and practices that help retain veterans once they are hired. Work is among the top sources of stress, even among civilian workers (American Psychological Association, 2012). Thus, stress resilience is likely to be a critical issue for returning veterans and may not be sufficiently well understood. Some vets may react more adversely to workplace stressors because of their cumulative history of trauma and the cultural tradition among veterans of hesitancy to admit mental health problems. Others may choose occupations (e.g., law enforcement, firefighting) that are likely to have similar trigger events. However, combat experiences likely strengthen the resilience of many veterans, enhancing their ability to cope with other kinds of demands. Many veterans develop attributes (physical fitness, self-confidence, leadership experience) that may even help foster resilience among their civilian coworkers. In our view, understanding both the positive and the negative aspects of veterans' return to civilian life constitutes one of the most important current challenges in military mental health research. The personal and organizational resilience factors described in this book likely play an important role in the resilience of soldiers throughout the rest of their lives.

Sinclair, Hammer, and Thomas (2012) made several recommendations to create what they termed *veteran-supportive workplaces*. Their recommendations most pertinent to resilience include recruiting and placing vets in high-quality jobs, increasing workplace flexibility, helping veterans develop peer support networks, developing veteran-focused supportive supervisor training (cf. Hammer & Brady, 2012; Hammer, Kossek, Anger, Bodner, & Zimmerman, 2011), encouraging help/treatment seeking (Britt & McFadden, 2012), and promoting behavioral health. Although some of these recommendations would be more suited for veterans, such policies and practices are also likely to benefit civilian workers in those organizations, as well as the organization itself (e.g., through company reputation, productivity, and retention).

CONCLUSION

Despite great progress in the science of military resilience, much work remains to be done. Moreover, with the large numbers of veterans returning home to garrison settings and in many cases to civilian life, the issues covered in this book will only grow in importance. Military issues and concerns have sparked some of the best research throughout the history of psychology, starting with World War I and the rise of the standardized testing movement and continuing into the 21st century; military researchers have made tremendously important contributions in areas such as leadership, job performance, occupational health, and the diagnosis and treatment of mental health disorders. We believe that military resilience researchers will make some of the next set of important contributions to applied psychology and that all of psychology will benefit from efforts to address some of the challenges inherent in military resilience research. We hope readers will find that this chapter—and, indeed, this entire volume—provides useful guidance on what we see as some of the most important issues in this literature. It has been a true privilege to edit this volume, and we are excited about the future of military resilience research.

REFERENCES

Adler, A. B., Britt, T. W., Castro, C. A., McGurk, D., & Bliese, P. D. (2011). Effect of transition home from combat on risk-taking and health-related behaviors. *Journal of Traumatic Stress, 24,* 381–389. doi:10.1002/jts.20665

Affleck, G., & Tennen, H. (1996). Construing benefit from adversity: Adaptational significance and dispositional underpinnings. *Journal of Personality, 64,* 899–922. doi:10.1111/j.1467-6494.1996.tb00948.x

Aldwin, C. M., Levenson, M. R., & Spiro, A., III. (1994). Vulnerability and resilience to combat exposure: Can stress have lifelong effects? *Psychology and Aging*, *9*, 34–44. doi:10.1037/0882-7974.9.1.34

Allen, E. S., Rhoades, G. K., Stanley, S. M., & Markman, H. J. (2010). Hitting home: Relationships between recent deployment, posttraumatic stress symptoms, and marital functioning for Army couples. *Journal of Family Psychology*, *24*, 280–288. doi:10.1037/a0019405

American Psychological Association. (2012). *Stress in America: Our health at risk.* Retrieved from http://www.apa.org/news/press/releases/stress/index.aspx

Azen, R., & Budescu, D. V. (2003). The dominance analysis approach for comparing predictors in multiple regression. *Psychological Methods*, *8*, 129–148. doi:10.1037/1082-989X.8.2.129

Bonanno, G. A., Mancini, A. D., Horton, J. L., Powell, T. M., LeardMann, C. A., Boyko, E. J., . . . Smith, T. C. (2012). Trajectories of trauma symptoms and resilience in deployed U.S. military service members: Prospective cohort study. *British Journal of Psychiatry*, *200*, 317–323. doi:10.1192/bjp.bp.111.096552

Britt, T. W., Adler, A. B., & Bartone, P. T. (2001). Deriving benefits from stressful events: The role of engagement in meaningful work and hardiness. *Journal of Occupational Health Psychology*, *6*, 53–63. doi:10.1037/1076-8998.6.1.53

Britt, T. W., & McFadden, A. (2012). Understanding mental health treatment seeking in high stress occupations. In J. Houdmont, S. Leka, & R. R. Sinclair (Eds.), *Contemporary occupational health psychology: Global perspectives on research and practice* (Vol. 2, pp. 57–73). Hoboken, NJ: Wiley-Blackwell. doi:10.1002/9781119942849.ch4

Bureau of Labor Statistics, U.S. Department of Labor. (2012). *Employment situation of veterans—2011.* Retrieved from http://www.bls.gov/opub/ted/2012/ted_20120323.htm

Chandra, A., Lara-Cinisomo, S., Jaycox, L. H., Tanielian, T., Burns, R. M., Ruder, T., & Han, B. (2010). Children on the homefront: The experience of children from military families. *Pediatrics*, *125*, 16–25. doi:10.1542/peds.2009-1180

Elder, G. H., & Clipp, E. C. (1989). Combat experience and emotional health: Impairment and resilience in later life. *Journal of Personality*, *57*, 311–341. doi:10.1111/j.1467-6494.1989.tb00485.x

Fikretoglu, D., & McCreary, D. R. (2012). *Psychological resilience: A brief review of definitions, and key theoretical, conceptual, and methodological issues* (Technical Report 2012-012). Toronto, Ontario, Canada: Defense R&D Canada.

Glasgow, R. E., & Emmons, K. M. (2007). How can we increase translation of research into practice? Types of evidence needed. *Annual Review of Public Health*, *28*, 413–433. doi:10.1146/annurev.publhealth.28.021406.144145

Hammer, L. B., & Brady, G. P. (2012, June). *NG/RC reintegration into the civilian workforce: Effects of post-9/11 deployment on veterans and their families.* Paper presented at the conference of the Work and Family Researchers Network, New York, NY.

Hammer, L. B., Kossek, E. E., Anger, W. K., Bodner, T., & Zimmerman, K. (2011). Clarifying work–family intervention processes: The roles of work–family conflict and family supportive supervisor behaviors. *Journal of Applied Psychology, 96*, 134–150. doi:10.1037/a0020927

Helgeson, V. S., Reynolds, K. A., & Tomich, P. L. (2006). A meta-analytic review of benefit finding and growth. *Journal of Consulting and Clinical Psychology, 74*, 797–816. doi:10.1037/0022-006X.74.5.797

Katz, D., & Kahn, R. (1978). *The social psychology of organizations* (2nd ed.). New York, NY: Wiley.

LeBreton, J. M., Hargis, M. B., Griepentrog, B., Oswald, F. L., & Ployhart, R. E. (2007). A multidimensional approach for evaluating variables in organizational research and practice. *Personnel Psychology, 60*, 475–498. doi:10.1111/j.1744-6570.2007.00080.x

LeBreton, J. M., & Tonidandel, S. (2008). Multivariate relative importance: Extending relative weight analysis to multivariate criterion spaces. *Journal of Applied Psychology, 93*, 329–345. doi:10.1037/0021-9010.93.2.329

Lester, P. B., Harms, P. D., Herian, M. N., Krasikova, D. V., & Beal, S. J. (2011). *The Comprehensive Soldier Fitness Program Evaluation: Report No. 3. Longitudinal analysis of the impact of master resilience training on self-reported resilience and psychological health data.* Retrieved from http://www.ppc.sas.upenn.edu/csftechreport3mrt.pdf

Meredith, S., Sherbourne, C., Gaillot, S. J., Hansell, L., Ritschard, H. V., Parker, A. M., & Wrenn, G. (2011). *Promoting psychological resilience in the U.S. military* (MG-966-OSD). Retrieved from http://www.rand.org/pubs/monographs/MG996.html

Nielsen, K., Randall, R., Holten, A., & González, E. R. (2010). Conducting organizational-level occupational health interventions: What works? *Work & Stress, 24*, 234–259. doi:10.1080/02678373.2010.515393

Nielsen, K., Taris, T. W., & Cox, T. (2010). The future of organizational interventions: Addressing the challenges of today's organizations. *Work & Stress, 24*, 219–233. doi:10.1080/02678373.2010.519176

Odle-Dusseau, H. N., Herleman, H. A., Britt, T. W., Moore, D. D., Castro, C. A., & McGurk, D. (2013). Family-supportive work environments and psychological strain: A longitudinal test of two theories. *Journal of Occupational Health Psychology, 18*, 27–36. doi:10.1037/a0030803

Park, C. L., & Fenster, J. R. (2004). Stress-related growth: Predictors of occurrence and correlates with psychological adjustment. *Journal of Social and Clinical Psychology, 23*, 195–215. doi:10.1521/jscp.23.2.195.31019

Reivich, K. J., Seligman, M. E. P., & McBride, S. (2011). Master resilience training in the U.S. Army. *American Psychologist, 66*, 25–34. doi:10.1037/a0021897

Ruvolo, C. M., & Bullis, R. C. (2003). Essentials of culture change: Lessons learned the hard way. *Consulting Psychology Journal: Practice and Research, 55*, 155–168. doi:10.1037/1061-4087.55.3.155

Shapiro, D. L., Kirkman, B. L., & Courtney, H. G. (2007). Perceived causes and solutions of the translation problem in management research. *Academy of Management Journal, 50,* 249–266. doi:10.5465/AMJ.2007.24634433

Sinclair, R. R., Hammer, L. B., & Thomas, J. L. (2012, June). *Military veterans as a vulnerable worker population: Occupational health challenges and opportunities.* Poster session presented at Research Translation With Vulnerable Worker Populations workshop, Fort Collins, CO.

Sledge, W. H., Boydstun, J. A., & Rabe, A. J. (1980). Self-concept changes related to war captivity. *Archives of General Psychiatry, 37,* 430–443. doi:10.1001/archpsyc.1980.01780170072008

Tedeschi, R. G., & McNally, R. J. (2011). Can we facilitate posttraumatic growth in combat veterans? *American Psychologist, 66,* 19–24. doi:10.1037/a0021896

U.S. Government Accountability Office. (2005). *Military personnel: Reporting additional servicemember demographics could enhance congressional oversight* (GAO-05-952). Retrieved from http://www.gao.gov/new.items/d05952.pdf

Wang, M., & Hanges, P. J. (2011). Latent class procedures: Applications to organizational research. *Organizational Research Methods, 14,* 24–31. doi:10.1177/1094428110383988

Wang, M., Sinclair, R. R., Zhou, L., & Sears, L. E. (2012). Person-centered analysis: Methods, applications, and implications for occupational health psychology. In R. R. Sinclair, M. Wang, & L. E. Tetrick (Eds.), *Research methods in occupational health psychology: Measurement, design, and data analysis* (pp. 349–373). New York, NY: Psychology Press/Routledge.

Weinrib, A. Z., Rothrock, N. E., Johnsen, E. L., & Lutgendorf, S. K. (2006). The assessment and validity of stress-related growth in a community-based sample. *Journal of Consulting and Clinical Psychology, 74,* 851–858. doi:10.1037/0022-006X.74.5.851

White, C. J., De Burgh, H. T., Fear, N. T., & Iversen, A. C. (2011). The impact of deployment to Iraq or Afghanistan on military children: A review of the literature. *International Review of Psychiatry, 23,* 210–217. doi:10.3109/09540261.2011.560143

Wood, M. D., Britt, T. W., Thomas, J. L., Klocko, R. P., & Bliese, P. D. (2011). Buffering effects of benefit finding in a war environment. *Military Psychology, 23,* 202–219. doi:10.1080/08995605.2010.521732

INDEX

Frame-of-reference effects in personality
        assessments, 60
Frederickson, B. L., 54
French, W. L., 78
Functional social support, 69–70
Fundamental attribution error, 68
Funder, D. C., 23

Gal, R., 176
Garber, B. G., 147
GAT (Global Assessment Tool),
        198–202, 241–242
Gelfand, L., 119–120
Gender
    and residential mobility, 169
    resilience research on, 68
    and resource availability for single
        parents, 178–179
    of single parents in the military, 177
George, J. M., 25
Gillham, J., 197
Global Assessment Tool (GAT),
        198–202, 241–242
Goleman, D., 98
González, E. R., 245
Gorman, G. H., 4
Graded return to work, 148–149
Gravino, K., 176
Griffith, J., 50
Group cohesion, military, 51
Group randomized trials of resilience
        training, 230–232
Group resilience, 232–233
Gudanowski, D. M., 74
Gulf War veterans, 72
Guzzo, R. A., 74

Hackman, J. R., 87
Haiti (deployment to), 71
Hammer, L. B., 248
Hardiness
    and cohesion, 99
    as composite personality trait, 28–30
    of leaders, 99–100
    as leadership attribute, 86
    modeling of, 74, 99
    and morale, 49–50
    resilience research on, 68
    and self-efficacy, 124
    and stress reactions, 100

Hardiness training, 74
Harland, L., 95
Harmony guidelines, 226
Harms, P. D., 240
Harrell, M. C., 169–170
Harris, M. A., 178
Harrison, D. A., 92
Health care
    behavioral, 195, 228
    for veterans, ix
Hendrix, C. C., 176
Herian, M. N., 240
Herzog-Simmer, P., 178
High-risk occupations, resilience in,
        224–225
Hisle-Gorman, E., 4
Hobfoll, S. E., 54, 58
Hogan, J., 36
Hoge, C. W., 52, 86
Holten, A., 245
Homecoming experience of veterans, 146
Hope, 30–31
Horizontal cohesion, 51
Huberts, L., 93
Huff, M. B., 31
Hypermasculinity, 76

Idealized influence behavior
    and ethical leadership, 96
    in leadership model, 94
    as stress buffer, 95
    in transformational leadership, 90
Inclusive taxonomies of personality
        traits, 24–26
Indirect resilience training, 225
Individual coping styles, 68
Individual factors, 230
    in morale, 49–50
    resilience research on, 68
    in resilience study framework, 10–11
    situational vs., 78–79
Individualization
    of CRMs, 206
    of resilience-building interventions,
        156
    of resilience training, 229–230
Individualized consideration behavior
    in proposed leadership model, 94
    as stress buffer, 95
    in transformational leadership, 90

in extremis, 86, 97–98
as predictor of cohesion, 51–52
proposed model of, 93–96
and psychological capital, 101–103
trait approach, 87
transactional, 51, 89–90
transactional–transformational
approach to, 88–89
transformational, 51, 90–91
undermining of resilience by, 226
Leadership factors, in morale, 49
Leadership training, 73
"Leading by example," 125
Lebanon War, 57
Lee, J. E. C., 34
Lensvelt-Mulders, G. M., 34
Lester, P., 4
Lester, P. B., 208, 240
Litz, B. T., 52
Locus of control, 28
Longitudinal research
on morale and unit cohesion,
59–60
on resilience, 239–240
Long-term mental health, short-term
performance vs., 154–155, 226
Luria, G., 27
Luthans, F., 30, 31, 102, 103
Lyons, J. B., 95

Maguen, S., 97
Makowsky, P. P., 169
Mancini, A. D., 7, 36
Manning, F. J., 48
Marine reservists, 119–120
Markman, H. J., 176
Marshall, G. N., 35
Masten, A. S., 75, 203
Master Resilience Trainer (MRT)
courses, 125, 200, 203–205
McAdams, D. P., 26
McBride, S., 208
McCreary, D. R., 6–8, 34, 120–121,
241
McCubbin, H. I., 174, 175
McCubbin, M. A., 175
McFadyen, J. M., 176
McGurk, D., 8, 86, 88, 238
McKee, A., 98
McMurray, J. J., 102

Mental health
performance and long-term,
154–155, 226
as unit responsibility, 143
Mental Health Advisory Team
(MHAT), 142
Mental health care
access to, 151
barriers to, during deployment, 142
facilitation of, 142–144
and military culture, 241
negative consequences of seeking,
227–228
Mental health problems
and combat stress, 76, 226
of combat veterans, 247
during deployment, 142
deployment as risk factor for,
149–150
and exposure to stressors, 21–22
as indicators of positive adaptation,
238
of military spouses, 170–171
and multiple traumatic events, 240
performance influenced by, 142
postdeployment education about, 148
predeployment psychological
screening to prevent, 138
reintegration and, 146
stigmatization of members with,
76, 120
"Mental readiness" model, 121
Meredith, S., 241, 245
Metacognitive skills, in CSF training,
195
MHAT (Mental Health Advisory
Team), 142
Mhatre, K. H., 31
Mikulincer, M., 57–58, 176
Military chaplains, 144, 211
Military culture
building resilience in, 240–241
changing, 207
as situational factor, 76–78
Military families, 167–184
CSF training for, 215
effects of combat deployments for, 4
resilience-building interventions for,
179–183
resilience in, 174–177

Positive affect (PA), 25–26, 48–49, 54
Positive outcomes, from adversity,
    243–244
Positive psychology, 100
    in CSF, 195
    limits of, 229
    in postdeployment interventions,
        153–154
Postdeployment educational programs,
    148
Postdeployment mental health screening,
    149–153
Postdeployment period (deployment
    cycle), 145–154
Posttraumatic growth, 243
Posttraumatic stress disorder (PTSD)
    benefit finding and, 244
    CBT for treatment of, 145
    civilian studies on, 145
    combat stress and, 57
    coping styles and, 116
    external locus of control and, 28
    hope and, 31
    morale during deployment and, 55
    negative appraisals of events and,
        123–124
    neuroticism and, 25
    in Operation Enduring Freedom/
        Operation Iraqi Freedom
        veterans, 124
    optimism and, 31
    personality traits and, 36–37
    predeployment psychological
        functioning and, 52
    primary prevention of, 213–214
    and regulation of stressors, 117
    research design for, 55–56
    screening for, 151
    self-esteem and, 27
    social support and, 70
Posttraumatic stress disorder (PTSD)
    symptoms
    assessment of, 55
    in children, 172
    and combat exposure, 4, 7, 31, 55, 244
    stress and, 58
Powell, J., 169
Predeployment briefings, 141
Predeployment period (deployment
    cycle), 138–141

Predeployment psychological function-
    ing, 52, 55–56
Predeployment psychological screening,
    138–141
Preparatory education, 121–123
Privacy, of GAT scores, 199
Proactive personality, 32–33
Professional support, 156
Protective family traits, 176
PRP (Penn Resilience Program),
    197–198
Psychological capital (PsyCap), 30–32
    and authentic leadership, 103
    and leadership, 101–104
    as second-order construct, 86–87
    and traumatic exposure, 68
Psychological disorders, 57, 70
Psychological distress, 7, 8, 122
Psychological functioning
    assessments of, 55
    predeployment, 52, 55–56
    in resilience research, 55–56, 59–60
    of returning soldiers, 3
    and unit cohesion, 56
Psychological injuries of war, ix–x
Psychological reactions to high-
        intensity combat courses, 129
Psychological resources, 53–54
Psychological well-being, 58, 171.
    See also Well-being
PsycINFO, 8–9
PTSD. See Posttraumatic stress disorder
PTSD symptoms. See Posttraumatic
    stress disorder (PTSD) symptoms

Quasi-experimental designs, 60–61

Randall, R., 245
READY (Resources for Education
        About Deployment and You)
        program, 78
Reappraisal process (for stressors), 24
Reed, M. G., 203
Reed, M. G. J., 75
Reichard, R. J., 31
Reintegration, 172–173
Reintegration programs, 146
Reivich, K. J., 75
Relative weights analysis, 242
Relaxation techniques, 127

ABOUT THE EDITORS

Robert R. Sinclair, PhD, is an associate professor of industrial and organizational psychology at Clemson University, where he also serves as the graduate program coordinator for the Department of Psychology. He completed his doctorate in industrial and organizational psychology at Wayne State University in 1995. Prior to moving to Clemson University in 2008, he held faculty positions at the University of Tulsa and Portland State University. Dr. Sinclair is a founding member and past president of the Society for Occupational Health Psychology. He currently serves as an editorial board member for the *Journal of Occupational Health Psychology*, the *Journal of Management*, and the *Journal of Organizational Behavior* and as a panel member for the Occupational Safety and Health Study Section of the National Institute for Occupational Safety and Health. His recent work includes an edited volume (2012, with Jonathan Houdmont and Stavroula Leka) titled *Contemporary Occupational Health Psychology: Global Perspectives on Research and Practice* (Vol. 2) and an edited volume (in press, with Mo Wang and Lois Tetrick) titled *Research Methods in Occupational Health Psychology: Measurement, Design, and Data Analysis*. Dr. Sinclair's research focuses on individual factors (e.g., personality) and organizational factors (e.g., leadership) that contribute to occupational health concerns faced by military personnel, nurses, and entry-level hourly employees. His specific interests include economic stress, the employment relationship, work schedules, counterproductive workplace behavior, and psychological resilience.

Thomas W. Britt, PhD, is a professor of social and organizational psychology at Clemson University. He received his doctorate from the University of Florida in 1994 before entering active duty as a research psychologist in the U.S. Army. Dr. Britt was stationed at the Walter Reed Army Institute of Research (WRAIR)–Heidelberg, Germany Unit from 1994 to 1997 and then at the WRAIR in Silver Spring, Maryland, from 1997 to 1999. Dr. Britt left active duty in 1999 (he received an honorable discharge as a major) and spent a year at King College before moving to Clemson University in 2000. He has published over 60 empirical articles and multiple book chapters and has been an editor for a book and four-volume series in areas of military psychology. His articles have been published in leading journals such as *Psychological Review, Psychological Bulletin,* the *Journal of Personality and Social Psychology,* the *Journal of Personality,* and the *Journal of Occupational Health Psychology.* Dr. Britt's research investigates the determinants of organizational stress and resiliency and stigma and other barriers facing individuals seeking needed mental health treatment. His research has been funded by multiple grants and contracts from the Department of Defense and Medical Research Command. He currently is being funded by a grant from the Department of Defense to comprehensively address the factors determining whether military veterans seek needed mental health treatment. His research in the area of military psychology has been conducted in collaboration with colleagues from the Walter Reed Army Institute of Research.